Practical Guide

to

HOME INSPECTION

T0204595

Sweet Rain Press Regional Office: Los Angeles, California

Library of Congress Catalog Card Number: 2011907487
ISBN-13: 978-0615486574
Printed in the United States of America.
Published by Sweet Rain Press
Los Angeles, California

Practical Guide

to

HOME INSPECTION

Jeffrey I. Charloff, P.E., F.ASCE
Consulting Engineer

This book is dedicated to:
my wife Monica,
and to my children,
Andrea, Michelle, and Perry.

Sweet Rain Press
Los Angeles

Preface

Throughout the course of my consulting engineering career on both the East and West coasts of the United States, I have detected numerous home and building problems while in the midst of conducting inspections. Some of these problems resulted from either poor or negligent workmanship. Indeed, the lack of good construction practice involves errors, omissions or even using inadequate or defective materials. Some other issues that I have encountered stemmed from mere aging. Many of these scenarios could have been avoided if only they were spotted early enough before they had caused damage or, if only homeowners had just known how to identify certain conditions which had later turned into serious conundrums.

From my collection of experiences of performing pre-purchase home inspections, I recommend this text to homebuyers, engineers, homeowners, real estate personnel, architects, builders and attorneys as an aid in determining the physical condition of a home. This text will assist homebuyers in making well-informed, insightful decisions when facing one of the most exciting, but nerve-wracking decisions of their lives - the purchase of their homes. The book includes house plumbing, electrical, roofing, heating, foundation and structural problems commonly encountered when inspecting a home. Some building code and safety items have been presented, too.

This easy-to-understand book was written to sharpen one's discernment on the subject of shelter, one of man's basic needs. I ultimately feel that this information will assist people to arm themselves with a unique, but useful knowledge base that will enable them to be proactive and well-equipped in finding the right home fit for their lifestyle.

Note that because building code requirements and construction details vary from locality to locality, and from year to year, this collection is intended to highlight a limited amount of information as a general guidebook only. Although some material discussed here might be appropriate for certain situations, nonetheless, it is recommended that readers consult with their local building department officials, architects or engineers upon seeking specific advice about building inspection or home construction matters for their particular needs.

Jeffrey I. Charloff,, P.E.

Los Angeles, California

April 2011

Contents

xiv   Practical Guide to Home Inspection

xvii   Practical Guide to Home Inspection

xxv   Practical Guide to Home Inspection

xxvii   Practical Guide to Home Inspection

Introduction

A pre-purchase home inspection is often regarded as one of many "hoops" that a buyer must jump through in order to secure a dream home. It is my goal to inform you that this "hoop" is probably going to be the most important in the home-buying process, and it deserves your time and energy as such. A thorough examination of a home now will prevent unwelcome surprises later, and it will behoove you to learn all that you can about the types of problems and conditions that a home has had, has at the present time, and may have in the future.

I aim to simplify this journey of discovery for you, although by no means is this portion of the home-buying process simple. Arming yourself with knowledge and information is the best weapon against having to take on potential problems and issues that a home may have lurking beneath its seemingly lustrous exterior.

Whenever possible in the beginning of my home inspections, I often meet with sellers and ask them questions regarding their residences. Most homeowners have been cooperative during my interviews with them and have furnished me with an array of information about their homes. They live in them. They know their homes well.

The first part of the book essentially outlines key questions I frequently ask sellers. The interview begins by asking them about the history of their dwellings in order to find out about any additions, changes, revisions, or alterations. With this information and while examining the home, I interpret what permits or other documentation should be on file with the local building department. *Part I, Advisory Concepts for Homebuyers* contains advice concerning certain facts that every homebuyer should learn about and advice about which documents, reports and items ought to be obtained. Further, *Advisory Concepts for Homebuyers* points to various construction characteristics which should be realized about many homes before purchase.

Part II, Highlights of Home Inspection, is loaded with discovery problems. Just like a pianist must know keys, notes, and chords, it will be your job to learn many home construction problems, conditions that the home may possess, as well as the causes of these various problems and conditions. This knowledge will enable you to recognize what you need to look for when determining whether a house is the right fit for you. It is worth your while to be as comprehensive as possible during your assessment of a particular home. Delving beneath the surface now could prevent unwanted responsibilities later, and it will enable your dream home to be a dream and not a nightmare.

Practical Guide

to

HOME INSPECTION

PART I.

ADVISORY CONCEPTS FOR

HOMEBUYERS

Chapter 1

PERMITS

This chapter introduces the homebuyer to the importance that approved permits be obtained. After all, the homebuyer should want to buy a legal house!

1.1 CERTIFICATE OF OCCUPANCY

Here's a simplified example of the 'how', the 'what' and the 'where' of a Certificate of Occupancy - the document that tells you the house was built as a legal dwelling:

A couple wishes to have a new custom home built on a graded lot they have recently purchased. They engage the services of a licensed architect who designs and prepares plans for the house. The architect shows his drawings to the couple who like the drawings, gets their approval of the design and then visits the building department for plan check approval. Once the plans are approved by the building department, a reputable licensed general contractor is selected to build the house pursuant to the plans and specifications which are furnished to him. During the course of construction, periodic inspections are made by the building department inspector. When the house has been completed, the building department inspector is called in to make a 'final inspection.'

If the inspector finds that the house has been built in accordance to the approved plans and specs and complies with all codal compliances, the building department deems the building fit for occupancy and issues a document called a "Certificate of Occupancy" or a "Final Approval." The purchasers can then move into and take occupancy of their new home.

Form 123

DEPARTMENT OF BUILDINGS
CITY OF USA

No. **1554**
Date 5/14/74

CERTIFICATE OF OCCUPANCY

(Standard form adopted by the Board of Standards and Appeals and issued pursuant to Section 127 of the USA Charter, and Sections C.33-189.8 to C34-144.0 inclusive Administrative Code 3.4.3.8. to 8.9.3.1. Building Code.)

This certificate supersedes C. O. No.

To the owner or owners of the building or premises:
THIS CERTIFIES that the new-xxxxxxxxxxxx-building-premises located at

456 Hoover St., CITY OF USA

Block 1520   Lot 3

, conforms substantially to the approved plans and specifications, and to the requirements of the building code and all other laws and ordinances, and of the rules and regulations of the Board of Standards and Appeals, applicable to a building of its class and kind at the time the permit was issued; and CERTIFIES FURTHER that, any provisions of Section 253 of the City of USA have been complied with.

Fig. 1.1 - Example

Determine with certainty that a 'Certificate of Occupancy' or a 'Final Approval' exists for the entire home as it is comprised at the present time by examining the file for the house which should be available at the local building department. It's important to view this document regardless of whether the home you're interested in purchasing is new or old.

1.2 CERTIFICATE OF OCCUPANCY - WHEN ELSE IS IT NEEDED?

A Certificate of Occupancy or a Final Approval is generally also needed for the following examples:

    a.   for the building's present usage (especially if it has been converted);

    b.   for the home following a significant fire;

    c.   or following an explosion;

    d.   for a revised interior layout;

    e.   for added rooms;

    f.   for a structurally remodeled kitchen or bathroom;

    g.   for an extended room;

    h.   and for an enclosed porch.

1.3 IS THE HOUSE A YEAR-ROUND DWELLING?

While examining the file of the house at the local building department,

determine that the house is considered to be a 'year-round dwelling.'

Example:

Fig. 1.2

There is no heat inside the beach house and, in the community in which this

home is located, the house fails to qualify for year-round occupancy.

1.4 ABOUT PERMITS IN GENERAL

When certain additions or revisions have been made to a home, approved permits should be on file with the local building department. Approved permits will help assure you that the building department has inspected and accepted the construction work as that of being safe and proper.

Building departments issue several kinds of permits for various kinds of work done to a home. The names of the kinds of permits needed differ from one building department in one locality to that in another, but they generally include:

a.   Grading Permit and Approval;

b.   Building Permit and Approval;

c.   Electrical Permit and Approval;

d.   Plumbing Permit and Approval;

e.   Mechanical - Heating and Air Conditioning Permits and Approvals.

Here are some examples of work items that building departments normally issue permits for:

Grading Permits: are normally required when there is significant movement of soil material (for example, that which might exceed 50 cubic yards of dirt), or when significant retaining/ drainage work is done.

Building Permits: are usually required for building or re-building a chimney, building a raised deck or patio overhang, for a later roofing cover installation, perhaps for later aperture work (such as a skylight, window or doorway installation), and for any newer structural/addition work done. Such permits should be in order for the construction of a swimming pool or spa, or even a tennis court, too.

Electrical Permits: The electrician should have ordered this kind of permit when he wired the house with new wiring (including 110 volt outdoor wiring and lighting), when a new circuit breaker panel has been installed, for the hookup of an electric self-cleaning oven, or for a 220 volt outlet which has been provided for an electric dryer.

Plumbing Permits: are usually required for the installation of an exterior underground lawn sprinkler system, the installation of a later hot water heater, for significant repiping of a house, a gas barbecue installation, for laundry equipment and dishwasher hookups, and some later plumbing fixture work.

Mechanical Permits: are usually required for

the installation work of a new furnace

and central air conditioning system, and

for a significant amount of climate

ducting work.

Your local building department can advise you of exactly what construction work requires permits. Remember, permits need approvals. This is mentioned since some permits might have been issued for a specific job, but that job was completed without having been inspected by the building department and, consequently, there is no approval. So be sure pertaining permits and approvals exist for all significant later work that has been done to the home. They should be on file with the local building department.

1.5 NO PERMITS?

If it should be found out that no approved permits are in order and could not be forthcoming because of illegal or makeshift construction, then the possible cost of legalizing/the cost of retrofitting could be quite costly. Moreover, insurance policies might not cover the homeowner against losses of bodily injury or of property damages that are caused by illegal construction.

Example:

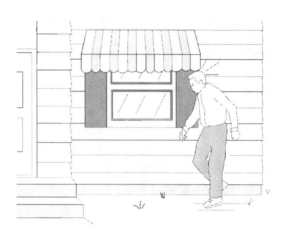

Fig. 1.3

The window awning in the above illustration was installed by an inexperienced, unlicensed contractor without the issuance of a building permit. Indeed, the awning had been placed too low on the building such that it offers little headroom clearance between soil grade and its underside. A guest walks by this awning and inadvertently scrapes his head against it. That guest sues the homeowner, but the homeowner's insurance company doesn't want to pay for damages. Later, the homeowner engages the services of an experienced licensed contractor to raise the height of this awning. The building department gets called out to inspect it, approves its installation and then issues the homeowner a 'Certificate of Compliance' (or an approved Building Permit) for this work.

Here are more example items in which approvals would not likely be forthcoming:

      a.   an illegal construction of a new incinerator in the backyard to burn gathered autumn leaves where that community no longer permits incinerator construction or use;

      b.   the exterior sink installation which drains its waste or 'grey' water onto the ground rather than into the house's plumbing waste system;

      c.   the existence of a cooking range inside a guest house;

      d.   the installation of a high-up placed exterior doorway having no steps outside it;

      e.   the installation of a kitchen garden window that dangerously protrudes into the pathway outside it that can inadvertently be walked into;

      f.   the installation of a ceiling light-fan that is hung dangerously low;

g. the hallway which has a narrow width;

h. the lack of an attached ladder to the attic where the forced air furnace is located;

i. the high step riser that leads from the garage up to the house;

j. the location of the electric meter having been placed high up on the exterior wall of the house;

k. some plumbing lines which run along grade and can cause tripping hazards;

l. the existence of a non-shatter resistant window not being at least 5 feet up from the bathtub floor for it is a safety hazard;

m. the lack of a hallway between the kitchen and the bathroom off of the kitchen;

n. the permanent cabinet closure of the space beneath the bathroom sink where one cannot gain access to this sink's plumbing;

o.   the lack of waste drainage cleanouts;

p.   the patio enclosure construction since it affects natural light and ventilation to several existing rooms;

q.   and the new attic hatch in the garage which could adversely affect the fire-rating of the ceiling between the house and garage.

Chapter 2

DOCUMENTS, REPORTS

AND ITEMS TO REQUEST

You have heard of the expression "what you see is what you get."

Well, in this chapter, what the purchaser asks for is what he or she might get.

Those requests which are listed here are considered to be reasonable requests.

2.1 GET THE BUILDING PLANS AND SPECS

Fig. 2.1

Ask the seller for a complete approved set of architectural, structural and mechanical plans of the house in addition to the building specifications. Ask, too, for any possible later addition and remodeling plans.

2.2 OBTAIN THE SOILS AND GEOLOGICAL REPORTS

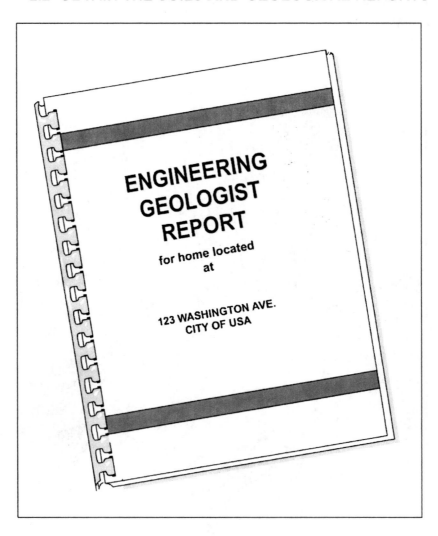

Fig. 2.2

Obtain the engineering soils and geological reports for the home site (if they, in fact, exist) and study them carefully. Make sure that there are no unfavorable soil or geological conditions which you cannot or do not wish to deal with.

2.3 OBTAIN SERVICE CONTRACTS

Fig. 2.3

Obtain all home service contracts which the seller might have. This includes contracts with possibly a heating contractor, appliance retailers, a pest control service, or perhaps even with a homeowners warranty program. Determine whether or not the contracts are transferable to you.

2.4 GET THE TERMITE CONTROL GUARANTEE

Fig. 2.4

Whether the house was tented and fumigated and/ or had been termite-proofed or treated, either work usually reflects past termite problems. Should the control job have been done recently, ask the seller for a possible guarantee that might still be in effect. Note that there could be damage caused by termites within wall sections and often such damage doesn't get corrected during the course of termite proofing or fumigating the house. The damage can be detected by probing through the walls or by removing the wall cover. However, as you can well realize, the probing and the wall cover removal doesn't fall within the normal work scope of a regular home inspection.

2.5   EXAMINE THE PAST HEATING BILLS

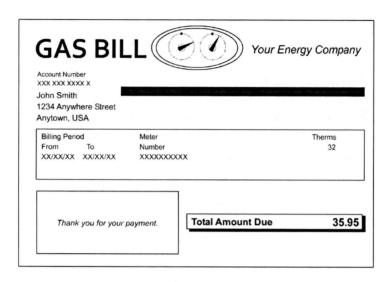

Fig. 2.5

Ask the owner to show you the past (gas or oil or electric) heating bills. You should be interested in knowing how much money the seller has been paying the utility company because

    a.   electric heat can be expensive;

    b.   the attic is not insulated, causing much heat loss from the dwelling;

    c.   the attic has some insulation, but, in these days, the amount of it is considered minimal and inadequate;

    d.   (in many older houses), insulation has not been provided inside the exterior walls;

    e.   the house doesn't utilize storm windows (which are appropriate in colder climate homes);

    f.   and the house uses generally drafty casement and jalousie windows.

Hence, the cost of heating your prospective home could just be more money than that which you have been anticipating.

2.6 REQUEST CLIMATE CONTROL INDEX

Request to review which rooms each thermostat control activates heating or air conditioning to. However, if the house is an older house that utilizes push-button furnace controls instead, then learn which rooms each such push- button control activates the generation of heat to.

Example 1:
The thermostat in the living room of this home controls the generation of warm and cool air to the main level, whereas the thermostat on the second floor of the house controls the generation of heat and cool air to the upper level.

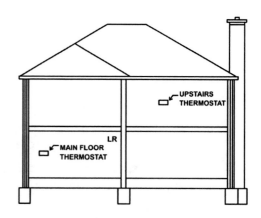

Fig. 2.6A

Example 2:
The push-button furnace control with red and white indication lights and high and low settings still used in the entrance vestibule of this older home activates the east basement's gravity furnace to warm the east portion of the house, while the push-button control in the library activates the west basement's gravity furnace to warm up the westerly portion of the building.

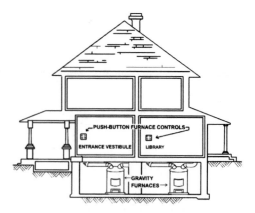

Fig. 2.6B

2.7 ACCOUNT FOR STORED DOORS

Fig. 2.7

Find out where all the stored doors come from. Should they still serve a useful purpose, you might want to have the owner re-install them before closing.

2.8 ACCOUNT FOR STORED SCREENS

Fig. 2.8

Ask for a list of all window screens which are being stored away and have the owner provide you with a directory indicating their placement locations on the house. Allowances should be made for those screens which can no longer be used as well as for any missing ones. Have the seller furnish you with a similar list for any and all stored storm windows.

2.9 REMOVAL OF STORED MATERIAL AND DEBRIS

Fig. 2.9

Ask the seller to remove all debris and material either being stored or observed to be lying about such locations of the dwelling as the garage, the attic, the basement and outside the house. Removal costs can be expensive. This should be done before closing.

2.10 GET THE AUTOMATIC GARAGE DOOR OPENERS

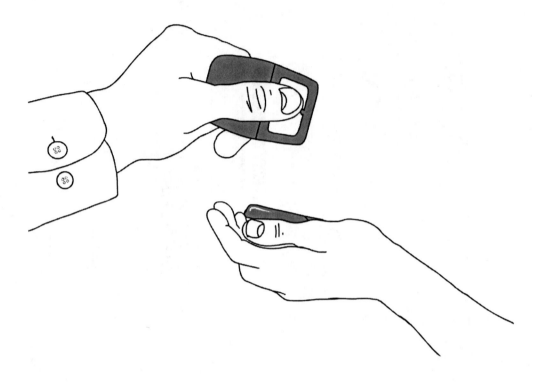

Fig. 2.10

Have all automatic garage door transmitters conveyed to you at closing time.

2.11 REQUEST ALL FOOD CENTER ATTACHMENTS

Fig. 2.11

Request that all built-in blender or "food center" attachments be conveyed to you at the time of closing. Food center attachments are costly to replace.

Chapter 3

LEARN SOME IMPORTANT FACTS

This chapter presents a host of factual items for the homebuyer to learn about in connection with his or her prospective home so as to become better informed about it.

3.1 LEARN YOUR LOCATION WELL

A good location is one of the foremost concerns you should have in the selection of your home.

Here are some examples of how different locations of houses could affect the homeowner:

Example 1:

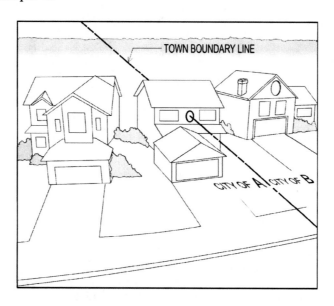

Fig. 3.1A

A town's boundary line can cross a property. The west section of the house in this illustration is legally located in the City of 'A', whereas the east portion of the home is located in the City of 'B.' This causes legal complications.

Example 2:

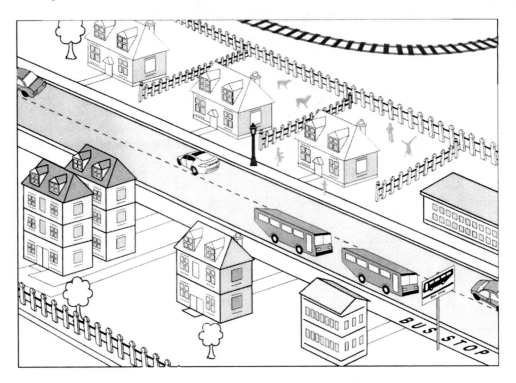

Fig. 3.1B

Make a survey of the surrounding area to determine whether the house is located within the sound range of any outstanding noises which could take away from the tranquility that is ordinarily anticipated in a residential environment. Here the house is situated on a mixed-use street having neighboring sites that could offer lots of potential distractions. Even vibrational effects from a passing train which travels the closeby railroad tracks is a serious problem to those attempting to sleep.

Example 3:

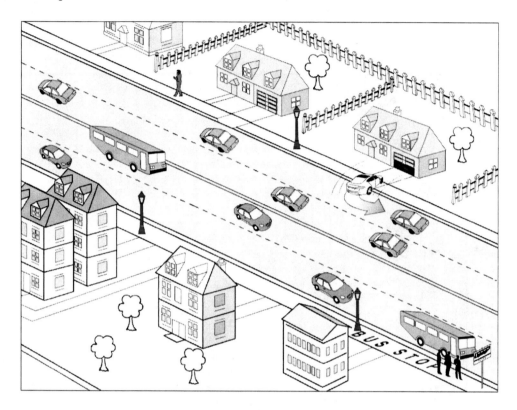

Fig. 3.1.C

Because this house is on a major thoroughfare, traffic noises are louder than

might be expected in a residential neighborhood. Realize, too, that backing

out of this home's driveway can be dangerous on account of the traffic.

Example 4:

Fig. 3.ID

This home is located not too far away from an airport. Although it is not

directly located below a flight pattern, disturbing sounds of low flying aircraft

could sometimes be heard, depending on how the wind blows.

Example 5:

Fig. 3.IE

For safety reasons, realize the location and elevation of the house you are considering to purchase relative to the street. This house is situated at the end of a 'T' street and was the subject of a severe collision from a speeding car whose drunk driver failed to observe the STOP sign and make the turn he was supposed to make. Unfortunately, a separating wall was absent in the front yard at the time to help protect the house from this unfortunate accident.

Example 6:

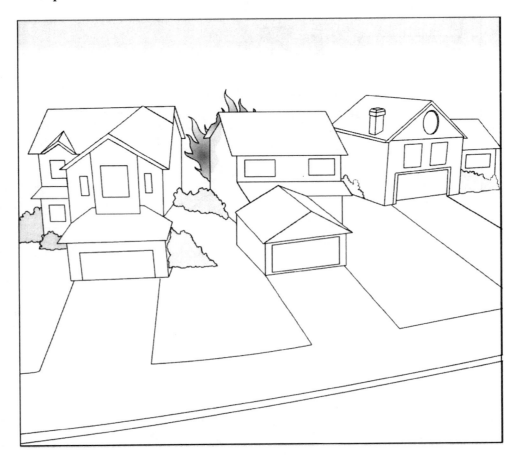

Fig. 3.IF

Determine where the closest fire hydrant is located in relationship to your
prospective home. For the home above, none was viewed in the immediate
sight; nor was one observed within 500 feet of the dwelling. Reflective blue
diamond-like markers are normally present along Los Angeles streets to serve
as an aid in finding them.

Example 7:

Fig. 3.1G

This street lacks adequate lighting provision. This would be considered unfavorable by many from the standpoint of security.

3.2 ARE THERE ANY BUILDING VIOLATIONS?

When purchasing a home, be sure to determine if there are any unsettled building violations or fire department violations of which you do not wish to be responsible for, or, simply can't handle. If it should turn out, however, that there are violations or citations against the property, make certain that they are removed or satisfied before Closing. Check this out with the local building department or perhaps with the local conservation bureau.

Example 1:

The fire department has issued a citation to the homeowner to clear nearby hillside brush which is closer than 100 feet to the house and which could easily catch on fire. They further placed a violation against this home's faulty furnace.

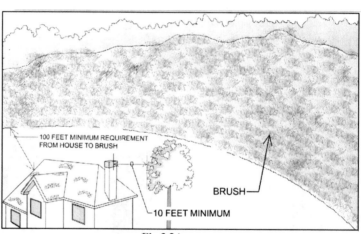

100 FEET MINIMUM REQUIREMENT FROM HOUSE TO BRUSH

BRUSH

10 FEET MINIMUM

Fig 3.2A

NOTICE OF VIOLATION
Inspection Finding:
House missing bathtub

A BUILDING INSPECTOR PASSED BY THIS HOUSE AND NOTICED THE STORED TUB.

Fig 3.2B

Example 2:

Because this home's only bathtub was removed from the house and because it is a building code requirement to have one, the building department inspector cited the homeowner with a building violation.

3.3   WHAT YOU CAN LEARN FROM THE BUILDING DEPARTMENT

Fig. 3.3

Besides being a place to obtain photocopies of permit records, a visit to the pertaining building department can inform you of:

a.   any known occurrences of neighborhood area flooding;

b.   the flood levels of nearby streams and waterways (for the high water levels should never surpass the ground elevation of the property which you are considering for purchase);

c.   and of any known active landslides, falling rock zones or other pertinent geological conditions in the neighborhood.

3.4 WHAT YOU CAN LEARN FROM THE FIRE DEPARTMENT

Fig. 3.4

If you are told of a past fire in the house you are considering to purchase, or if you should notice evidence indicating the possibility of one, contact the local fire department to find out the magnitude and nature of it. Be certain that the fire had no effect upon the Certificate of Occupancy or, a new Certificate of Occupancy was obtained after any possible significant fire.

3.5 FIRE EVIDENCE CAN AFFECT RE-SALE PRICE

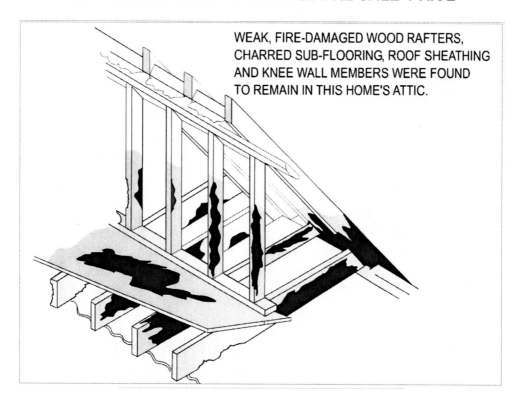

WEAK, FIRE-DAMAGED WOOD RAFTERS, CHARRED SUB-FLOORING, ROOF SHEATHING AND KNEE WALL MEMBERS WERE FOUND TO REMAIN IN THIS HOME'S ATTIC.

Fig. 3.5

Realize that the occurrence and evidence of a past fire can negatively affect the re-sale value of a home. In fact, it has often been found that houses which have suffered fire damage tend to have lower selling prices even though they have since been re-built or repaired pursuant to building department requirements.

3.6 LEARN OF ZONING RESTRICTIONS

Determine whether there are any special zoning restrictions in the event that future construction additions or changes be desired.

Example 1:

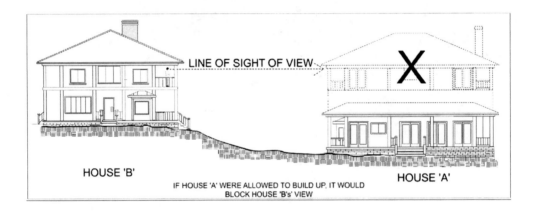

Fig. 3.6A

In the above illustration, homeowners in the neighborhood are restricted from extending their homes up to a height limitation set not to exceed 35 feet. This was done to respect the beautiful views which are being offered by these homes in this development.

Example 2:

Fig. 3.6B

On one side of the street, only single family residences are permitted.

However, on the other side of the street, local zoning allows apartment

buildings to be built.

Example 3:

THIS HOME'S GARAGE WAS ILLEGALLY CONVERTED TO A DEN

Fig. 3.6C

Zoning regulations might require the existence of a garage or a carport on a residential property. It is not uncommon to find that a garage has been later converted to another use and no new garage or carport has since been built to suit the locality's covered car parking requirement. As such, this conversion would be in violation of local zoning regulations.

Example 4

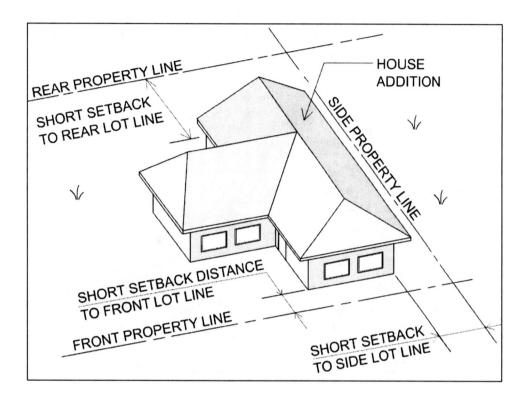

Fig. 3.6D

Permitted setbacks of buildings on properties vary with zoning. The addition that was later made to the illustrated one-family residence is an illegal addition for it was built without a building permit and doesn't conform to the locality's zoning which requires a minimum setback distance of 20 feet of the house in the front yard, a minimum 15 feet rear yard setback clearance and minimum 5 feet wide side yard widths.

Example 5:

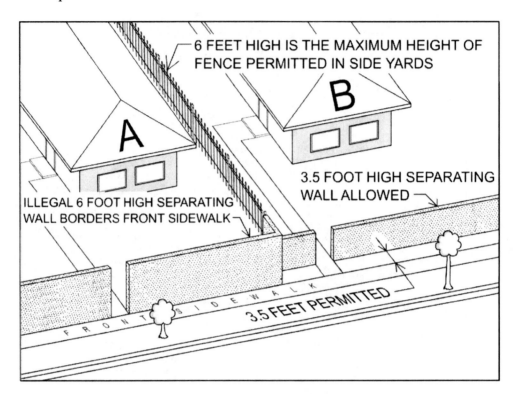

6 FEET HIGH IS THE MAXIMUM HEIGHT OF
FENCE PERMITTED IN SIDE YARDS

B

A

3.5 FOOT HIGH SEPARATING
WALL ALLOWED

ILLEGAL 6 FOOT HIGH SEPARATING
WALL BORDERS FRONT SIDEWALK

FRONT SIDEWALK

3.5 FEET PERMITTED

Fig. 3.6E

Since height and setback requirements of fence installations vary from locality

to locality, it is wise to check with your local zoning regulations for all the

particulars. In this illustration, home A's 6'-0" high fence wall which borders

the front sidewalk is considered to be an illegal installation, whereas home B's

front fence wall that is shorter and has been set back a distance from the

sidewalk is legal in that community.

Example 6:

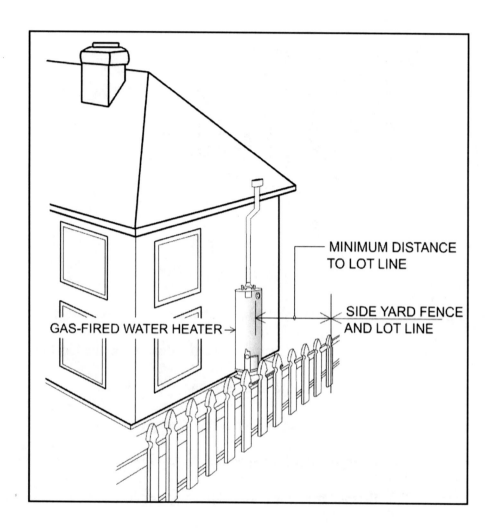

MINIMUM DISTANCE
TO LOT LINE

SIDE YARD FENCE
AND LOT LINE

GAS-FIRED WATER HEATER →

Fig. 3.6F

Many communities permit a fuel-fired water heater outside the house to be
located a certain minimum distance away from the side lot lines. In this
instance, that allowable minimum distance is 3'-0".

Example 7:

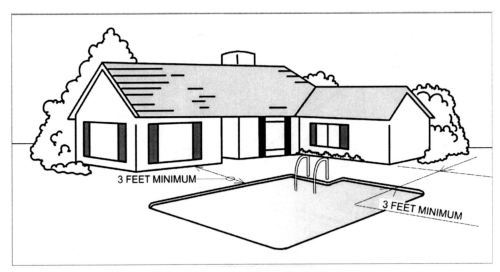

3 FEET MINIMUM

3 FEET MINIMUM

Fig 3.6G

Zoning codes require that swimming pools or spas be located to meet permissible minimum setback distances. In the illustration, the location of the swimming pool is not allowed to be closer than 3'-0" from the exterior rear wall of the single-family house or from an accessory structure or patio overhang. The zoning code which specifies this also requires that there be a minimum 3'-0" distance from the pool or spa to its water heater. Note that, in this locality, the heater itself is required to be set at least a 4'-0" distance from the middle of its exhaust flue to the back or side lot lines.

Example 8:

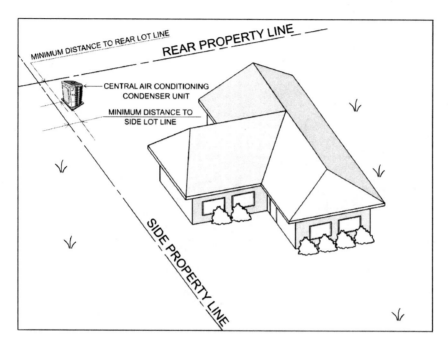

Fig. 3.6H

Zoning regulations in this community specify minimum setback distances to side and back lot lines for mechanical equipment which produce noise. Specifically, for instance, for a single family home, the figure was set at 4'-0" to its side lot line in this home's neighborhood. Some such common mechanical equipment found outside houses include central air conditioning condenser units, and swimming pool and spa motors.

Example 9:

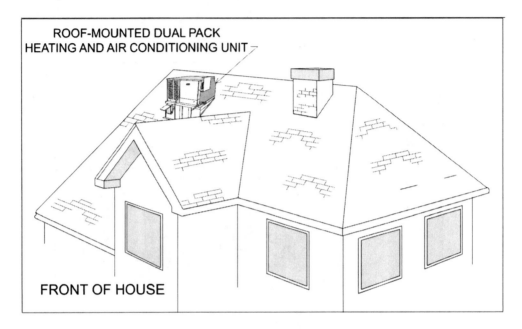

ROOF-MOUNTED DUAL PACK
HEATING AND AIR CONDITIONING UNIT

FRONT OF HOUSE

Fig. 3.6I

The zoning code in this community doesn't allow mechanical equipment to be placed outside the house in such a manner that that equipment can be observed from the street. A building department inspector who happened to be driving down a residential street cited a 'dual-pack' combination gas heating plant and electric air conditioning unit installation mounted on the front section of a house roof. Later, the inspector requested that the unit be relocated to the rear section of the house. See your local zoning regulations to learn of your prospective home's specific local zoning code requirements.

3.7 LEARN YOUR LEGAL RIGHTS

One of the primary rights which homeowners should be aware of is their "non-conforming rights." When a house was built in a legal fashion long ago, that house is entitled to stay in the fashion in which it was built regardless of whether there have been changes made in the newer building codes. Indeed, a homeowner generally doesn't have to update the home each time the building code gets revised. However, the homeowner has a duty to adequately maintain the home. In doing so, the owner is permitted to use the same kind of construction materials that the home had originally been built with (although, in some circumstances, 'retroactive laws' that later come into effect dictate the installation of new items in the building or, perhaps, the need to change some existing building conditions).

Note that if building maintenance was abandoned to where the house was allowed to become in very poor and unsafe condition, the homeowner could virtually loose all his or her non-conforming rights. The building department might require the owner to either retrofit the building or perhaps even have it demolished entirely.

Examples of Non-Conforming Rights:

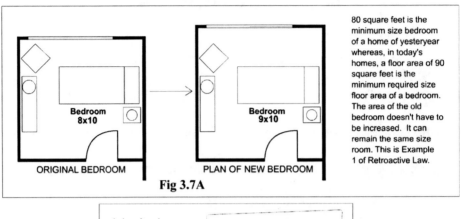

80 square feet is the minimum size bedroom of a home of yesteryear whereas, in today's homes, a floor area of 90 square feet is the minimum required size floor area of a bedroom. The area of the old bedroom doesn't have to be increased. It can remain the same size room. This is Example 1 of Retroactive Law.

ORIGINAL BEDROOM   PLAN OF NEW BEDROOM

Fig 3.7A

In Los Angeles, built-in unvented gas heaters are no longer permitted since they are deemed unsafe for use. This is Example 2 of Retroactive Law.

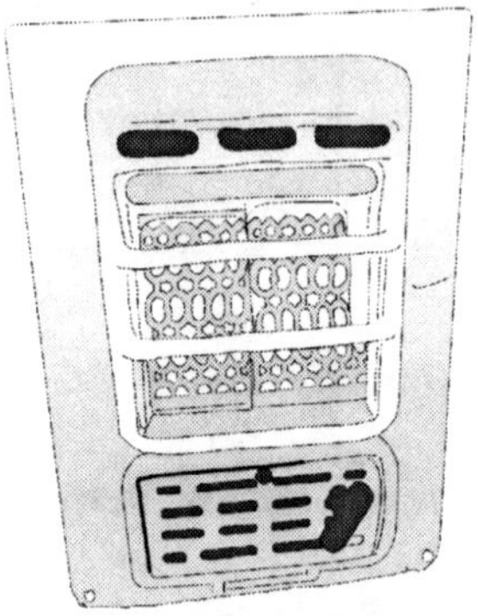

Fig 3.7B

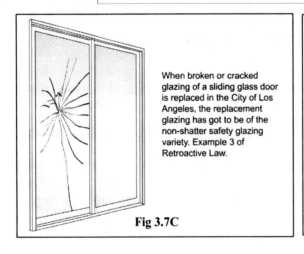

When broken or cracked glazing of a sliding glass door is replaced in the City of Los Angeles, the replacement glazing has got to be of the non-shatter safety glazing variety. Example 3 of Retroactive Law.

Fig 3.7C

Smoke detectors are required to be installed inside bedrooms and hallway locations outside the bedrooms in the City of Los Angeles in a change of home ownership.

Fig 3.7D

Moreover, learn your legal responsibilities and your rights in connection with the following example conditions:

Example 1:

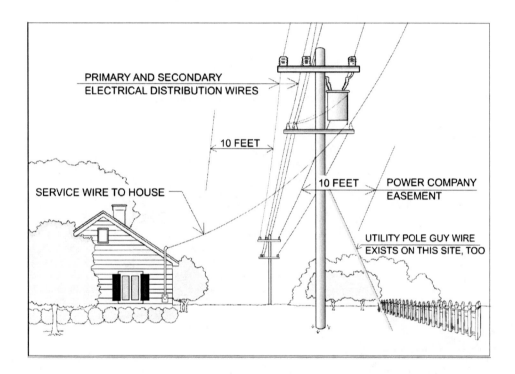

Any utility company or other easements which might exist for the right of way on or across the property. Shown in the illustration are overhead electrical lines which run above the backyard to a power pole located there. The electric company has a right to conduct their maintenance and repair work a limited number of feet beyond the edges of their lines.

Example 2:

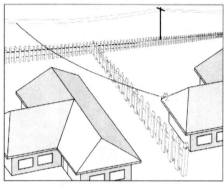

Fig. 3.7F

Utility lines which cross the site to service the neighboring house.

Example 3:

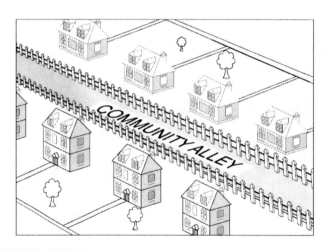

Fig. 3.7G

The community alley that is located behind the site.

Example 4:

Fig. 3.7H

Tree branch and root growth that cross neighboring sites. Here, the

neighboring tree's root is uprooting this property's walkway and some of that

tree's branches enter in the way of the same walkway. Who is responsible to

trim back this tree growth? Neighbor laws vary for different states, but

generally the property owner has the right to do this cutting when such

vegetative growth strays to his land. The procedure has got to be accordingly

performed within legal means, however.

Example 5:

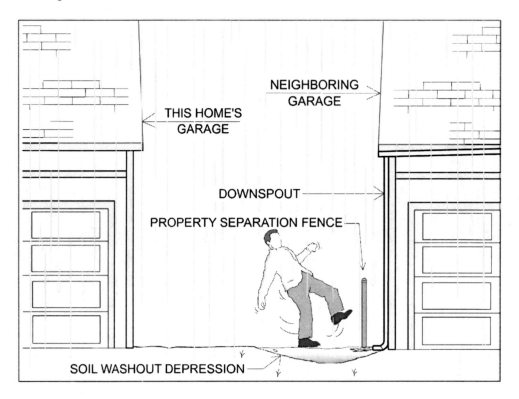

Fig. 3.7I

Water drainage or water run-off conditions with respect to your prospective

neighboring properties. In the illustration, discharge water from a neighbor's

garage downspout enters this home site and causes a washout soil depression

in the yard that, in turn, poses a slipping or tripping hazard.

Example 6:

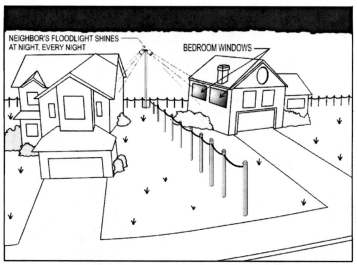

Fig. 3.7J
Light encroachments from neighboring sites.

Example 7:

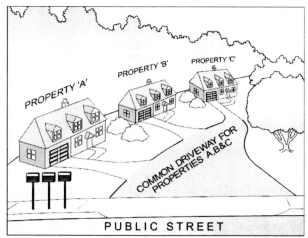

Fig. 3.7K
The common driveway. Learn who responsible to clean, repair or to repave it.

3.8 LEARN THE AGE OF THE HOUSE

UNDERSIDE OF TOILET TANK
LID WAS STAMPED THIS DATE

OCTOBER 1995

Fig. 3.8

    Determine the age of the house. The condition of a dwelling depends upon how old the house is. One way to find out the approximate age of the building would be to locate an original toilet in the house. If one does exist, remove its lid. The date which is found stamped on the lid (or possibly inside the tank) indicates the manufacturing date of that plumbing fixture. You can approximate the age of the house then since usually toilets are shipped out to houses within the year they are manufactured.

3.9 LEARN THE EXACT PROPERTY SIZE

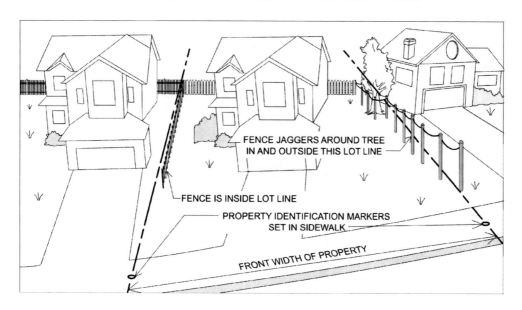

FENCE JAGGERS AROUND TREE
IN AND OUTSIDE THIS LOT LINE

FENCE IS INSIDE LOT LINE

PROPERTY IDENTIFICATION MARKERS
SET IN SIDEWALK

FRONT WIDTH OF PROPERTY

Fig. 3.9

Learn the exact property size and the boundary locations. Sometimes

property lines do not follow perimeter fences. Perhaps a land survey was

made for the home whereby survey "stakes" and "benchmarks" have been set

about the site which actually identify the whereabouts of the lot lines.

3.10 LEARN WHO OWNS THE FENCES

Fig. 3.10

Ask the seller who owns all the perimeter fences. Are they a part of the seller's property or could they have been paid for by the neighbors? Perhaps one or more fences are being shared with the neighbor(s) . You will need to know this since these exterior improvements will require maintenance.

3.11 DEFINE ITEMS INCLUDED WITH THE HOUSE SALE

Fig. 3.11

Determine exactly which appliances, equipment and furnishings are a part of the seller's property and included along with the property sale. Some sellers agree to the above illustrated example items to remain with the house, while others do not. And here are two more examples:

The telephone instruments inside the house which control the driveway's security gate do not stay with the house, nor does the security alarm system which is being leased.

3.12 LEARN WHAT ITEMS ARE NOT IN USE

THE DOORBELL IN THIS ILLUSTRATION IS INOPERATIVE.

Fig. 3.12

For instance, a doorbell.

Perhaps it has NO HOOKUP at the present time.

-or-

Perhaps it is presently DISCONNECTED and, thus, not operative. For instance, many homeowners need to reconnect their bathroom exhaust fans they disconnected because they could not tolerate the noise they produce.

-or-

Perhaps the item is just INEFFECTIVE.

Question the seller about what is not being used.

3.13 WHEN THE SELLER REPORTS INOPERATIVE EQUIPMENT

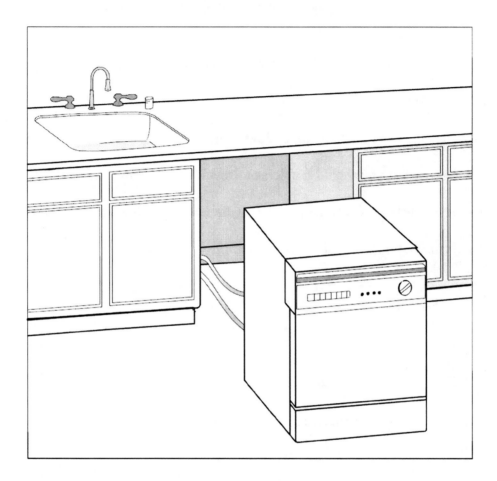

Fig. 3.13

When the seller advises you of a faulty appliance and makes no claims about it, consider getting a separate estimate of repair from an appliance repairman. If you feel that the estimate is much too costly, perhaps you should request that the seller have the appliance carted away before closing so you won't be faced with substantial removal costs.

3.14 LEARN WHAT'S NEW TO THE HOME

Learn what's new to the home and have the seller furnish you with the bills of sale for those items. As an example, newer kitchen appliances might have guarantees or possible implied warranties. Sometime later the bills of sale could assist you should problems arise with those items. Look at the purchase dates to see that the possible guarantees are still in effect and check whether they could be transferred to you.

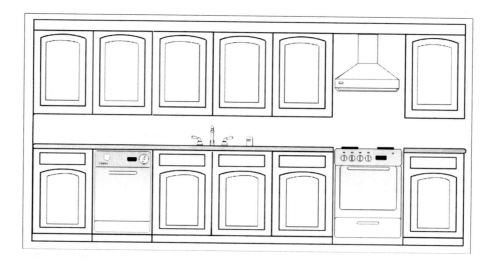

Fig. 3.14

In the above illustration, the seller had replaced an old dishwasher and a stove just a few months back and knows that the new appliances are guaranteed up to one year for both himself and for the purchaser of his home.

3.15 LEARN THE EXTENT OF HOME'S CENTRAL AIR CONDITIONING

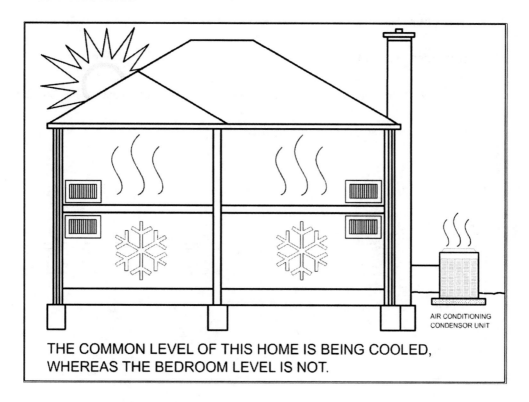

THE COMMON LEVEL OF THIS HOME IS BEING COOLED, WHEREAS THE BEDROOM LEVEL IS NOT.

AIR CONDITIONING CONDENSOR UNIT

Fig. 3.15

Realize that many homes do not have air conditioning. In those homes which reportedly are centrally air conditioned, the purchaser should determine exactly which rooms are cooled. You might be surprised to learn that the climate cooling system only serves one floor of the house or, perhaps, merely a portion of one floor.

3.16 IS THE HOUSE BURGLAR-SAFE?

A burglar alarm system connected to the police station is helpful as a security measure, but not all homes are so equipped. That's why it is so important to think out all the weak security links of your prospective home so that you could do something about them.

Example:

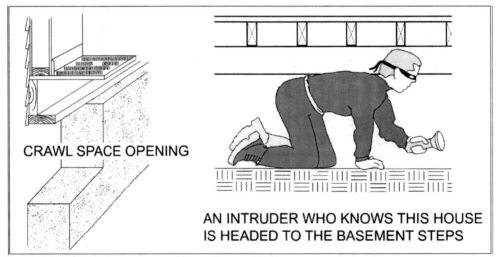

CRAWL SPACE OPENING

AN INTRUDER WHO KNOWS THIS HOUSE IS HEADED TO THE BASEMENT STEPS

Fig. 3.16

There is no security alarm system associated with the above illustrated house. Realize that an intruder could enter the house through the exterior wall's crawl space opening which then leads to the basement steps or to a floor hatch opening. In fact, the intruder could more easily gain access to the interior of the dwelling through the house's rear door pet opening.

3.17 LEARN IF SECURITY SIGN INDICATES ALARM SYSTEM

Fig. 3.17

Signs in front yards and decals placed in front windows which indicate the presence of security alarm systems are often used as deterrents to discourage would-be intruders from illegally entering the houses that have them. Check the home you are considering to buy to see whether it has these signs and, if so, whether the house is actually provided with a fully operative security system. Ask the seller about this.

Chapter 4

VARIOUS CONSTRUCTION

CHARACTERISTICS

This chapter was written to acquaint you with various characteristics of home construction. Not all characteristics are necessarily good nor are all necessarily bad, but they have been presented to you so that they will become meaningful to you when you come across them.

4.1 STEEPLY SLOPED DRIVEWAYS

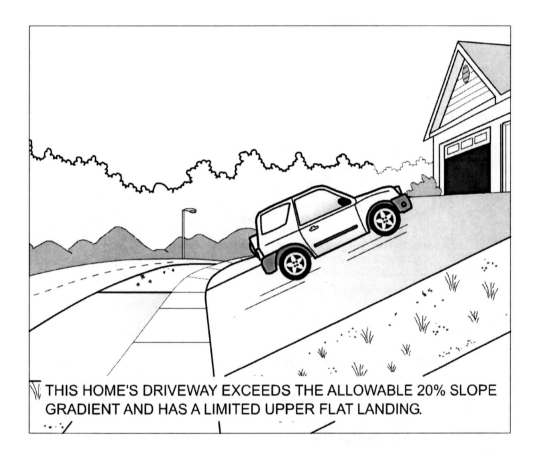

THIS HOME'S DRIVEWAY EXCEEDS THE ALLOWABLE 20% SLOPE
GRADIENT AND HAS A LIMITED UPPER FLAT LANDING.

Fig. 4.1

To drive up or down a home's steeply sloped driveway, particularly on
icy pavement, can be both difficult and dangerous. Building codes might
limit driveways to have up to a 20% gradient, but additionally in having
transitions of lesser slope pitches along their top and bottom lengths.

4.2 TREES NEARBY HOUSES COULD CAUSE DAMAGE

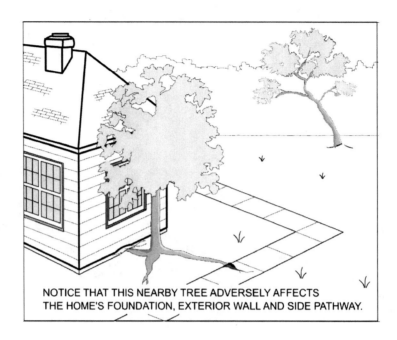

NOTICE THAT THIS NEARBY TREE ADVERSELY AFFECTS
THE HOME'S FOUNDATION, EXTERIOR WALL AND SIDE PATHWAY.

Fig. 4.2

Mature, towering trees which are located next to or nearby houses can cause all sorts of property damage. These damages might include uprooting damage, structural damage resulting from tree leaning or fall action, downward foundation movement caused by soil subsidence when tree roots have absorbed lots of moisture from the soil as well as tree root fracture and penetration damage to underground pipes. In fact, the latter damage can eventually further lead to possible blockage of underground pipes. Because of this, consider checking whether your homeowner's insurance policy would compensate you in the event of losses from such surrounding trees.

4.3 STUCCO USED AS A WALL SURFACE MATERIAL

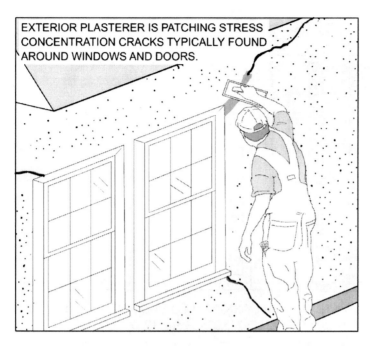

EXTERIOR PLASTERER IS PATCHING STRESS CONCENTRATION CRACKS TYPICALLY FOUND AROUND WINDOWS AND DOORS.

Fig. 4.3

Stucco can serve as a good material to surface exterior walls of houses. It has the advantage of being applied to wide, uninterrupted areas of the building in a variety of textures and colors. However, care must be exercised to patch and repair cracks and holes which develop in the siding to help stop distress growth there in addition to helping obstruct the possibility of insect and moisture penetration into the building.

Note that homebuyers of existing stucco houses face the risk of purchasing homes with wood rot /or mold inside exterior walls. This is because former homeowners might have left their patch maintenance work unattended. After all, why bother fixing walls if there are no outward indications of rot apparent? Indeed, when indications of structural rot damage become evident, or when the walls are probed or opened, then this possible damage can be found.

4.4 WOOD WINDOWS VS. METAL WINDOWS

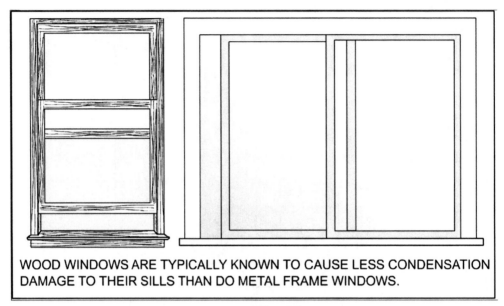

WOOD WINDOWS ARE TYPICALLY KNOWN TO CAUSE LESS CONDENSATION DAMAGE TO THEIR SILLS THAN DO METAL FRAME WINDOWS.

Fig. 4.4

Besides the warm look of wooden windows, these windows are actually considered to be "warmer" windows for they transmit less heat and cold loss through them than do metal windows.

What's more about wood windows is that there tends to be less frequent maintenance needed to paint or repair their window sills which might become damaged by window condensation water like metal windows often do.

4.5 CASEMENT AND JALOUSIE WINDOWS - OFTEN NOT SO AIRTIGHT

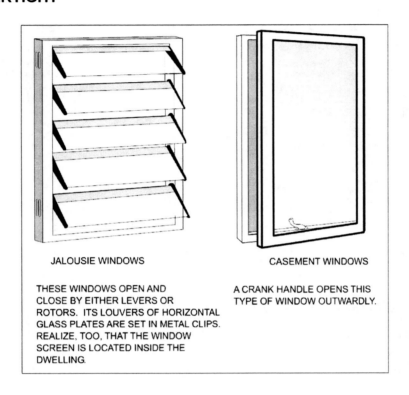

JALOUSIE WINDOWS

THESE WINDOWS OPEN AND CLOSE BY EITHER LEVERS OR ROTORS. ITS LOUVERS OF HORIZONTAL GLASS PLATES ARE SET IN METAL CLIPS. REALIZE, TOO, THAT THE WINDOW SCREEN IS LOCATED INSIDE THE DWELLING.

CASEMENT WINDOWS

A CRANK HANDLE OPENS THIS TYPE OF WINDOW OUTWARDLY.

Fig. 4.5

If you are interested in a house that has jalousie windows, you should know that many of these windows do not close well enough to be considered airtight and, hence, transmit heat and cold loss through them. Casement windows, on the other hand, frequently warp and, consequently, don't always close properly, either. In fact, the ones which are significantly warped cannot be straightened out, but will have to be replaced instead.

Moreover, jalousies don't offer ready exit egress routes through them like double hung or horizontal sliding glass windows do in the event of fire or other emergencies.

4.6 SLAB-ON-GROUND HOUSES

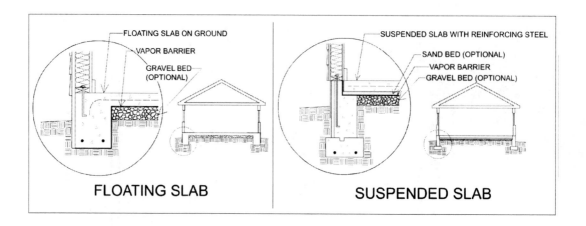

Fig. 4.6

"Slab-on-ground" or (also called) "slab-on-grade" houses have no basements and no crawl spaces that run beneath them.

For the popular 'floating' slab variety, which is used on favorably drained soils, a bed of crushed rock or gravel is prepared on the ground and then covered with a moisture barrier of polyethylene sheeting before the slab is poured. A typical slab is 4 inches in thickness and thickened more at the house footings that are monolithically poured with the slab. Note that with the 'suspended slab' type, however, the slab is not poured together with the foundation walls, but separately. In fact, the latter-mentioned slab sits atop these walls.

Note, too, that some plumbing piping might run below the floor slab's surface. Indeed, should leakage occur from this plumbing, repair might involve breaking up some areas of the floor slab.

4.7 'RAISED' FOUNDATION HOUSES

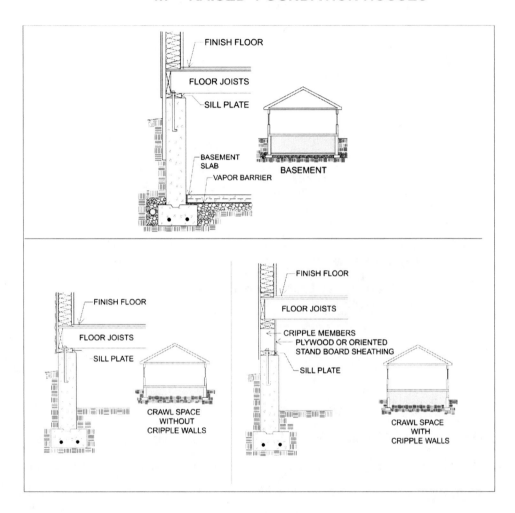

Fig. 4.7

Houses having a full basement, a crawl space, upper and lower crawl spaces (the latter on hillsides), or possibly a combination of underfloor basement and crawl space locations are considered to be houses built on "raised foundations." Note that with any such combinations of underfloors, plumbing is generally accessible.   Know what kind of underfloor exists under your prospective home!

4.8 SUMP PUMP ONLY CONTROLS BASEMENT FLOODING

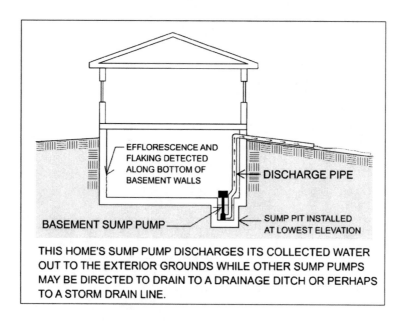

EFFLORESCENCE AND FLAKING DETECTED ALONG BOTTOM OF BASEMENT WALLS

DISCHARGE PIPE

BASEMENT SUMP PUMP

SUMP PIT INSTALLED AT LOWEST ELEVATION

THIS HOME'S SUMP PUMP DISCHARGES ITS COLLECTED WATER OUT TO THE EXTERIOR GROUNDS WHILE OTHER SUMP PUMPS MAY BE DIRECTED TO DRAIN TO A DRAINAGE DITCH OR PERHAPS TO A STORM DRAIN LINE.

Fig. 4.8

When you detect a sump pump in the basement of a house, it might reflect that the home's underfloor location suffers from a chronic water penetration problem; but the sump pump could also have been provided to control occasional basement flooding, or merely to get rid of some collected water in the underfloor during periods of heavy rains. The pump doesn't arrest the entry of water into the basement or underfloor crawl space although, perhaps, corrective drainage/possible regrading and waterproofing the basement would. What's also important to remember here is the fact that a serious water seepage condition that becomes neglected can adversely affect concrete, concrete block or other masonry foundation walls by flake-deteriorating them.

Sump pumps should be demonstrated to your satisfaction before closing to see that they work well. Still, however, there are risks of basement flooding taken with the use of these pumps since they run on electricity that may go out during stormy weather.

4.9 STEEPLY BUILT STEPS

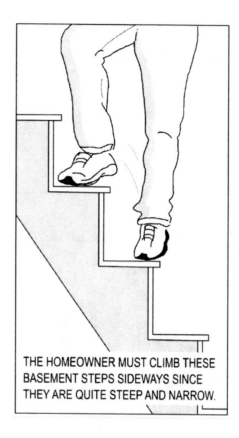

THE HOMEOWNER MUST CLIMB THESE
BASEMENT STEPS SIDEWAYS SINCE
THEY ARE QUITE STEEP AND NARROW.

Fig. 4.9

Realize that in many older homes, steps which lead to basements and attics are found to be quite steep and narrow. Therefore, be careful when climbing up or going down such steps. Be sure to inform all family members and visitors of this condition before they use them.

4.10 NO DIRECT ACCESS ROUTES FROM INSIDE THE HOUSE

Do not be surprised to find that a house lacks interior access routes to certain locations of the dwelling as one might normally expect for convenience.

Example:

Fig. 4.10

In the above illustration there are no direct access routes to the example home's basement, attic space or to the garage from inside the house. To gain access to these locations, the homeowner must go outside the house to enter them.

4.11 KITCHEN'S LOCATION POSES EXTRA CHORE

A house whose kitchen has been situated at a higher elevation than the garage and the home's entry poses an added chore for shoppers to bring bags of grocery items up to the kitchen. Here's an example:

Fig 4.11

In the picture, the homeowner finds that it is quite an effort for her to climb up the flight of steps to the kitchen either from within or from without while carrying heavy grocery packages she just purchased.

4.12 OLD REMAINING APPLIANCES

Fig. 4.12

The appliances which stay with the house in the illustrated example kitchen are old appliances. Often, appliance repairmen cannot get parts for old appliances and, consequently, they cannot be repaired because of this. Note that even when parts can be obtained, they frequently are more costly than the worth of the appliance.

4.13 BEDROOM UTILIZES SLIDING GLASS DOOR

Fig. 4.13

Some bedrooms lack windows but, instead, have been provided with sliding glass doors. As such, when fresh air is desired in those rooms, the sliding doors must be opened. What's considered to be unfavorable about this by many from a security standpoint is the use of sliding screen doors during evening and night hours.

4.14 KNOB AND TUBE WIRING IS OLD, EARLY WIRING

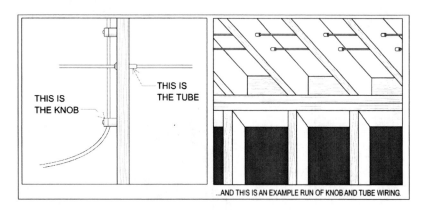

THIS IS
THE TUBE

THIS IS
THE KNOB

...AND THIS IS AN EXAMPLE RUN OF KNOB AND TUBE WIRING.

Fig. 4.14

Before today's plastic sheathed cable or flexible armored cable had been used to wire up houses, the early system of house electrical wiring was comprised of 2 individual strands of wire that run parallel to and closeby one another. This wiring is known as 'knob and tube wiring' and it was held secure to the house's framework with knob insulators and tubes made of porcelain. It might still be (wholly or partially) used in the older house you are considering to buy.

If it should be found that this type of wiring does, in fact, exist and is still being used, its condition should be carefully examined for torn, brittle or missing insulation along the cables, or for possible broken strands so as to prevent fire hazards from taking place or possible electrical shock. You don't have to change old, undamaged knob and tube wiring just because it exists.

4.15 INSUFFICIENT NUMBER OF OUTLETS IN OLDER HOUSES

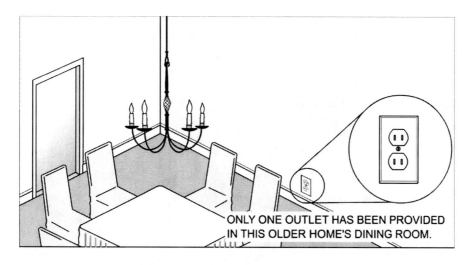

ONLY ONE OUTLET HAS BEEN PROVIDED
IN THIS OLDER HOME'S DINING ROOM.

Fig. 4.15

When you are searching for general purpose electrical outlets in a room and can't readily find one, you will then probably realize that you're in an older home and will likely want to budget for the cost of more "convenience outlets."

For today's homes there is one outlet required for every 12 feet of long wall space. For a shorter length wall 2 feet in length or longer, an outlet is required to be located along that wall. Also, an outlet should be located within 6 feet of a door. Outlets are normally found to start 1 foot up from the floor. Electrical codes offer these rules as their minimum requirements. But note for your convenience, too, that you should locate closer spacing of outlets over kitchen counter backsplashes to serve small appliances.

4.16 USE OF ORDINARY EXTENSION CORDS

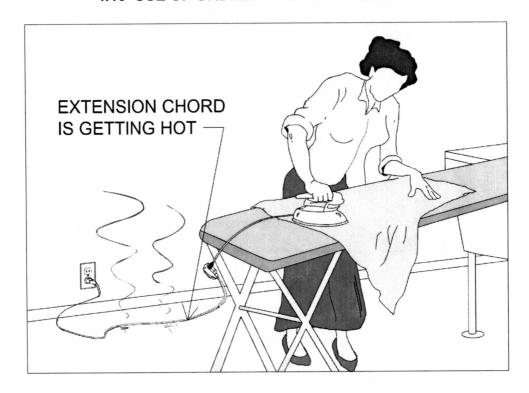

EXTENSION CHORD
IS GETTING HOT

Fig. 4.16

Common extension cords contain a normally small size diameter wire. Such wiring can overheat when carrying more amperes than it is intended for and can consequently cause a fire. In fact, ordinary extension cords are normally not recommended for use on such example appliances as irons and toasters. Homeowners tend to use extension cords when few electrical outlets are available in a room.

4.17 OLDER OUTLETS AND THEIR WIRING

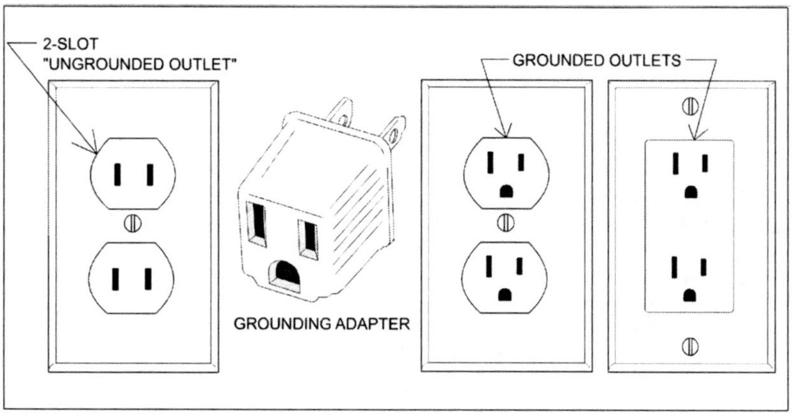

Fig. 4.17

Modern electrical convenience outlets installed in houses of today are 120 volt receptacles of the 3-hole variety. They accept 3 prong plugs and are known as "grounded" outlets. The 2-slot "ungrounded" outlets which are found in older houses are also 120 volt receptacles.

Whenever the 2-slot outlets are needed to serve an electrical tool, a 120 volt room air conditioner or other such appliances having 3 prong plugs, the installation of a grounding adapter then becomes required. This way, the tool or appliance that gets plugged into the adapter becomes grounded to earth. This is applicable, however, for houses that have 3 wire circuits. In fact, if the house has 3 wire circuits and 2 slot type outlets, one might consider replacing the old kind of outlets with the newer 3 hole type so as to avoid the use of outlet adapters altogether.

Upon observation, if it should be determined that the older home you are considering to purchase merely has 2 wire circuits instead as many old houses do, you may be faced with the prospect of having each of the outlets where the use of 3 prong plugs are needed re-wired. Conversion of the 2 slot receptacles to 3 hole receptacles does no good in this case.

4.18 GROUND FAULT INTERRUPTERS PROVIDE SAFETY

Fig. 4.18

Ground fault interrupters are electrical devices which help to protect people against the possibility of getting shocked through current leakage to ground. They do this when current leakage is detected by shutting off the electrical power to circuits or to receptacles controlled by them within a split second of time.

If, for example, one were to inadvertently or unknowingly attempt to retrieve a working electric toaster or hair blower that happened to accidentally fall into a sink basin that is filled with water, that person could badly suffer from a 'ground fault' shock without ground fault interrupter protection. Indeed, in some severe wet situations, such shocks could even be fatal.

The two main ground fault interrupter devices found today are the G.F.I. type circuit breaker and the G.F.I. outlet receptacle. The former being in an electrical panel offers protection to a circuit (such as the circuit breaker for a swimming pool or spa light), while the latter offers protection to that particular outlet and possibly some more outlets, too. You can recognize G.F.I.s by their little 'test' and 'reset' buttons.

In new homes, ground fault interrupters are required, for example, for those outlets nearby kitchen and bathroom sinks, for garage-located outlets, for outside outlets, as part of a swimming pool or spa light circuit breaker, and to control an inside tub spa motor, etc. Many homeowners of older homes have replaced their conventional outlets located nearby sinks with them already.

4.19 EVAPORATIVE COOLER - GOOD FOR LOW HUMIDITY PLACES

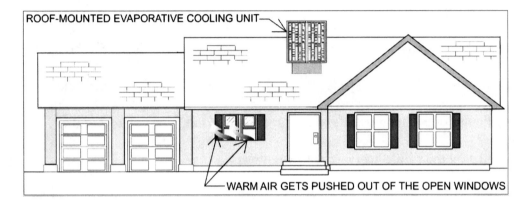

ROOF-MOUNTED EVAPORATIVE COOLING UNIT

WARM AIR GETS PUSHED OUT OF THE OPEN WINDOWS

Fig. 4.19

A roof-mounted evaporative cooler is being used to cool the illustrated house. This appliance, which is electrically operated, was chosen because the example house is located in the southwestern region of the United States where the humidity is normally low. An evaporative cooler cools on the principle of blowing outdoor air through water into the house.

Essentially, the unit is comprised of an absorbing pad, a blower, a motor and a pump. During its operation the pump is used to keep the absorbing pad wet. The blower's job is to move outside air through the pad to the interior of the house. When the outside air passes through the pad, it evaporates the water whereby losing heat and enters the inside somewhat cooler. The directed cool air then pushes the warm air out through vents and windows that are left open.

4.20 INEFFICIENT COOLING REGISTERS NEAR THE FLOORS

COOLING SUPPLY REGISTER

Fig. 4.20

Central air conditioning duct registers are sometimes installed at or near the floors. This could be the case when the central air conditioning system was later introduced to the home. However, this is not typically a very efficient arrangement for cooling the dwelling simply because cold air doesn't rise. On hot summer days, cold air is really most necessary near or at the ceilings.

4.21 INEFFICIENT HEAT REGISTERS NEAR THE CEILINGS

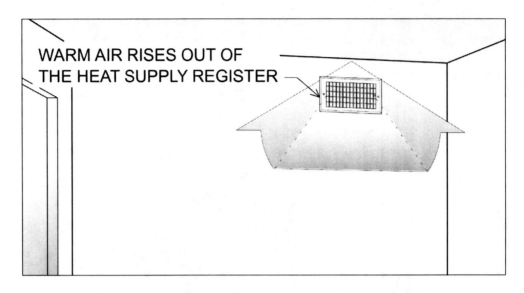

WARM AIR RISES OUT OF
THE HEAT SUPPLY REGISTER

Fig. 4.21

Forced warm air duct registers are sometimes installed close to or at

the ceilings. In fact, for homes in warm climates which are both heated and

cooled and use the same ducting for both purposes, this kind of installation is

typically chosen. Nonetheless, because warm air rises, the location of the

registers is not a very efficient arrangement for heating the home. In this

sense, separate air conditioning systems are more efficient.

4.22 DAMAGE CAUSED BY DUCT CONDENSATION

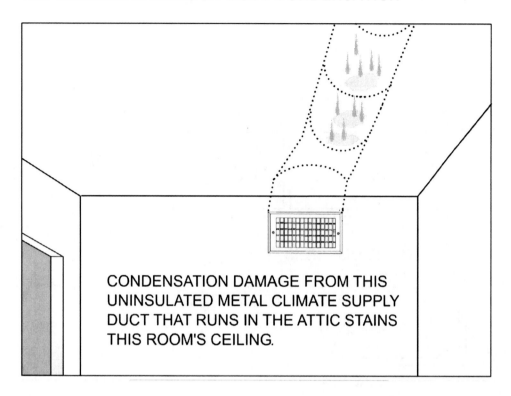

CONDENSATION DAMAGE FROM THIS UNINSULATED METAL CLIMATE SUPPLY DUCT THAT RUNS IN THE ATTIC STAINS THIS ROOM'S CEILING.

Fig. 4.22

Realize that there is a tendency for uninsulated metal climate ducts which are used for both heating and cooling the house to 'sweat.' This "sweat" or condensation formed around ducts decreases their life expectancy. What's more, the condensation might cause water stain damage to areas of ceilings and walls. Be out on the lookout for this!

4.23 ONE-ZONE HEATING - HIGHER TEMPERATURE UPSTAIRS

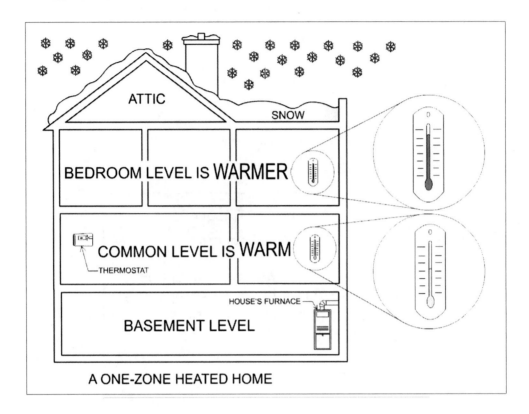

ATTIC

SNOW

BEDROOM LEVEL IS WARMER

COMMON LEVEL IS WARM

THERMOSTAT

HOUSE'S FURNACE

BASEMENT LEVEL

A ONE-ZONE HEATED HOME

Fig. 4.23

A home having one central heating plant which is activated and controlled by one thermostat is considered to be a 'one-zone' heated home. In such heat-controlled houses, don't be surprised to learn that there's higher temperatures upstairs than downstairs. This is typical for one-zone heated homes.

4.24 ELECTRIC BASEBOARD HEAT - CLEAN HEAT, BUT EXPENSIVE

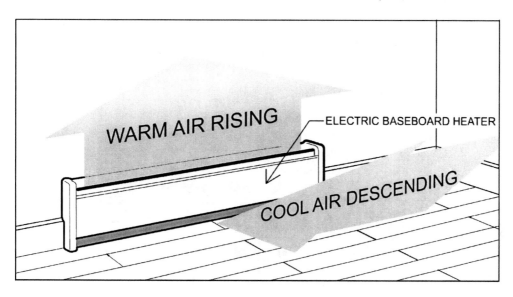

Fig. 4.24

Electric baseboard resistance heating consists of electric heater units that are fastened at wall base level around the house. It's the type of heating system that could be considered for use if no central heating is chosen. Indeed, that often means that there is no desire for heating ducts or plumbing pipes which normally serve furnaces to be installed inside houses. Baseboard heaters are favored for use in later added or finished off rooms for houses that do have central heating, but whose heating systems have not been extended to generate heat to these new rooms.

Basically what happens in such a heater's operation is that the unit's heating tube and fins heat up the cool air at the unit. As the warmed air rises, cool air travels down toward the floor to also become warmed.

Certainly heating up an entire house can be expensive energy-wise, but this type of heating is controllable by room and, moreover, produces uniform heat that's clean.

4.25 RADIANT HEAT - SLOW, EVEN HEAT

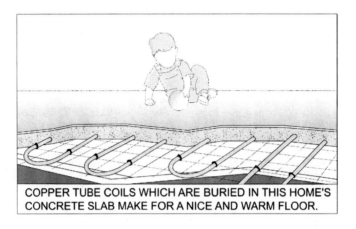

COPPER TUBE COILS WHICH ARE BURIED IN THIS HOME'S
CONCRETE SLAB MAKE FOR A NICE AND WARM FLOOR.

Fig. 4.25

Some popular means of generating radiant heat is from warmed water that circulates through copper tube coils which run in the ceilings or which are buried in the concrete floor slab. Also popular radiant heat is that which can be generated from grids of electrical resistance heat cables contained inside the ceilings.

Irrespective of which source of radiant heat the house has, radiant heat is known to spread evenly throughout rooms without producing noticeable drafty convection currents. However, since this type of heating system heats slowly, it does take a considerable lengthy time to warm up a rather chilly house. Additionally, should water leakage develop from the heating pipes, the floor or ceiling must be broken or torn open in order to fix the leak.

4.26 ELECTRIC HEAT PUMP - BEFITS WARM CLIMATES BETTER

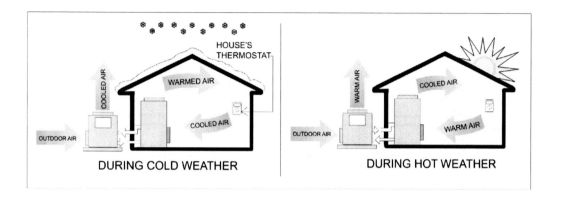

Fig. 4.26

Electric heat pumps are known to be efficient for they "move" heat rather than generate heat. In winter, a heat pump removes warmth from outside air and directs it to the interior of the home. This can be achieved since there is heat in air - even in cold air.

An electric resistance furnace generally costs more to heat up a cold home as do an electric radiant ceiling heating system or baseboard heaters. Remember, though, that when temperatures fall real low, expensive-to-run supplemental electric resistance heaters then work in the heat pumps. That's why it is more economical to operate heat pumps where climates are warm and temperatures seldom go down very low.

Note that the pump works like an air conditioner taking heat from inside air to the outside in summertime.

4.27 COOL FLOORS EXIST OVER UNHEATED GARAGES

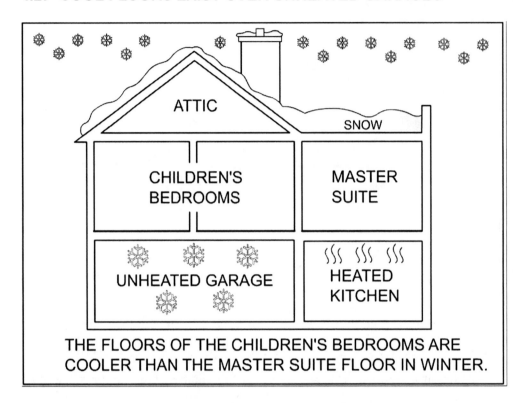

Fig. 4.27

Quite commonly, garages lack heating provision. Because of this, the floors in those rooms which are located directly over unheated garages become comparatively cooler than other floors which exist on the same level of the house. This becomes particularly noticeable in cold weather.

4.28 HOUSE IS IN A LIMITED STATE OF RENOVATION

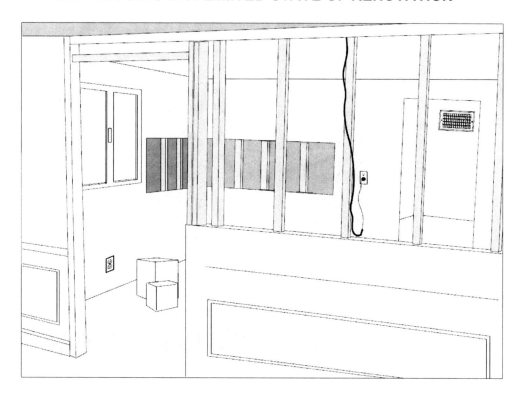

Fig. 4.28

If the house you are considering for purchase is in a limited state of renovation, it will require considerable work ahead. Because the problems with completing a renovation project are many, consider on-site general contracting management supervision. This should ultimately save you from getting "stressed out."

Chapter 5

ADVICE FOR BUYERS OF

NEW HOMES

This chapter is intended to offer advice specifically

to buyers of new homes.

5.1 WHAT THE BUILDER MAY NOT PROVIDE

Here is a list of some items that many builders do not provide:

a.   A furnace humidifier. (It's used to increase the relative humidity in the house since the inside air becomes rather dry when a forced warm air system is used);

b.   A mailbox;

c.   Storms and window screens;

d.   Perimeter fencing;

e.   A back patio;

f.   An underground lawn sprinkler system;

g.   A lawn, shrubbery and other landscaping;

h.   A washer and a dryer.

Some builders might consider these items as 'optional' items. So know exactly what items are included along with the sale of your new home.

5.2 AGREED ALLOWANCE FOR A NEW HOUSE

When builders bid on the construction of a new house after they have worked off plans and specifications which are incomplete or are not specific enough, they do this by making some stipulations and allowances. The allowance in an agreement with the builder is an estimate that the builder gives for what a certain construction item would cost. This dollar amount is made over and above the builder's fixed bid. Allowances are usually made for hardware items, cabinetry, finish flooring and electrical lighting fixtures as well as other finish items. With this cost estimate, the builder establishes his judgement of the total cost of the construction job.

Example 1:

The builder has allowed $750.00 over his bid for the cost of a dining room chandelier since the maker and model of the chandelier were not specified.

Example 2:

Because of an agreed allowance with the builder for the sum of $25,000.00, the purchaser provides the installation of all finish flooring.

5.3 WHAT BUILDERS NORMALLY GUARANTEE

A buyer of a new home should also request guarantees against defective workmanship and defects in materials on the following items:

    a.   Roofing;

    b.   Plumbing;

    c.   Electrical work;

    d.   Heating, ventilating and air conditioning work.

Usually builders offer buyers a one year guarantee on these items. Many builders provide a one year guarantee against building water seepage as well. You might note that a number of manufacturers of building materials provide longer than a one year guarantee on their products and so, for awhile, buyers are accordingly protected by these guarantees.

5.4 GET APPLIANCE GUARANTEES AND MANUALS

Fig. 5.1

Ask the builder to supply you with the manufacturers' guarantees for the appliances, the appliance instruction manuals and any instructional videos which come along with the appliances. In case the builder doesn't have them, demand that they be gotten from the suppliers or from the manufacturers directly.

5.5 GET NAMES OF SUPPLIERS AND SUBS

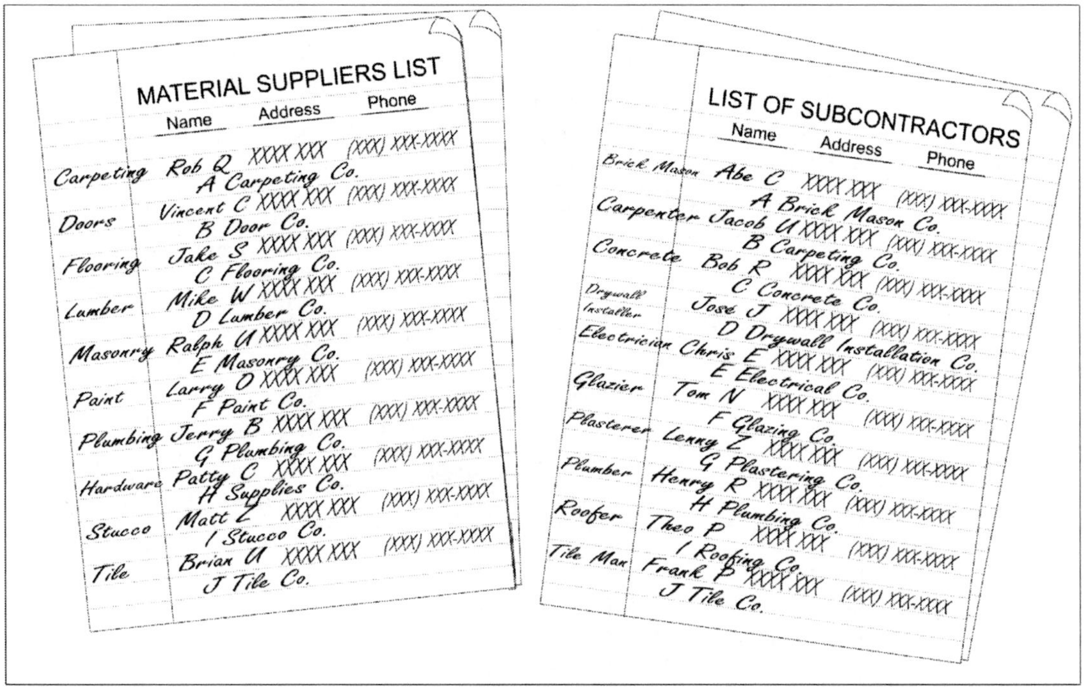

Fig. 5.2

Get the names of the material suppliers and subcontracting firms that were involved with the construction of the house. Get their telephone numbers and addresses, too. This information could prove to be helpful to you should the event of problems arise. That way, you do not need to go directly to the builder.

5.6 OBTAIN SAMPLE MATERIALS

Fig. 5.3

If you wish, request that the builder furnish you with samples of
roofing cover material, tiling, some wood and masonry, wallpaper, paint, stain
and carpeting. These samples just might come in handy to you in the future.

Chapter 6

INQUIRY GUIDE

Part of every complete pre-purchase home inspection includes the rite of asking questions. This chapter can serve as your guideline of sample questions that you may wish to inquire answers about.

6.1 INQUIRE ABOUT YOUR CONCERNS

Homebuyers should consider inquiring about some of the following concerns of interest:

a. determining whether mineral rights come along with the sale of the property;

b. learning whether there are any underground utilities and plumbing supply and waste lines which cross the home site to any of the neighboring properties;

c. more about the history and use of the site and additional information about the site's subdivision. For instance, was the property part of an orange or walnut grove?

d. determining whether the house has been later equipped with a new water main;

e. additional information about the adequacy of street drainage in the neighborhood, especially in front of the house;

f.   the cost of fire insurance for the house and learning whether it would be difficult to obtain. Ask if there has been any known fire to have occurred in the locality of the home. For instance, the known "Malibu Fire" burned the neighbor's house down. You may also wish to learn more about the extent of water spray action from the irrigation sprinklers present;

g.   more about the neighboring parcels of land, including what they have been zoned for and who owns them. For instance, the seller spoke of zoning for 2-family homes across the street from this house. Ask if there are any neighboring land parcels which are presently landlocked;

h.   more about the environmental locality of this dwelling. This includes, for example, determining with certainty whether the nearby electrical transformer vault, the not-too-distant utility pole and wiring pose any possible harmful health effects to the residents of the house such as during seismic activity or by means of possible radiation;

i.   additional information about the nearby water channel. For example, learn who cleans and maintains this channel. Ask, too, if water which runs along it attracts insects or emits odors;

j.   determining whether gnats or other flying insects frequent the home's yards where a multitude of such insects are noted to hover about the property;

k.   determining whether a vehicle has ever run into the home and, if so, learn exactly what damage did it do;

l.   determining whether the street storm drain in front of the house poses a safety hazard to small children for it has a wide unprotected opening. Learn, too, whether foul odors are emitted from this storm drain or whether it attracts insects at times;

m.   more about the lot size relative to the minimum size zoned lot permitted in the locality;

n. determining whether cable television is now possible in the neighborhood or, perhaps, will be possible in the near future;

o. learning whether the exterior tiles have been recently sealed;

p. determining that sewage which exits the house is done by gravity flow and does not require pumping through the waste lines. If this is so, is there a hermetically sealed pump to do this work;

q. determining whether it is required for the house to be connected to city sewers when they are installed along the street in front of the house;

r. determining the exact route of the home's sewer lines in exiting the home site;

s. why the street curb in front of the house has been marked with painted numerals;

t. learning of any possible encroachments;

u.   how the perimeter fences, walls and curbing run relative to the property lines. For example, one fence doesn't run straight, but juts to one side at its mid length;

v.   where the collected water from the outside area drains exit. Could it be to the drainage outlet in the street curb?

w.   determining whether the swimming pool has been equipped with overflow drains;

x.   determining whether the planter along the outside wall of the house has been waterproofed;

y.   learning whether the close-to-grade wood used in the construction of this home utilizes pressure-treated wood with an approved preservative, or is of a durable variety;

z.   determining whether anchor bolts have been used along mud sillplates to help secure the house framing (called the superstructure) to its respective foundation in the event of seismic activities. The finished walls prohibit examination of this condition;

aa.   learning for what kind of pests does the extermination service treat against;

bb.   learning the age of the house's tile roof, including learning whether it has a new underlayment (since many homeowners of tile roofs merely replace the old underlayment and any damaged tiles);

cc.   determining whether tub, door and shower glazing as well as low-to-floor window and transom window glazing consist of safety tempered glazing which is appropriate for these glass sections;

dd.   how well secure is the climate control unit mounted upon the roof;

ee.   how well the mirrored panels have been fastened to the wall. Are they glue-adhesive fastened?

ff.   determining whether the tile finish floors become hazardously slippery when wet;

gg.   verifying the existence of vinyl asbestos tile finish flooring in this home. A laboratory can make a positive identification of it;

hh.   learning whether the mineral asbestos is present in all acoustical ceiling spray material. Again, a laboratory can make a positive identification of it;

ii.   learning whether acoustical ceiling spray, which was reportedly recently removed from the house, was performed by a certified or licensed asbestos abatement contractor (if asbestos was, in fact, found to be present in that acoustical spray material);

jj.   additional information about the community's shared well water supply system that the house is connected onto. This was provided by a private company with each homeowner having been granted transferable shares of well usage. The home's private well was disconnected and is not in use;

kk.   determining whether the efflorescence which was seen in the fireplace chamber reflects a chimney water penetration problem possibly because of faulty flashing. A chimney contractor/or a roofer will have to check this out;

ll.   determining whether the self-cleaning oven requires exterior venting and, if this is so, learn whether it has been so equipped;

mm.   determining if there is pre-wiring already installed underground to serve an outside post lamp. If so, ask then if all that would be required is the post lamp itself;

nn.   what the timer controls;

oo.   what some electrical switches control. Are some switches extra ones that have not been connected to control anything?

pp.   determining whether or not the firm which architecturally designed the home or the home's remodeling work is a duly licensed architectural firm and, further, had been engaged to oversee the construction;

qq.   determining whether belonging to the local homeowners association is mandatory or not;

rr.   (new home) determining whether any possible design changes conform to the issued plans (which should, of course, be approved plans). If not, then request to see possible final amended documentation or addenda for any possible changes. For instance, the builder spoke of a shared connecting bathroom to serve two bedrooms but, instead, it was later decided after the plans were building department - approved that each bedroom was to have its own bathroom and was so accordingly built that way. The building department inspector 'red-lined in' and signed off this change at the job site;

ss.   (new home) determining whether there is a longer period than one year guarantee on the roof;

tt.   (new home) for what length of time is the structural integrity of the house guaranteed for;

uu.   (new home) determining if the builder offers guarantees relative to paint and cabinet touch-ups;

vv.   (condominium) learning whether the homeowners of the building are involved in any possible existing litigation matters or other possible action taken with respect to possible building defects and deficiencies;

ww.   (condominium) requesting verification of the fact that the common walls which separate the apartment units are of the correct fire-rated wall variety;

xx.   (condominium) and determining whether guarantees exist for the building's fire sprinkler system and elevators, or possibly whether there are service contracts to maintain them.

Chapter 7

LIMITATIONS ON YOUR

INSPECTION

Simply, the greater amount of time that is spent in conducting your home inspection, the more will be your findings. I strongly recommend investing in the time to have a thorough pre-purchase examination performed. Of course, it must be realized that limitations do exist in every inspection as to what can be examined and what cannot. Relative to this, in the following pages you will see some 'whats' which were not done, some 'hows', some 'whens' and some 'whys.'

7.1 DEMONSTRATE APPLIANCES AND OTHER ITEMS

Be sure to demonstrate all equipment and appliances before closing - although, at times, this may not be possible because of weather or other conditions. The sample suggestions below might help you in your demonstration endeavors:

Exterior Drainage Devices: perhaps on a rainy day or possibly at best by simulating the flow of water by using a garden hose to check how effective is their water acceptance ability.

Underground Lawn Sprinkler System: in springtime since in cold weather in cold climates sprinkler systems are often kept winterized.

Automatic Garage Door Opener: by the use of its transmitters.

Air Conditioner: on a warm day since testing this type equipment during cold weather may not be possible below preset levels of temperature and because demonstrating in low temperatures can possibly cause damage to the equipment. The outdoor temperature should be warm for a meaningful demonstration.

Exhaust Fans: when they are re-connected or re-opened.

Fireplace Gas Main: without the cap on its line.

Light Fixtures: when their faulty or missing bulbs are replaced.

Refrigerator: that was off during the home inspection. A refrigerator takes a considerable amount of time to reach its ultimate temperature. Ask the owner to turn on this appliance a day before the demonstration.

Security Alarm System: by the owner or by the owner's security alarm company. During the demonstration determine which apertures and entrances are 'trapped' secure, which locations are 'shunted' and learn if the smoke detectors are a part of the system.

Self-cleaning Oven: with sufficient time because it takes a lengthy time for a self-cleaning "pyrolytic" oven to clean itself.

Swimming Pool and Spa Pump Motor, Filter and Heater Equipment: in warm weather when the pool and spa are in operating condition and are no longer winterized. Or, perhaps, merely the heaters demonstrated when their gas pilot lights are turned on.

7.2 DEMONSTRATION LIST WHEN ELECTRICITY IS OFF

During the home inspection, if the electricity is off or if there is no electrical service available, one could not completely determine general electrical problems and demonstrate the following:

[] the outlet and fixture performances

[] the air conditioning system(s)

[] the automatic overhead garage door opener(s)

[] the electric doorbell

[] the electric _____ heating system or the furnace(s)/fan(s)

[] the electric heater fan in the _____

[] the electric hot water heater

[] the furnace emergency switch operation (if one exists)

[] the exhaust fan(s) of the _____

[] the heat lamp(s)

[] the intercom

[] the electric oven

[] the range hood

[] the trash compactor

[] the dishwasher

[] other remaining appliances

[] and other electrical equipment

7.3 DEMONSTRATION LIST WHEN GAS IS OFF

If the gas is off, or if there is no gas available during the home inspection, one could not determine the hot water temperature(s) [should domestic water be heated by gas-fired hot water tank(s)], nor determine whether gas odors exist. One also could not demonstrate the following:

[] the gas-fired furnace(s) and heating (including

    the thermostat(s) for heating)

[] the gas furnace's hot water heating capability

[] the gas-fired hot water heater

[] the gas barbecue

[] the _____ fireplace gas main(s)/loglighter(s)

[] the gas cooktop/range

[] the gas wall oven

[] the gas dryer

[] the heating capability of the swimming pool/spa

    heater

[] the gas heater in the _____

[] and the outside gas lantern

7.4 DEMONSTRATION LIST WHEN THERE IS NO WATER

If there is no water to the house during the home inspection, one could not observe the water pressure, nor could one demonstrate the following:

[] the operation of the plumbing fixtures

[] the hot water heating capability

[] the dishwasher

[] the washing machine

[] the laundry drain

[] the swimming pool equipment

[] the underground lawn sprinkler system

[] the well

7.5 LOCATE THE UTILITY METERS

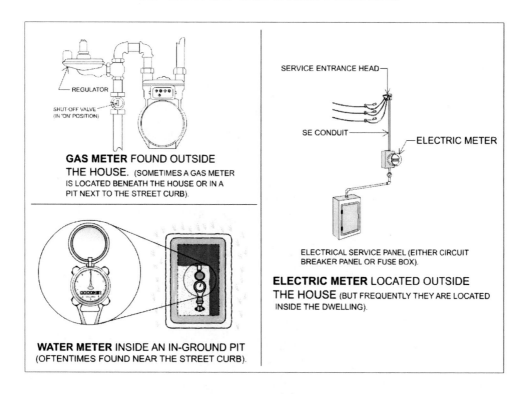

Fig. 7.1

Learn how to identify your utility meters and then locate them.

7.6 HAVE THE WELL WATER CHECKED

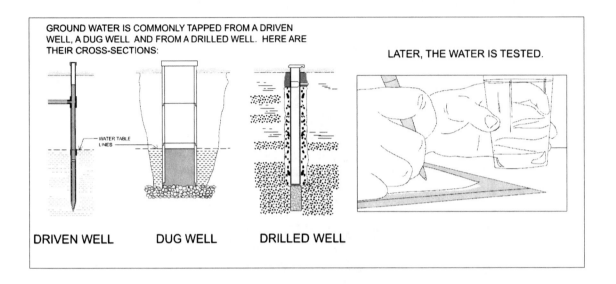

GROUND WATER IS COMMONLY TAPPED FROM A DRIVEN WELL, A DUG WELL AND FROM A DRILLED WELL. HERE ARE THEIR CROSS-SECTIONS:

LATER, THE WATER IS TESTED.

WATER TABLE LINES

DRIVEN WELL   DUG WELL   DRILLED WELL

Fig. 7.2

Contact a qualified local water testing laboratory to determine whether the well water is potable. Ask that they check out the water's mineral and bacteria content.

7.7 EXAMINE HOME'S INDEPENDENT SEWAGE DISPOSAL SYSTEM

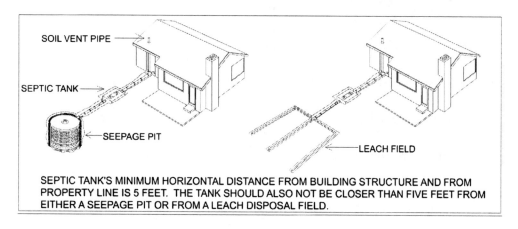

SOIL VENT PIPE

SEPTIC TANK

SEEPAGE PIT

LEACH FIELD

SEPTIC TANK'S MINIMUM HORIZONTAL DISTANCE FROM BUILDING STRUCTURE AND FROM PROPERTY LINE IS 5 FEET. THE TANK SHOULD ALSO NOT BE CLOSER THAN FIVE FEET FROM EITHER A SEEPAGE PIT OR FROM A LEACH DISPOSAL FIELD.

Fig. 7.3

Before one examines the home's independent sewage disposal system, learn exactly what the system actually consists of and where it is located. For example, does it consist of one or more septic tanks connected to leach field(s) that are located outside the house (and not beneath the house)? Are the tank(s) and disposal field set back properly? (Some are not. See the minimum defined setbacks in the sketch above of which distances might vary with local codes). Also, learn the gallon size capacity of each tank and whether it conforms to the minimum capacities recommended by your local building code. (Tanks are normally sized in accordance to the number of bedrooms the house has. For a two bedroom house there may be a 750 gallon capacity tank; for three bedrooms, 900 gallon size tank; for four bedrooms, 1,000 gallon size; and for five bedrooms, a minimum of 1,250 gallons might be the required capacity size tank).

What would be helpful in this investigation would be to obtain the possible layout plans for this matter, the permit(s) and other possible prepared documentation, including the bill of sale for this work. If possible, view within the cleanout or inspection openings. A "scum stick" and a "sludge stick" measure scum and sludge levels, respectively. These measurements together with a special chart table help determine whether the tank needs to be pumped. Lastly, ask the age of the septic system and whether the tank has been cleaned out of late.

7.8 EXAMINE THE FLOORS UNDER THE CARPETS

Before closing, ask the seller for permission to move back area rugs and view the floors under the carpets. Doing this will allow you to see the type of floors being covered over and to discover possible existing floor problems. Here's an example:

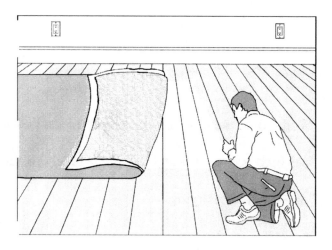

Fig. 7.4

This purchaser noticed the yellowing effect of the bleached wood finish floor beneath the area rug's base mat that he just lifted. In another room, cork material was found used under the center area rug.   And, finally, slab cracking was detected under the lifted portion of the bedroom closet's wall-to-wall carpet.

7.9 EXAMINE IT ALL

Make sure that all areas of the house have been thoroughly examined prior to the time of closing. Of course, in reality, this can't be completely achieved in a normal home inspection for there are areas which are inaccessible and unobservable. The sample suggestions below will help you in your continued examination:

Remainder of the Garage: after the material has been removed.

Some Venting/Flue Work out to the Exterior: including for the fuel-fired furnace, the fuel-fired hot water heater, the range hood fan, all other exhaust fans, and for clothes drying.

Remainder of the Attic: look for evidence of past fires, evidence of roof leaks, any condensation damage, the structural integrity of the rest of the framing members and any evidences of rodent and termite infestation.

Tub Plumbing Access: should there be one.

Viewing the Water and Waste Connections within the Plumbing Accesses provided for the Bathtubs: for their covers were painted and sealed shut.

The balance of the Underfloor Crawl Space: where ductwork, structural members in addition to plumbing and drain lines blocked access to view all areas.

Locating the Central Air Conditioning Condensate Line.

Locating the Climate Air Return Register.

Locating any Plumbing Waste Drainage Cleanouts.

Some Roof and Chimney Areas.

Other lengths of the Perimeter Fences: where they were largely covered by vegetative overgrowth/ such as on the neighboring sides.

Some Hillside Property: which had not been climbed.

7.10 RE-EXAMINE AFTER THE SNOW MELTS

When snow covers the exterior, re-examination of outside areas

becomes necessary.

Example:

Fig. 7.5

Because it snowed heavily during the inspection, details of the roof, the

sidewalk, the driveway and other exterior improvements could not be directly

examined. When the snow melts, the roof, the grounds and these

improvements will have to be carefully looked at.

7.11 AVOID RISKS WHEN DEMONSTRATIONS ARE NOT POSSIBLE

Up to the time when all appliances and items can be demonstrated and checked to your satisfaction, you could be taking a big risk. This is why it is so important to have everything demonstrated and be satisfied that all is in working order.

For example, if you should find that a furnace doesn't work properly after you move in, there may be a serious repair problem the cost of which might fall upon your shoulders. Hopefully you will not be faced with the prospect of the need for a new heating plant altogether, the cost of which is likely even higher.

If possible, evaluate the risk. A new furnace alone could be as much as $2,500.00 or higher. Try to protect yourself against the risk by requesting that that dollar amount evaluated be held in an escrow account until all details can be entirely evaluated. Note that if there are problems, the money would be available for repair; and if no problems are found, then that money would be given back to the seller of the home. Speak to your attorney about this.

PART II.

HIGHLIGHTS OF HOME

INSPECTION

Chapter 8

ELECTRICAL AND

LIGHTING CONCERNS

The basics of inspecting a home electrically involves determining what electrical service the house has and comparing it to the building's existing electrical load requirements; determining the kind and size of wiring that's being used in the home; and performing some simple circuit testing and evaluating circuits. There's more, such as spotting electrical hazards that pose fire or shock hazards. Lighting must be examined, too.

8.1 NEARBY LEANING UTILITY POLES

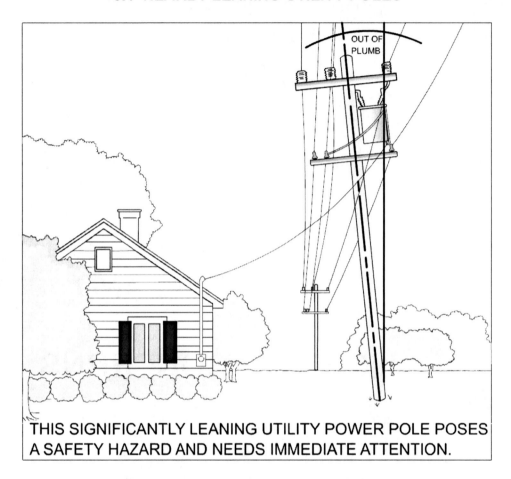

THIS SIGNIFICANTLY LEANING UTILITY POWER POLE POSES A SAFETY HAZARD AND NEEDS IMMEDIATE ATTENTION.

Fig. 8.1

Nearby significantly leaning utility poles can pose safety hazards. When one such pole is cited, the homeowner should call the utility company to further check the leaning pole and plumb and secure it as deemed necessary.

8.2 ELECTRICAL SERVICE LINES CROSS POOL

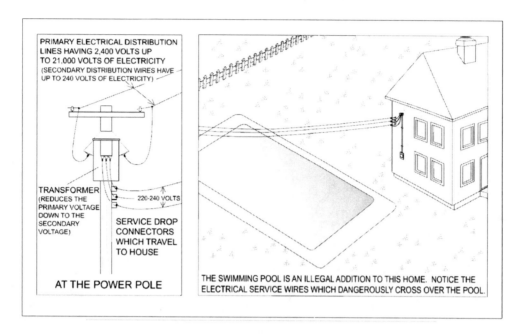

Fig. 8.2

Separate electrical service lines which cross a later added, non-permitted swimming pool or spa could be a real killer to a swimmer if one or more of these lines should snap and enter the pool or spa water. Electric companies may accept instead bundled service wires to run above pools and spas since, when they snap, there is much less chance of a voltage differential to occur to cause electrical shock.

8.3 FRAYED OVERHEAD SERVICE LINES

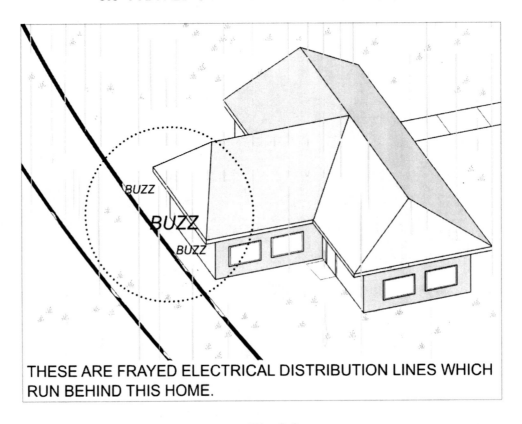

THESE ARE FRAYED ELECTRICAL DISTRIBUTION LINES WHICH RUN BEHIND THIS HOME.

Fig. 8.3

The homeowner should immediately call the local electric company to check out nearby overhead electrical lines that appear to be badly frayed so that the electric company's workmen can make corrective work measures as necessary. This includes attending to those electrical service lines which travel to the house.

8.4 LOW OVERHEAD ELECTRICAL SERVICE LINES

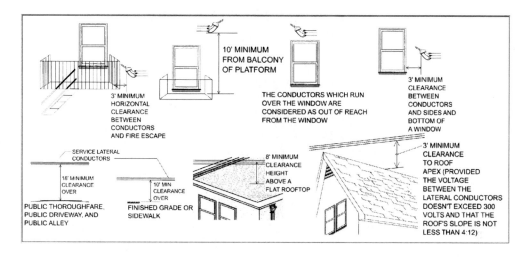

Fig. 8.4

Sometimes, incoming overhead electrical service lines offer dangerously low clearance height, although there are minimum required clearance heights for these lines. In fact, your local electrical code might specify a 12 feet clearance height for an electrical service drop above a home's driveway. The code might also specify their minimum clearance height of not less than 10 feet above the ground. Anything less than these heights pose safety hazards and either the electric company or an electrician would have to be called in to make the correction.

8.5 SMALL ELECTRIC SERVICE

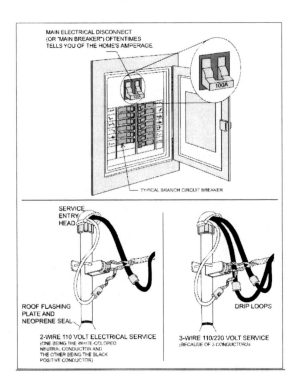

Fig. 8.5

A house's total electric service is dependent upon the size of the home and what electrical equipment it contains.

You can often determine what the house's electrical amperage service is by reading its amp rating on the electrical panel that's usually marked with it. The number of amps could also possibly be observed on the main circuit breaker or electrical disconnect. To learn of the home's voltage, see if there are 3 wires which enter the house (which are easily seen at an overhead service mask) for 110/220 volt service, or whether there are just a 2- wire entry that provides 110 volt service. Electricians identify the house's electrical service as "'x'- many wire, 'y'- many volt, 'z'- many amp, overhead or underground service."

An electrician could calculate the home's electrical load and compare it to the home's existing service. This is especially important to be done if the house was added onto or if the dwelling has had later electrical requirements introduced to it to serve major electrical appliances (such as an electric dryer or a self-cleaning oven) and equipment (such as central air conditioning, a sauna, or even an electric hot water heater).

Small or marginal service should be increased for such service could result in an electrical fire in the event the main breaker fails to trip. Hopefully the electrical service panel is not found warm when it is being test-touched. Even if the service is sufficient for the limited existing electrical requirements of the house, you may wish to increase the service if you have intentions of adding significant electrical loading, including to accommodate appliances and equipment that have been mentioned above.

8.6 NO ELECTRICAL MAIN DISCONNECT

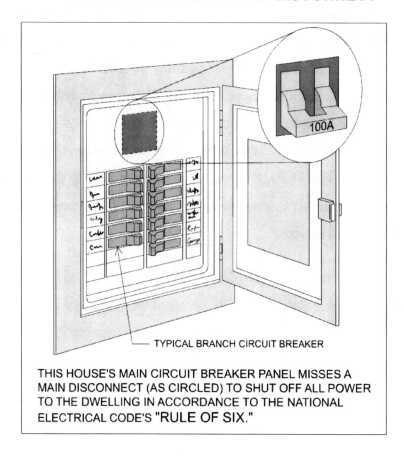

TYPICAL BRANCH CIRCUIT BREAKER

THIS HOUSE'S MAIN CIRCUIT BREAKER PANEL MISSES A
MAIN DISCONNECT (AS CIRCLED) TO SHUT OFF ALL POWER
TO THE DWELLING IN ACCORDANCE TO THE NATIONAL
ELECTRICAL CODE'S "RULE OF SIX."

Fig. 8.6

Some old circuit breaker panels with more than 6 circuit breakers have
not been equipped with a main breaker. The presence of a 'main' at the
service panel box is helpful and needed in an emergency. You can then shut
off all the electricity to the home in a hurry. Normally, a main circuit breaker
is not required for homes having 6 or lesser number of circuit divisions.

8.7 ACCESS TO THE ELECTRICAL MAIN DISCONNECT

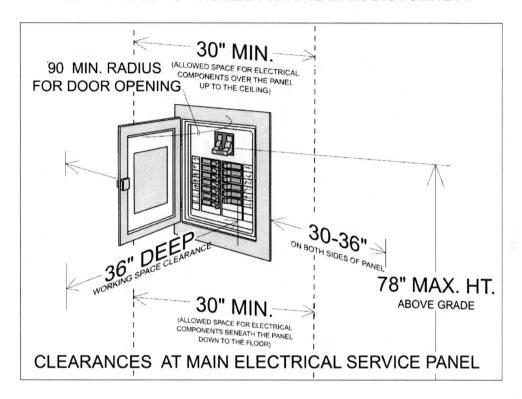

Fig. 8.7

Be sure that there is a 36 inch clear working space provided in front of the electrical service panel. Your local electrical code probably specifies that dimension as it likely does a 6'- 6" maximum height dimension above grade for the house's main electrical disconnect so that there is reasonable access to it. Indeed, it's smart not to build or store anything directly in front of this panel.

8.8 ELECTRICAL REMOTE DISCONNECT

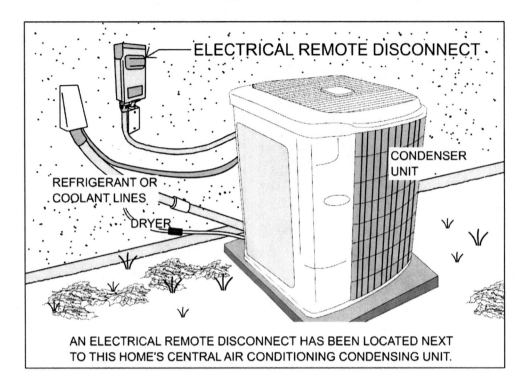

AN ELECTRICAL REMOTE DISCONNECT HAS BEEN LOCATED NEXT TO THIS HOME'S CENTRAL AIR CONDITIONING CONDENSING UNIT.

Fig. 8.8

An "electrical remote disconnect" should be found located nearby the central air conditioning condenser unit, but sometimes it is not. An air conditioning serviceman depends upon this disconnect to shut off the electrical power to this equipment so that he can safely work on the air conditioning system without risk of shock hazard, even if someone inside the house were to unknowingly attempt to activate the home's cooling system.

8.9 A HOUSE MUST BE ELECTRICALLY GROUNDED

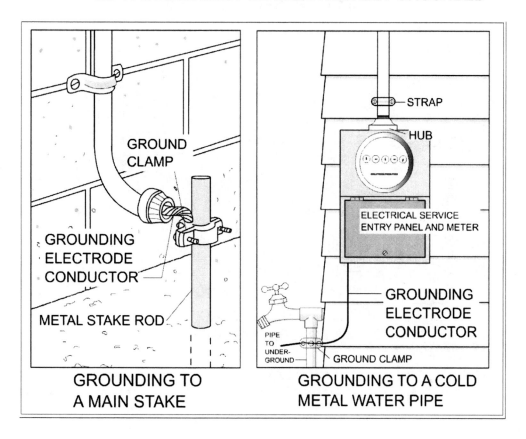

Fig. 8.9

A house is required to be electrically grounded. Usually electrical

grounding is by a "grounding conductor" (wire) that clamps onto a cold metal

water pipe. Another ground is a wire which connects onto a "stake" (metal

rod) that is driven into earth. The supplement rod is now required because of

the possibility of the use of plastic water pipes that some houses use today.

There could be a grounding problem when one feels a 'tingling' sensation

while touching an appliance.

8.10 UNDERGROUND WIRING

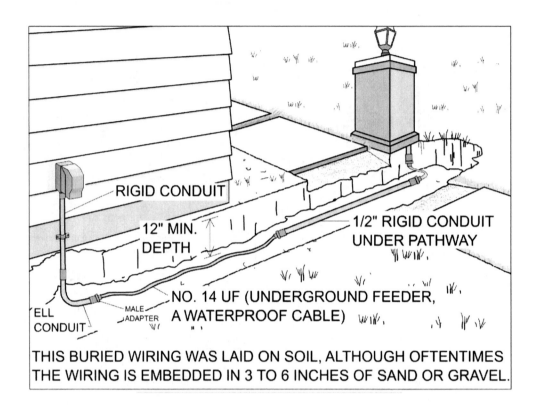

RIGID CONDUIT

12" MIN. DEPTH

1/2" RIGID CONDUIT UNDER PATHWAY

NO. 14 UF (UNDERGROUND FEEDER, A WATERPROOF CABLE)

ELL CONDUIT

MALE ADAPTER

THIS BURIED WIRING WAS LAID ON SOIL, ALTHOUGH OFTENTIMES THE WIRING IS EMBEDDED IN 3 TO 6 INCHES OF SAND OR GRAVEL.

Fig. 8.10

Oftentimes, wiring outside the house that is buried underground to serve a post lamp or an outdoor outlet, for example, has been run by a homeowner or another party who is not proficient in correct wiring methods. Perhaps the wiring has been laid directly along the ground (producing a hazardous condition) or has been buried in too shallow a trench of less than 12". (Burying the wires deeper helps to avoid accidental damage when digging). Then, too, there are those who unknowingly run non-metallic sheathed cable or BX type wiring underground. They should have known that wiring placed below ground might likely be required to run through rigid conduit. Note that there are many municipalities which also allow the underground use of the waterproof plastic-sheathed underground feeder ("UF") cable kind. As for the electrical receptacle boxes, splice boxes and fixtures themselves, they should be checked to see that they are rated for exterior usage and are of the weatherproof variety.

8.11 PROTECTION OF OUTSIDE RECEPTACLES

NOT ONLY IS THIS HOME'S BACKYARD PATIO OUTLET GFI-CONTROLLED, BUT IT IS WEATHERTIGHT AND, AS SUCH, PROTECTED FROM THE ELEMENTS.

Fig. 8.11

Check whether any of the outdoor electrical outlets and switches are absent of protection from the elements. If they do lack protection the cost of correction is not a capital expense, but the work should be attended to.

8.12 KNOW YOUR SIZE AND TYPE OF WIRING

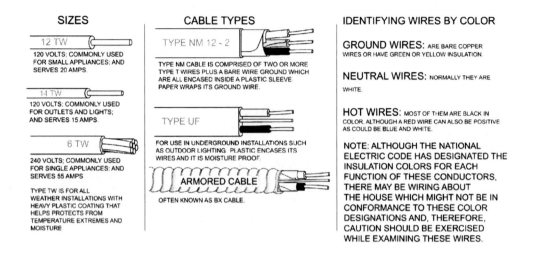

SIZES

12 TW
120 VOLTS; COMMONLY USED FOR SMALL APPLIANCES; AND SERVES 20 AMPS.

14 TW
120 VOLTS; COMMONLY USED FOR OUTLETS AND LIGHTS; AND SERVES 15 AMPS.

6 TW
240 VOLTS; COMMONLY USED FOR SINGLE APPLIANCES; AND SERVES 55 AMPS

TYPE TW IS FOR ALL WEATHER INSTALLATIONS WITH HEAVY PLASTIC COATING THAT HELPS PROTECTS FROM TEMPERATURE EXTREMES AND MOISTURE

CABLE TYPES

TYPE NM 12 - 2
TYPE NM CABLE IS COMPRISED OF TWO OR MORE TYPE T WIRES PLUS A BARE WIRE GROUND WHICH ARE ALL ENCASED INSIDE A PLASTIC SLEEVE. PAPER WRAPS ITS GROUND WIRE.

TYPE UF
FOR USE IN UNDERGROUND INSTALLATIONS SUCH AS OUTDOOR LIGHTING. PLASTIC ENCASES ITS WIRES AND IT IS MOISTURE PROOF.

ARMORED CABLE
OFTEN KNOWN AS BX CABLE.

IDENTIFYING WIRES BY COLOR

GROUND WIRES: ARE BARE COPPER WIRES OR HAVE GREEN OR YELLOW INSULATION.

NEUTRAL WIRES: NORMALLY THEY ARE WHITE.

HOT WIRES: MOST OF THEM ARE BLACK IN COLOR, ALTHOUGH A RED WIRE CAN ALSO BE POSITIVE AS COULD BE BLUE AND WHITE.

NOTE: ALTHOUGH THE NATIONAL ELECTRIC CODE HAS DESIGNATED THE INSULATION COLORS FOR EACH FUNCTION OF THESE CONDUCTORS, THERE MAY BE WIRING ABOUT THE HOUSE WHICH MIGHT NOT BE IN CONFORMANCE TO THESE COLOR DESIGNATIONS AND, THEREFORE, CAUTION SHOULD BE EXERCISED WHILE EXAMINING THESE WIRES.

Fig. 8.12

With respect to residential wiring, wire sizes vary from a small size wire (perhaps #16 gage) to a comparatively large size (such as #6 gage wire); but sizes 12 or 14 are common sizes to wire up rooms. Number 12 wire is advisable (over #14) because it is capable of carrying more current (20 amps as opposed to 15 amps). Thinner wires than these are prone to heat up with high resistance and become overloaded. That creates a real fire hazard.

Identify the type of wiring which is being used in the house. Is it copper wire, copper-clad or aluminum wire? Just about everyone knows that copper is a good conductor of electricity. It's even more efficient than aluminum. In fact, aluminum wiring used throughout a house is no longer considered to be safe wiring because the current that travels through it causes oxidation which results in loose connections between the wiring and the receptacle terminal screws. Those loose connections can overheat and turn into a fire. So be careful of problem wiring signs such as circuit breakers that trip, lights that flicker or outlets that feel warm to the touch.

Note that electrical codes today do not allow #12 and #14 gage aluminum wires to be used in new homes. Some owners of homes which contain aluminum wire tighten the screws in the receptacles, 'pigtail' the wiring or replace the wiring completely. The latter is expensive. That's why it's a good idea to have some receptacles opened for inspection of the size and type wiring that is being used.

Lastly, learn, too, whether the house wires run through rigid conduit or whether "flex" conduit or BX flexible armored cable, "knob and tube" wiring, nonmetallic sheathed cable, or even whether "romex" (cable of plastic sheathing) has been the choice wiring variety used in the building. Many times, newer areas of the home have a completely different type of wire than the home's original wiring.

8.13 SECURE UNSUPPORTED ELECTRICAL CONDUIT

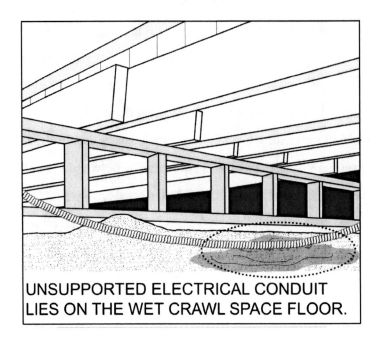

UNSUPPORTED ELECTRICAL CONDUIT
LIES ON THE WET CRAWL SPACE FLOOR.

Fig. 8.13

Both unsupported and improperly supported electrical conduit pose a safety hazard. Look for wiring which dangles from floor joists in underfloor locations. It's not uncommon to find that some lengths of cable actually run along wet or moist soil there. Your local electrical code probably specifies that non-metallic sheathed cable (romex) or flexible metal cable needs to be secured at least every 4 feet - 6 inches.

8.14 OCTOPUS WIRING

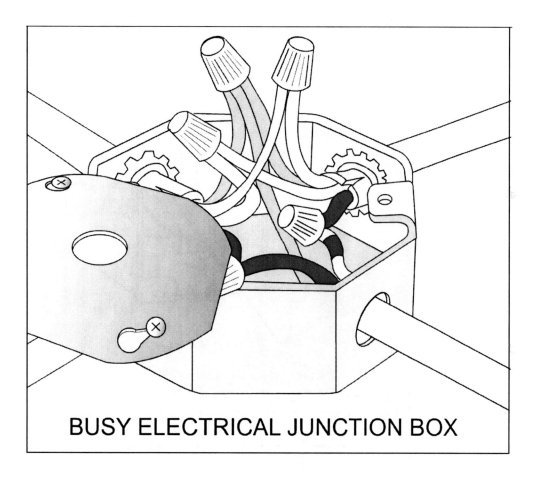

BUSY ELECTRICAL JUNCTION BOX

Fig. 8.14

An electrician should be engaged to check and make corrective work measures as necessary to 'octopus wiring' which is sometimes seen in underfloor and attic spaces.

8.15 CLOSE OFF OPEN J-BOXES AND RECEPTACLES

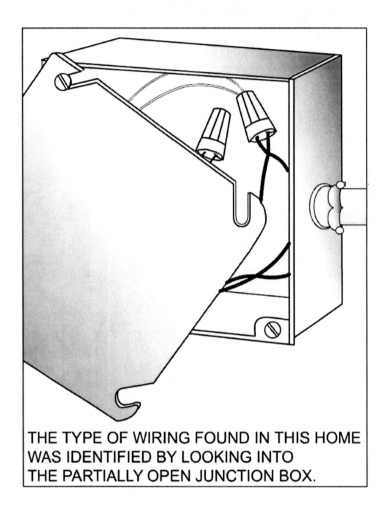

THE TYPE OF WIRING FOUND IN THIS HOME
WAS IDENTIFIED BY LOOKING INTO
THE PARTIALLY OPEN JUNCTION BOX.

Fig. 8.15

Electrical junction boxes are often left open. This is especially observed in underfloor and attic spaces which are spaces that are not much frequented. They should be covered closed as should missing receptacle covers be provided.

8.16 DANGEROUSLY LOCATED RECEPTACLES

Fig. 8.16

Electricity and water don't mix safely. Yet, it's not unusual to find a low hanging light fixture that has been installed directly over a bathtub, an electrically hazardous condition. In fact, switches and outlets are not even supposed to be located within arm's reach of a bathtub.

It is also not a very good idea to have an outlet located directly behind a kitchen cooktop, either, since the wiring of a small appliance which plugs into the outlet could easily get caught on fire from either an operating gas cooktop burner or an electric cooktop element.

8.17 WORN OUT OUTLETS

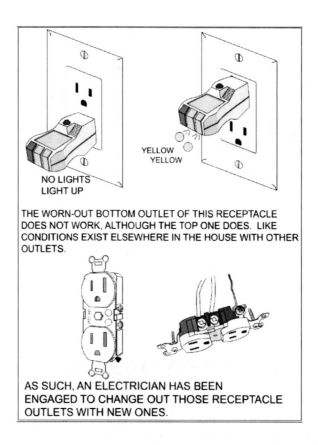

NO LIGHTS
LIGHT UP

YELLOW
YELLOW

THE WORN-OUT BOTTOM OUTLET OF THIS RECEPTACLE
DOES NOT WORK, ALTHOUGH THE TOP ONE DOES. LIKE
CONDITIONS EXIST ELSEWHERE IN THE HOUSE WITH OTHER
OUTLETS.

AS SUCH, AN ELECTRICIAN HAS BEEN
ENGAGED TO CHANGE OUT THOSE RECEPTACLE
OUTLETS WITH NEW ONES.

Fig. 8.17

As outlets and switches get old, they can wear out. Perhaps you'll find

this by noting that one outlet of the 2 outlets at a receptacle no longer

operates. Replacement receptacles then become necessary.

8.18 TIGHTEN RECEPTACLES' INTERNAL SCREWS

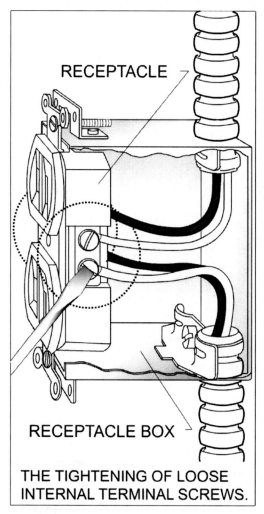

RECEPTACLE

RECEPTACLE BOX

THE TIGHTENING OF LOOSE
INTERNAL TERMINAL SCREWS.

Fig. 8.18

The internal terminal screws of old outlets in 35 year old or older

homes should be tightened. In some old outlets, the screws tend to loosen

from the wires. As such, loose wire connections can overheat and become on

fire.

8.19   SOME PROBLEMS WITH 3-HOLE OUTLETS

Electrical outlets of the 3-hole variety can have the following sample problems:

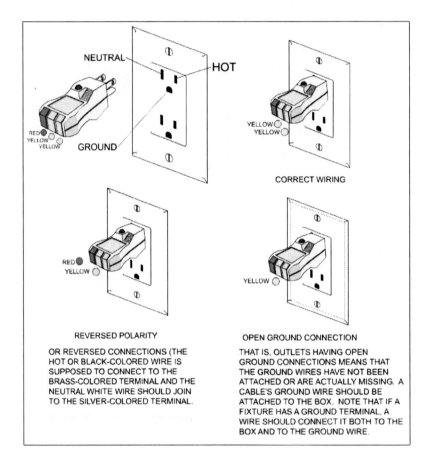

Fig. 8.19

It is easy to check out the condition of these outlets with a relatively inexpensive circuit tester that you can purchase from your local electrical supply store.

8.20 NEEDED LIGHT SWITCHES

Fig. 8.20

To avoid personal injury while entering a dark room, it is important to have a switch located at the room's entryway so that you could operate a light fixture in that room or else control the operation of an electrical outlet to which an electric lamp could be plugged into. Some homeowners, however, replace a ceiling light with an electric ceiling fan, removing that room's light source.

Look, too, for the existence of a light to illuminate a stairway and check whether upper and lower level 3-way switches control that fixture.

8.21 OUTDOOR LIGHTS

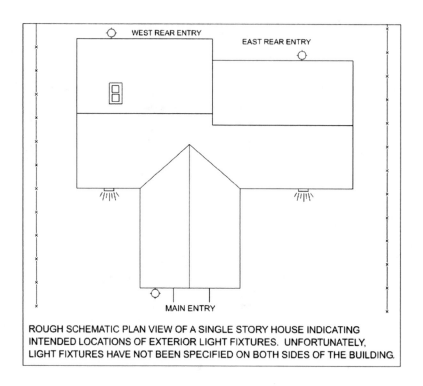

WEST REAR ENTRY

EAST REAR ENTRY

MAIN ENTRY

ROUGH SCHEMATIC PLAN VIEW OF A SINGLE STORY HOUSE INDICATING INTENDED LOCATIONS OF EXTERIOR LIGHT FIXTURES. UNFORTUNATELY, LIGHT FIXTURES HAVE NOT BEEN SPECIFIED ON BOTH SIDES OF THE BUILDING.

Fig. 8.21

Outdoor lights help make a home more favorable from the standpoint of security and visual safety. Therefore, be sure to check for adequate outdoor lighting provision, including along the sides of the house. Indeed, today's electrical codes today generally require that the location of each house entry receive illumination, although it is not necessary to place a light at each exterior doorway.

8.22 LOCATION OF HANGING LIGHTS

Fig. 8.22

Watch out for some hanging light fixtures! The exterior one pictured

above hangs rather low and likely someone could inadvertently walk into it.

Moreover, wind or seismic forces could cause this light to sway against a

wall. As a matter of prudent precaution, correction should be made at such

lights since falling, broken glass can cause critical harm.

8.23 SOME LIGHTS CAN POSE FIRE HAZARDS

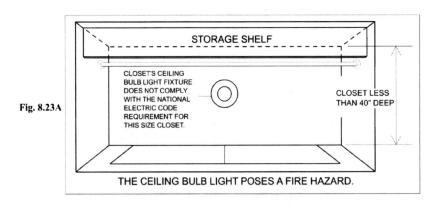

STORAGE SHELF

CLOSET'S CEILING
BULB LIGHT FIXTURE
DOES NOT COMPLY
WITH THE NATIONAL
ELECTRIC CODE
REQUIREMENT FOR
THIS SIZE CLOSET.

CLOSET LESS
THAN 40" DEEP

Fig. 8.23A

THE CEILING BULB LIGHT POSES A FIRE HAZARD.

In today's electrical codes, exposed electric bulb lights are generally not permitted to be used in closets having a depth of less than 40 inches. Where the closet is deeper than that dimension, an exposed bulb type light must be located a minimum of 18 inches away from materials which are combustible. Further, an unobstructed space is required to exist between the bulb and the closet floor.

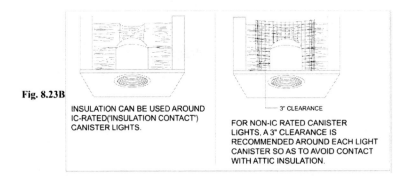

Fig. 8.23B

INSULATION CAN BE USED AROUND
IC-RATED('INSULATION CONTACT')
CANISTER LIGHTS.

3" CLEARANCE

FOR NON-IC RATED CANISTER
LIGHTS, A 3" CLEARANCE IS
RECOMMENDED AROUND EACH LIGHT
CANISTER SO AS TO AVOID CONTACT
WITH ATTIC INSULATION.

Recessed ceiling 'can' lights which are 'low heat-rated' lights and which are not protected by guards to shield away combustible material from them can cause such material to ignite when in contact with them. Specifically, a fire could develop from a hot light touching some cellulose insulation that was later blown into the attic space. And that's why lighting fixtures must be approved. Approved fixtures are supposed to be both rated and insulated.

8.24 SOME COMMONLY ENCOUNTERED LIGHTING PROBLEMS

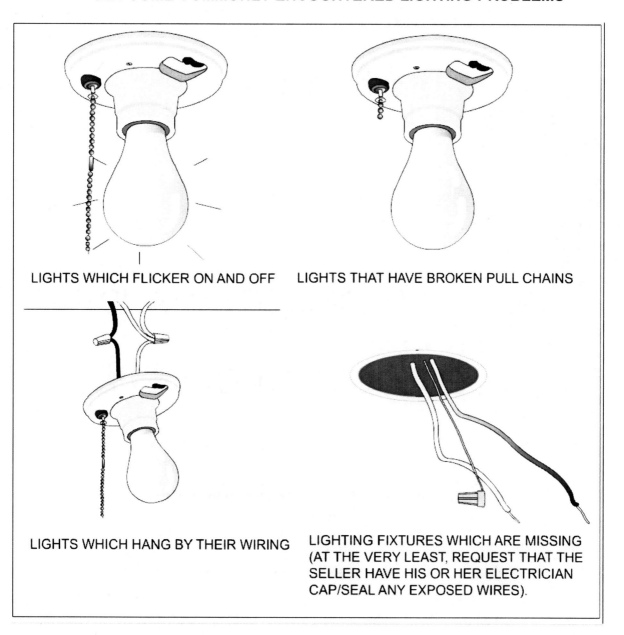

LIGHTS WHICH FLICKER ON AND OFF

LIGHTS THAT HAVE BROKEN PULL CHAINS

LIGHTS WHICH HANG BY THEIR WIRING

LIGHTING FIXTURES WHICH ARE MISSING (AT THE VERY LEAST, REQUEST THAT THE SELLER HAVE HIS OR HER ELECTRICIAN CAP/SEAL ANY EXPOSED WIRES).

Fig. 8.24

Chapter 9

ENVIRONMENTAL AND

GEOLOGICAL CONCERNS

I have presented in the pages ahead many of today's primary environmental concerns relative to residential living. Be on the lookout for the existence of any health and safety hazards on or about the site.

Learning about health hazards involves asking questions and doing research. You could consult with specialists, like an environmental engineer, a geotechnical engineer or a geologist, too.

9.1 ENVIRONMENTAL CONCERNS

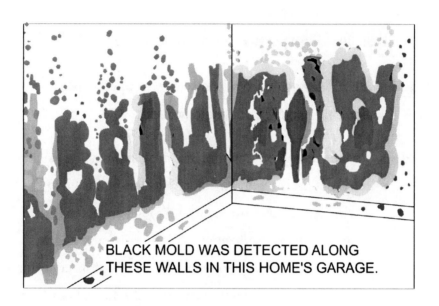

BLACK MOLD WAS DETECTED ALONG
THESE WALLS IN THIS HOME'S GARAGE.

Fig. 9.1

The following is a list of some of today's leading residential
environmental concerns:

Asbestos: Many experts claim that old asbestos can be a health hazard
in the sense that the mineral is a cancer-causing agent. There
is a health risk if asbestos fibers are released into the air such as
by decay.

Lead-base Paint: Ingested particles or flakes of lead-base paint could
possibly cause lead poisoning in a person. It is sometimes
found in old houses. Getting rid of lead paint is expensive and
should be done by a specialist who does this work.

Urea Foam Insulation: Is considered to be an agent that causes cancer.
It was used to insulate outside walls. The cost of its removal is
also expensive since the inside of the walls must be broken into.

Underground Toxic Wastes: Soil, for example, that comes from an old landfill and has been used as earth fill on the property might be contaminated with toxic substances. There could be contaminated soil and ground water on your prospective property from a possible nearby toxic waste dump.

Lead in Water: May come from lead solder in copper pipes. Now lead solder is no longer permitted to be used.

Radon: From the decay of uranium, radon is a radioactive gas that is odorless. It is also without color. The gas builds up to high levels in some houses by entering through cracks in the floor slab or through cracks in basement walls. The provision of cross ventilation is often used to reduce the levels of its concentration. Radon is an environmental threat since the gas is known to be a cancer-causing agent.

Mold and Mildew: Mold is simply tiny fungi which forms on both animal matter and vegetable matter. Basically, one associates mold with dampness or decay. Black mold is of particular concern because it can be a health risk. The formation of black mold can usually be prevented by lowering the humidity inside a house and by improving the house's ventilation. Mildew, on the other hand, is usually a whitish coating caused by fungi that one sees on such materials as paper, leather and fabrics when they are exposed to moisture. Indeed, oftentimes within houses, the air might contain too much moisture. Mildew can frequently be stopped from forming by raising the home's temperature and by improving ventilation.

9.2 ASBESTOS WRAP THERMAL INSULATED DUCTING

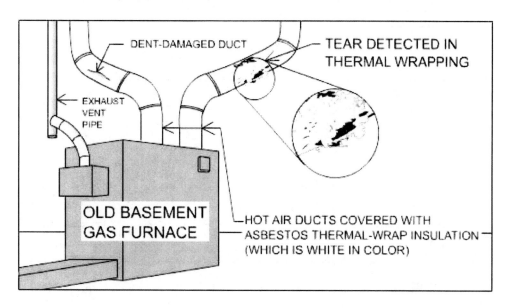

Fig. 9.2

Of particular concern with this mineral is that many older houses still utilize asbestos thermal wrap insulation around their heating ducts. Asbestos insulation can also be found on old heating plants. Asbestos fibers can be discharged into the air either by decay or by workmen in the house who puncture- damage it, or who abrade it, or perhaps disconnect the ducting. When tests disclose evidence of pulverisable or "friable" asbestos inside the house, sealing or "encapsulating" the mineral might be appropriate. But, in fact, entire removal could be deemed to be more favorable or even necessary. Licensed asbestos abatement contractors are specialists in the procedure of this work. They work with the mineral when it is wet. They use plastic chambers called "glove bags." And, these contractors know well enough not to vacuum it up. Responsible licensed asbestos abatement contractors also know not to leave the remains of the removed duct insulation in (attic or underfloor crawl spaces of) the home as unfortunately it is occasionally found.

9.3 PAINTED FIREPLACE CHAMBERS

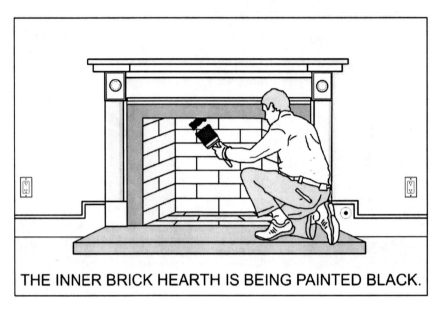

THE INNER BRICK HEARTH IS BEING PAINTED BLACK.

Fig. 9.3

Painted fireplaces (which are often painted white or black) may look nice but, before use, determine whether the paint is a heat tolerant paint that can be used in fireplace chambers without emitting toxic fumes when heated.

9.4 MORE ENVIRONMENTAL CONCERNS

Some additional environmental hazards are shown in Figure 9.4. Because these examples can pose potential health and safety hazards to you and your family, consider consulting with an environmental engineer more about them.

HAZARDOUS WASTES:
STORAGE TANKS, WHETHER OF FUEL OR OF OTHER CHEMICALS, CAN CONTAMINATE SOIL AND GROUND WATER. SEE EXAMPLE TO THE RIGHT OF THIS WRITING.

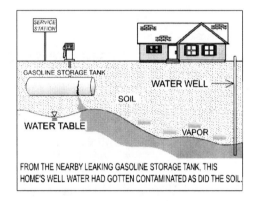

FROM THE NEARBY LEAKING GASOLINE STORAGE TANK, THIS HOME'S WELL WATER HAD GOTTEN CONTAMINATED AS DID THE SOIL.

AND

HOUSEHOLD HAZARDOUS PRODUCTS: CAN BE POISONOUS WHEN SWALLOWED, INHALED OR EVEN TOUCHED. A HOUSEHOLD HAZARDOUS WASTE PRODUCT MIGHT IGNITE EASILY, OR IT MAY BE CORROSIVE. IN FACT, IT'S POSSIBLE THAT SUCH A PRODUCT CAN EVEN EXPLODE IF IT IS NOT PROPERLY STORED, IF IT IS MIXED WITH ANOTHER OR OTHER PRODUCTS, OR PERHAPS EVEN SPILLED.

CLEANING PRODUCTS, PAINT SUPPLIES, AUTOMOBILE SUPPLIES AS WELL AS GARDENING SUPPLIES ARE EXAMPLES OF HOUSEHOLD HAZARDOUS PRODUCTS WHICH REQUIRE SAFE STORAGE AND PROPER DISPOSAL.

Fig. 9.4

9.5 BARE SLOPE INVITES EROSION

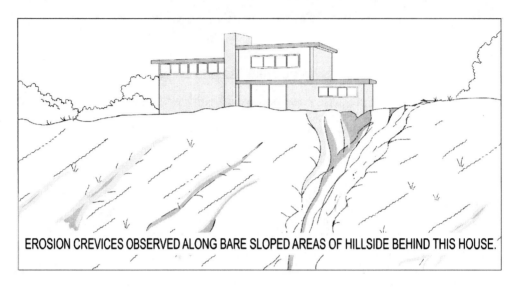

EROSION CREVICES OBSERVED ALONG BARE SLOPED AREAS OF HILLSIDE BEHIND THIS HOUSE.

Fig. 9.5

Where hillsides have bare sloped areas, soil erosion is possible. Proper ground cover should be planted there to help control this destructive process.

9.6 CONSULT WITH GEOLOGIST BEFORE COMMITMENT

Fig 9.6

Consider having a licensed geologist or a geotechnical engineer carefully examine the premise grounds before commitment. You don't want to see failure from any geological occurrences such as:

Hillside Sloughing/Debris or Rock Slides - the casting of soil, debris and rocks down a hillside;

Slump - another geological downward displacement;

Subsidence - or the lowering or sinking of a ground area;

Creep - a slow downward superficial material movement;

Soil Erosion - the wearing away of soil such as aggravated by water or by wind;

Or other geological conditions.

Expensive retaining and /or extensive soil control work may need to be instituted, but that work could turn out to prove to be only partly helpful.

Be sure to discuss with the engineer or geologist the following:

-the possibility of underground springs that may run through or about the site;

-whether the house is on a "cut and fill" lot and, if so, learning what parts are what in addition to learning whether the soil fill material has been compacted (say to 90% relative compaction);

-the possibility of poor soil compaction;

-the possibility of poor soil absorption that could affect a septic system;

-the closeness of the house to a hillside slope for favorable geological setback requirements;

-differential settlement of the swimming pool and spa. Check if the water surface line appears closer to a coping joint at one end of the pool than that along the other end. What's more, locate the existence of any possible large gaps at the jointing between the pool coping and pool deck;

-house settlement cracks and some other structural damages, including walls that have become unplumb or perhaps floors that are no longer level. Search for any doors which swing from a stationary position or doors that do not close;

-the proper type of hillside ground cover;

-any hazardous hillside instability or hillside landslide possibility and direction of any fault planes. Is the hillside not comprised of rock but of compacted earth instead which, as a result of heavy precipitation, will loosen in time from water seeping in it and slide?

-the possibility of water seepage problems that can undermine foundations, deteriorate foundation walls, upheave the building and consequently cause cracking and adversely affect wood structural members;

-rodent control (since, for example, gophers could loosen up hillside soil and cause hillside failure);

-tall trees being close to the house that could also adversely affect the home's foundation and structure;

-the area of any soil depression, including determining whether a tree or large plant has possibly been removed from that location;

-and, if in earthquake country, the possibility of an earthquake fault running through or nearby the site;

-etc..

Chapter 10

EXTERIOR IMPROVEMENTS

Consider addressing the exterior improvements to the property first. You would be outdoors, so the air would stimulate you. And with each improvement inspected, there's usually a sense of accomplishment since you are constantly moving about.

Just remember that repairs made to exterior improvements can substantially add up in costs.

10.1 CONCRETE PAVEMENT CRACKS

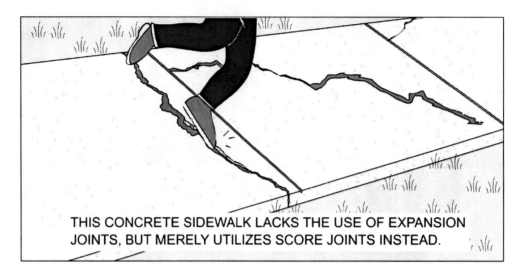

THIS CONCRETE SIDEWALK LACKS THE USE OF EXPANSION JOINTS, BUT MERELY UTILIZES SCORE JOINTS INSTEAD.

Fig. 10.1

Heat causes concrete pavements to expand. During the course of expansion, tensile stresses are exerted in the pavement. Because concrete is comparatively weak in tension, it cracks. Concrete slabs need room to expand. That's why regularly spaced "expansion joints" are placed along concrete pavements to reduce the chance of concrete from developing cracks.

Besides "temperature cracks," cracks in concrete can develop from impact, from tree roots pushing up the pavement, from settlement of support as well as because of weak concrete that was made up of an improper mix, or from concrete that lost a significant amount of moisture during its time of curing.

Accordingly, patching or repaving distressed concrete helps to prevent potential tripping hazards. Indeed, if the corrective work measures are not performed along finely cracked pavements in a timely manner, expansive soil that gets wet through the cracks can swell and aggravate the scope and size of the cracks further. Most homeowners prefer to repave severely affected pavements.

10.2 WORN BLACKTOP PAVEMENT

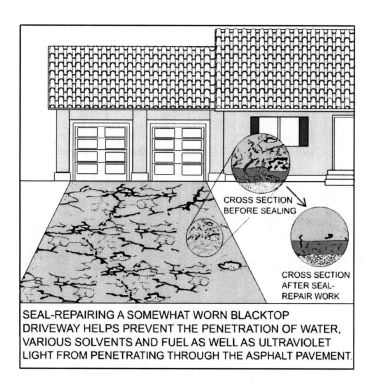

CROSS SECTION
BEFORE SEALING

CROSS SECTION
AFTER SEAL-
REPAIR WORK

SEAL-REPAIRING A SOMEWHAT WORN BLACKTOP
DRIVEWAY HELPS PREVENT THE PENETRATION OF WATER,
VARIOUS SOLVENTS AND FUEL AS WELL AS ULTRAVIOLET
LIGHT FROM PENETRATING THROUGH THE ASPHALT PAVEMENT.

Fig. 10.2

Slurry sealing a blacktop driveway is needed when such pavements begin to age and deteriorate. In fact, sealing helps to prevent the driveway from eventually becoming gravel.

10.3 OIL STAINS MARK THE DRIVEWAY

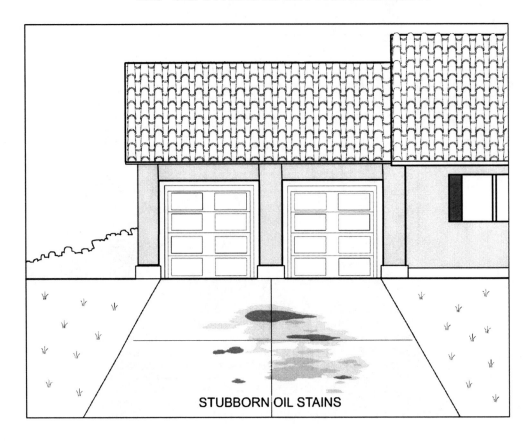

STUBBORN OIL STAINS

Fig. 10.3

It's hard to get rid of stubborn oil stains which mark concrete driveways even though appropriate cleansing action is taken. A few months could pass by before you're even happy that the stains are gone. Try scrubbing them off using an emulsifying agent.

10.4 PROVIDE ACCESS ROUTE TO YARD

THE HOMEOWNER REALIZES THAT IN ORDER TO CREATE A SAFE AND
EASY ACCESS ROUTE FROM HIS BACKYARD TO HIS FRONT YARD,
HE NEEDS TO ADD STEPS, RAILINGS, AND A PAVED WALKWAY IN HIS SIDE YARD.
THIS RETROFITTING WORK ALSO INCLUDES THE REMOVAL OF TWO EXISTING
SIDE YARD TREES WHICH ARE IN THE WAY OF THE PROSPECTIVE PATHWAY.

Fig. 10.4

With some hillside properties, proper access routes to side yards or to backyards have not been provided. Or, it could be that the existing routes to these locations are hazardous ones. Easy access is important, especially when there is a need for quick egress in the event of emergencies. Expensive exterior improvement work to correct this condition at many homes would include the provision of steps, railings and walkways.

10.5 UNRETAINED STEEP GRADE EARTH EMBANKMENT

Fig. 10.5

The construction of a retaining wall along a length of steeply sloped earth embankment might be (or soon become) necessary even though the soil grade has been unretained like that for years.

10.6 HYDROSTATIC PRESSURE EXERTED ON RETAINING WALL

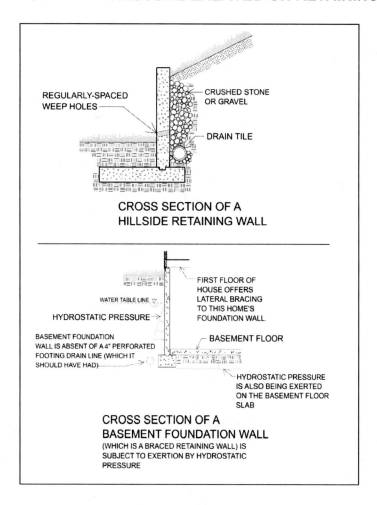

Fig. 10.6

Learn what type of drainage system has been provided behind retaining walls because significant hydrostatic pressure can be exerted on such walls without proper drainage. Look for evidences of cracks in the wall, wall leaning, bowing-out effects and wall bulging, too. Is there the presence of drainage weepholes along the bottom of the retaining wall? Learn, too, whether drainage piping has been located behind the wall as shown in the drawing above.

10.7 LEANING RETAINING WALLS

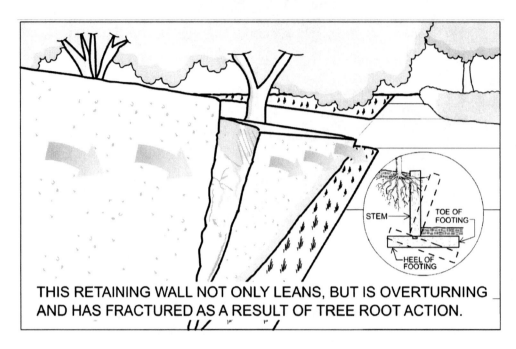

THIS RETAINING WALL NOT ONLY LEANS, BUT IS OVERTURNING AND HAS FRACTURED AS A RESULT OF TREE ROOT ACTION.

Fig. 10.7

Retaining walls which lean might have to be rebuilt. Leaning could be caused by such factors as earth movement, hydrostatic pressure that is exerted on the walls, tree root action, or possibly even by poorly designed, undersized walls.

Additional modes of retaining wall failure include lateral and shift displacement failure as well as wall bowing or wall bulging and serious cracking.

10.8 INCREASE RETAINING WALL

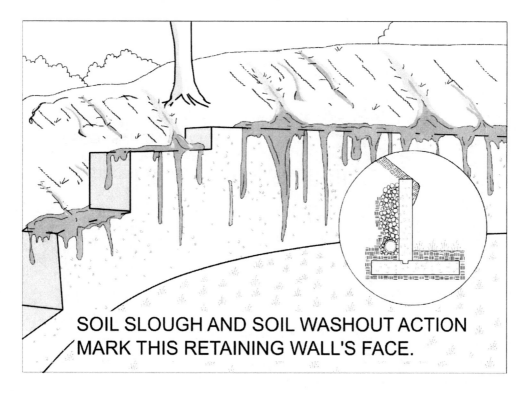

SOIL SLOUGH AND SOIL WASHOUT ACTION MARK THIS RETAINING WALL'S FACE.

Fig. 10.8

It might be necessary to increase the height and length of a retaining wall, or possibly even provide debris fencing due to some soil conditions. Specifically, this could be because of soil sloughage or soil wash-down action. However, first check whether your municipality requires you to obtain a permit before this work is begun.

10.9 POOR CONDITION OF FENCES

THIS PICKET FENCE IS IN A STATE OF DISREPAIR FOR IT HAS LOOSE, FALLEN PICKETS, PARTIALLY LEANS AND IS AFFECTED BY TERMITES.

Fig. 10.9

Look for fences which lean and are in worn, damaged condition.

Look, too, at other fences which are in such a state of disrepair that they ought to be discounted entirely. Repair or replacement of fences can be costly.

10.10 FENCE OFF EMBANKMENT

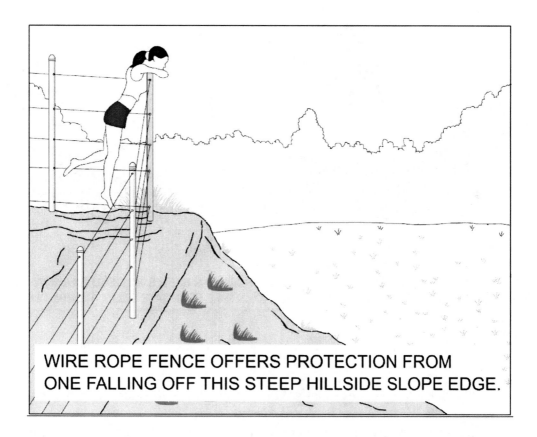

WIRE ROPE FENCE OFFERS PROTECTION FROM
ONE FALLING OFF THIS STEEP HILLSIDE SLOPE EDGE.

Fig. 10.10

Falling down a steep embankment could be dangerous or even be fatal.

For this reason, the installation of fencing alongside the foot edge of an

unprotected hillside slope embankment is recommended.

10.11 FENCE OFF A SWIMMING POOL

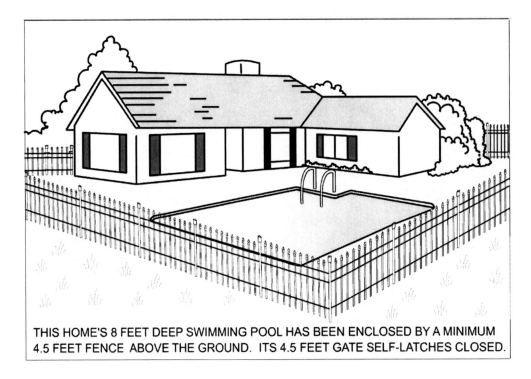

THIS HOME'S 8 FEET DEEP SWIMMING POOL HAS BEEN ENCLOSED BY A MINIMUM
4.5 FEET FENCE ABOVE THE GROUND. ITS 4.5 FEET GATE SELF-LATCHES CLOSED.

Fig. 10.11

Building codes usually require that bodies of water which are more
than 18 inches deep be fenced off and gated. Fences protect young children
by keeping them from wandering into an unwatched swimming pool or spa
and drowning.

10.12 DIFFERENTIAL SETTLEMENT OF SWIMMING POOL

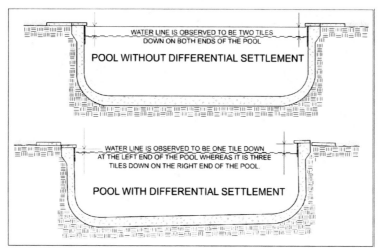

WATER LINE IS OBSERVED TO BE TWO TILES DOWN ON BOTH ENDS OF THE POOL

POOL WITHOUT DIFFERENTIAL SETTLEMENT

WATER LINE IS OBSERVED TO BE ONE TILE DOWN AT THE LEFT END OF THE POOL WHEREAS IT IS THREE TILES DOWN ON THE RIGHT END OF THE POOL.

POOL WITH DIFFERENTIAL SETTLEMENT

Fig. 10.12A

In the illustration, the in-ground swimming pool has evidently gone through some differential settling action since the water surface line along one end appears to be closer to the coping joint than that which was seen at its other end. Check the water line in your prospective swimming pool to see if it is about the same distance down along a wall tile all around the pool.

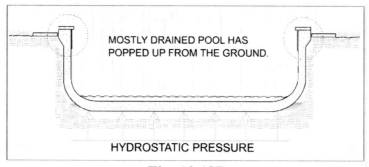

MOSTLY DRAINED POOL HAS POPPED UP FROM THE GROUND.

HYDROSTATIC PRESSURE

Fig. 10.12B

An in-ground swimming pool could possibly lift or pop-up from the ground due to hydrostatic pressure exerted on it while it is being drained when there is little water weight to hold the pool down. Note that there's less risk of a pool lifting during dry seasons than during rainy ones. One reason why a homeowner drains the pool would be to replace the pool water that has mineral saturation and has become too hard.

10.13 RUSTED DIVING BOARD BOLTS

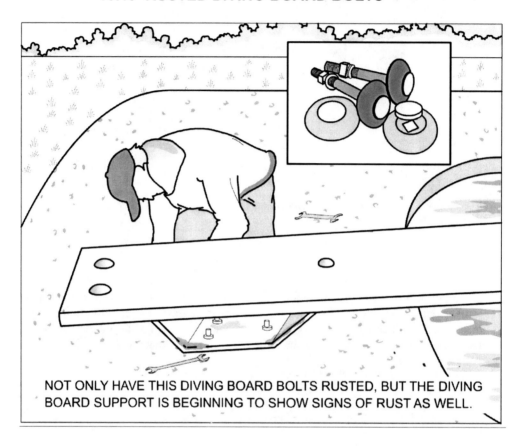

NOT ONLY HAVE THIS DIVING BOARD BOLTS RUSTED, BUT THE DIVING BOARD SUPPORT IS BEGINNING TO SHOW SIGNS OF RUST AS WELL.

Fig. 10.13

Because diving board bolt connections rust and weaken, they should not be neglected to be examined periodically for their structural condition for safety reasons. A diver jumping on a diving board that snaps off its support from such a connection failure could get seriously hurt. Replacement bolts are not considered to be a capital expense.

10.14 HEIGHT RESTRICTIONS OF PATIO COVERS

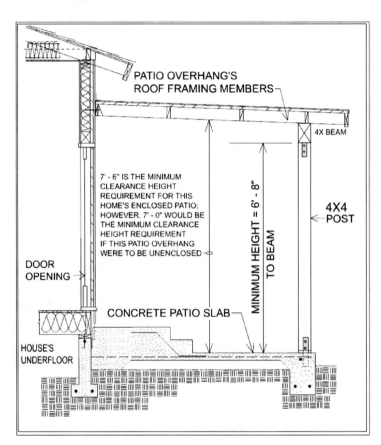

Fig. 10.14

There are building codes which specify the maximum height that a patio cover can be built and a minimum clearance height along the end of its projection, too.   See if your prospective patio cover falls within those guidelines set by the local building department.

Chapter 11

FIREPLACE AND CHIMNEY

There's a host of items to check for while inspecting a fireplace and chimney. But, remember, your primary concern would be to determine whether the fireplace and chimney have been built correctly. This includes checking whether the chimney has been equipped with a flue liner which might be needed for fire safety reasons (depending on how thick the chimney walls are); whether the stack extends a proper height above the roof; and whether it has a separate flue to serve either another fireplace or a heating plant. It's important to see that a smoke shelf exists above the fireplace (since it helps to deter downdraft action of the fire) as does a damper door.

11.1 RELOCATE LOG LIGHTER'S GAS VALVE

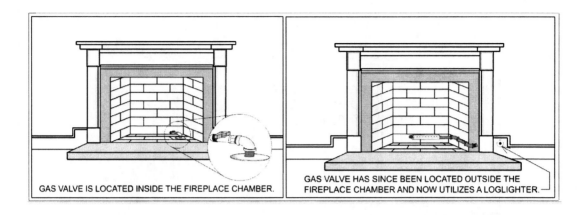

GAS VALVE IS LOCATED INSIDE THE FIREPLACE CHAMBER.

GAS VALVE HAS SINCE BEEN LOCATED OUTSIDE THE FIREPLACE CHAMBER AND NOW UTILIZES A LOGLIGHTER.

Fig. 11.1

In many older homes, log lighter gas valves which have been provided to help ignite a fire have often been positioned inside the fireplace chamber. Once the fire starts, it would not be safe nor easy to shut off the gas with a flame being in the way. Very little can be done about this short of engaging a plumber to relocate the gas valve outside the chamber and outer hearth area altogether.

11.2 OUTER FIREPLACE HEARTHS

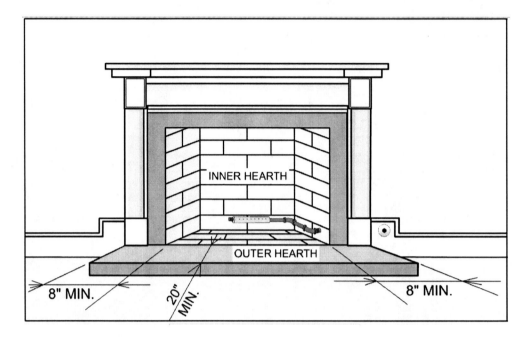

INNER HEARTH

OUTER HEARTH

8" MIN.   20" MIN.   8" MIN.

Fig. 11.2

Most fireplaces require an outer hearth. Remember, when kindling a fire in a fireplace, sparks can fly out of the chamber. It's good to know that a safe fireplace has been built with a hearth which projects a minimum of 20 inches into the room from the face of the opening in addition to being 16 inches wider than the inner hearth opening. In fact, many masonry contractors build the outer hearth at least 2 feet wider than the fireplace opening.

11.3 EQUIP FIREPLACE WITH FIRESCREENING

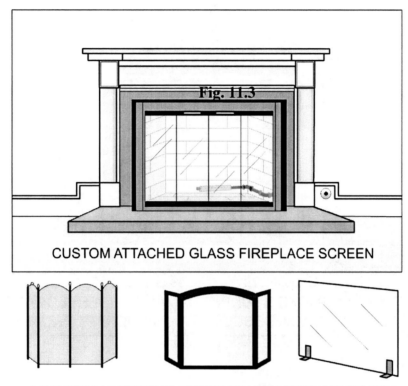

Fig. 11.3

CUSTOM ATTACHED GLASS FIREPLACE SCREEN

SOME POPULAR EXAMPLES OF FREE-STANDING FIREPLACE SCREENS

Non-attached wire mesh or safety glass fireplace fire screens are not always included with the sale of the house. This is because sellers take them with them to their new homes. In that case, for fire safety reasons, budget for a replacement fire screen when you first move in. New homes are now required to be equipped with fire screens.

11.4 WHAT SMOKE STAINS OVER THE FIREPLACE OPENING MEAN

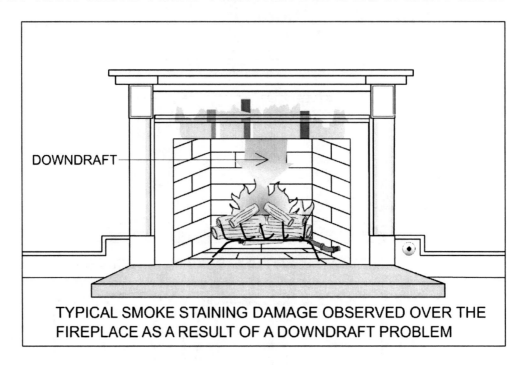

TYPICAL SMOKE STAINING DAMAGE OBSERVED OVER THE
FIREPLACE AS A RESULT OF A DOWNDRAFT PROBLEM

Fig. 11.4

Smoke staining which is observed above a fireplace opening may merely be an indication that someone neglected to open the damper door when igniting a fire in the fireplace. However, the staining could be indicative of an occasional downdraft problem. (A downdraft problem takes place when the outdoor air gets sucked down a chimney due to air pressure inside the house being lower than that which is outside). If there is a downdraft problem, chimney hood work may then be in order to remedy the condition. No one wants to experience flames lipping out of the fireplace chamber and allow gases of combustion to spread into the house.

11.5 WOOD FINISH OVER A FIREPLACE

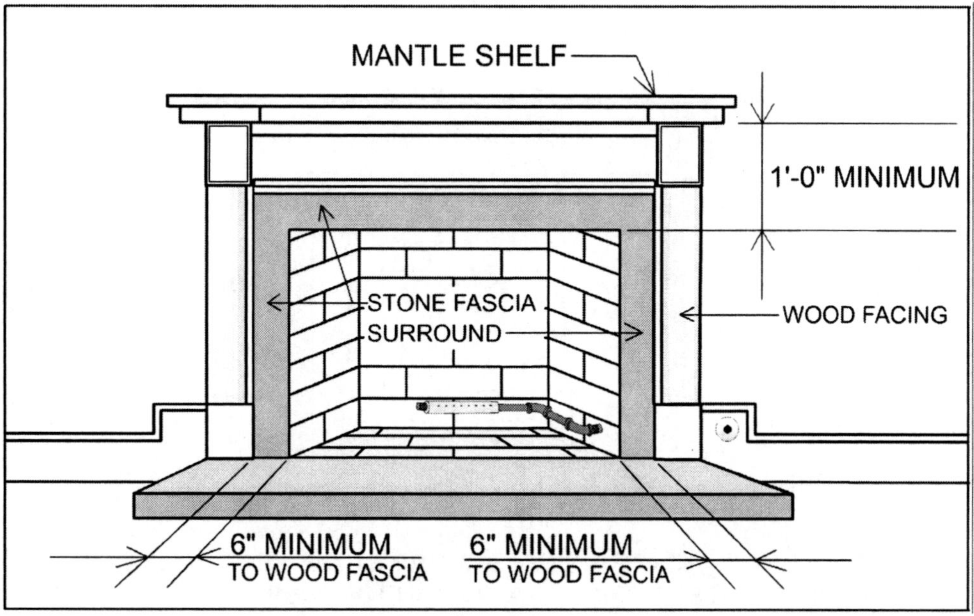

MANTLE SHELF

1'-0" MINIMUM

STONE FASCIA
SURROUND

WOOD FACING

6" MINIMUM
TO WOOD FASCIA

6" MINIMUM
TO WOOD FASCIA

Fig. 11.5

For fire safety reasons, finishes of wood or other combustible material should not be placed less than 6" of the fireplace opening. In fact, if wood is desired to be used as a facing, many consider 8 inches as the proper minimum distance that it be away from the fireplace opening. Additionally, many consider it proper for a wood mantle shelf or other projection to be installed at least 12 inches above the fireplace recess just in case a fire were to lip out of the fireplace chamber.

11.6 REPAIR MASONRY FIREPLACES

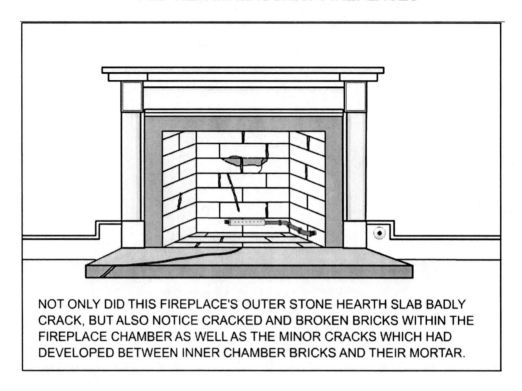

NOT ONLY DID THIS FIREPLACE'S OUTER STONE HEARTH SLAB BADLY CRACK, BUT ALSO NOTICE CRACKED AND BROKEN BRICKS WITHIN THE FIREPLACE CHAMBER AS WELL AS THE MINOR CRACKS WHICH HAD DEVELOPED BETWEEN INNER CHAMBER BRICKS AND THEIR MORTAR.

Fig. 11.6

Repairing masonry fireplaces could involve the replacement of badly cracked marble or other stone outer hearth slabs and repointing the masonry joints of the fireplace's inner chamber.

11.7 WHEN A FIREPLACE BEGINS TO SMOKE

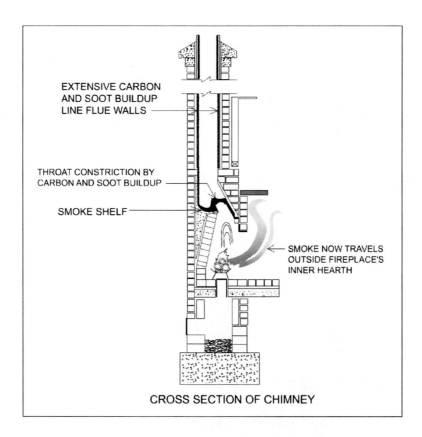

EXTENSIVE CARBON
AND SOOT BUILDUP
LINE FLUE WALLS

THROAT CONSTRICTION BY
CARBON AND SOOT BUILDUP

SMOKE SHELF

SMOKE NOW TRAVELS
OUTSIDE FIREPLACE'S
INNER HEARTH

CROSS SECTION OF CHIMNEY

Fig.11.7

When a fireplace begins to smoke and has not done so in the past, this reflects the possibility of carbon and soot build-up inside the chimney at its stack throat location. By cleaning the smoke shelf and the chimney, the problem will likely be arrested.

Note that a chimney should be cleaned yearly if it is to be used daily, or almost daily. For occasional usage, it's more likely necessary to have the stack cleaned once in every 5 or 10 years.

11.8 NO FIREPLACE DAMPER DOOR

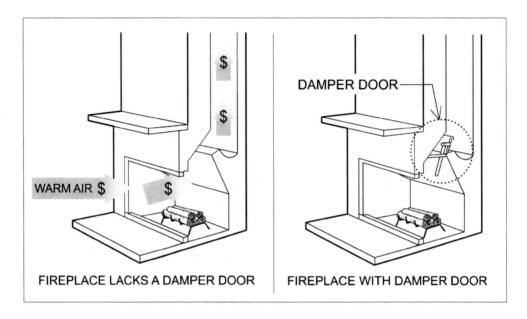

Fig. 11.8

Without a damper door in a fireplace, warm air inside a house during the winter time tends to be drawn to the outdoors. To save on your future heating costs, a damper in the fireplace is recommended. Today's building codes do require their presence in new homes as tight-fitting dampers that have ready access and that open and close.

11.9 SOME COMMON DAMPER DOOR PROBLEMS

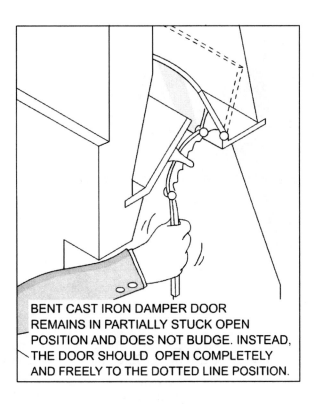

BENT CAST IRON DAMPER DOOR
REMAINS IN PARTIALLY STUCK OPEN
POSITION AND DOES NOT BUDGE. INSTEAD,
THE DOOR SHOULD OPEN COMPLETELY
AND FREELY TO THE DOTTED LINE POSITION.

Fig. 11.9

Damper doors sometimes need adjustments to open and close easily.

Some may be stuck, bent and do not quite fit right, or are rusted.

11.10 IS THERE A CHIMNEY ASH PIT?

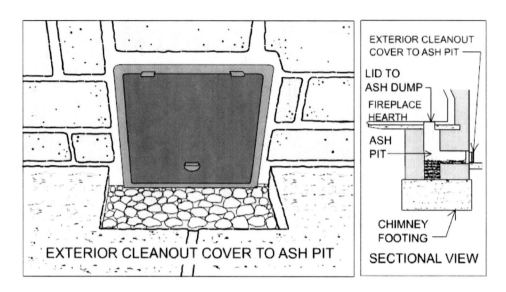

EXTERIOR CLEANOUT COVER TO ASH PIT

EXTERIOR CLEANOUT
COVER TO ASH PIT

LID TO
ASH DUMP

FIREPLACE
HEARTH

ASH
PIT

CHIMNEY
FOOTING

SECTIONAL VIEW

Fig. 11.10

Some chimneys have ash pits, while others do not. A chimney ash pit

is located below the fireplace chamber where burnt ashes collect.

11.11 CHIMNEY'S AIR INTAKE OPENING HELPS COMBUSTION

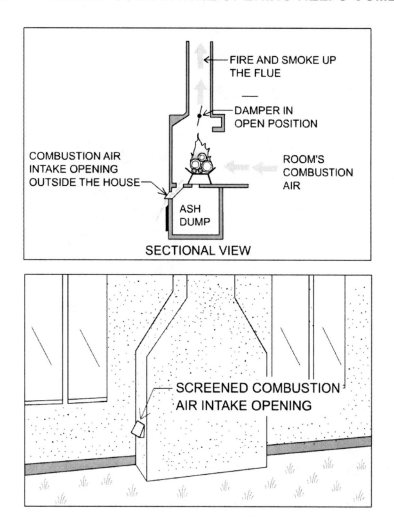

Fig. 11.11

Many new chimneys which are located on exterior walls are required to be equipped with air intake openings. They allow outside air to enter the fireplace chamber to aid in combustion. Your local building code might specify these openings to be a minimum of 6 square inches in size.

11.12 WHEN WALLS OF THE CHIMMNEY FEEL HOT

Fig. 11.12

When the walls of a chimney feel hot, this could mean that there's leakage in the flue. When such leaks develop, it is normal to find that the brickwork around the flue is in poor condition. Until the stack is checked by a chimney contractor, no one should use the fireplace. The chimney contractor, in his investigation, might video-tape the flue and, additionally, might light a fire in the fireplace, cover the chimney top with a wet blanket and look for smoke to exit through the walls of the chimney.

11.13 BENT CHIMNEY

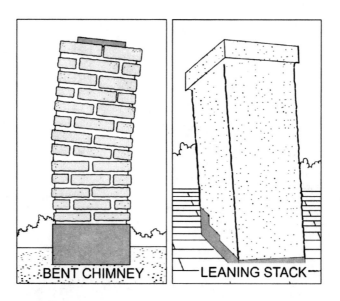

Fig. 11.13

Some masonry chimney stacks lean or bend into the wind. If the chimney serves an oil-fired heating plant, the bending action could be caused by expansion of some masonry joints from fuel oil having a high sulfur content.

Leaning chimney stacks, whether used for a fireplace or to serve a heating plant, should be checked out by a chimney contractor before use. Hopefully chimney re-building costs don't turn out to be needed since the cost of that work can be expensive. Even if leaning stacks do check out, they should be periodically measured and re-inspected so as to be certain they don't seriously worsen.

11.14 CHIMNEY NEEDS PROPER HEIGHT

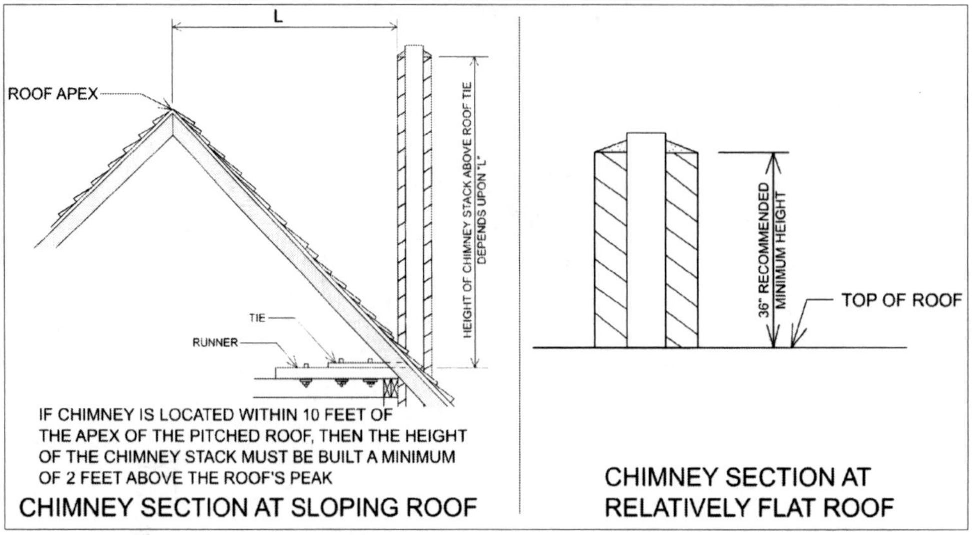

L

ROOF APEX

HEIGHT OF CHIMNEY STACK ABOVE ROOF TIE DEPENDS UPON 'L'

TIE

RUNNER

IF CHIMNEY IS LOCATED WITHIN 10 FEET OF
THE APEX OF THE PITCHED ROOF, THEN THE HEIGHT
OF THE CHIMNEY STACK MUST BE BUILT A MINIMUM
OF 2 FEET ABOVE THE ROOF'S PEAK

CHIMNEY SECTION AT SLOPING ROOF

36" RECOMMENDED MINIMUM HEIGHT

TOP OF ROOF

**CHIMNEY SECTION AT
RELATIVELY FLAT ROOF**

Fig. 11.14

Chimneys should be built to a proper height. This helps to prevent
fireplace smoking problems.

11.15 CHIMNEY TOP NEEDS A SPARK ARRESTER

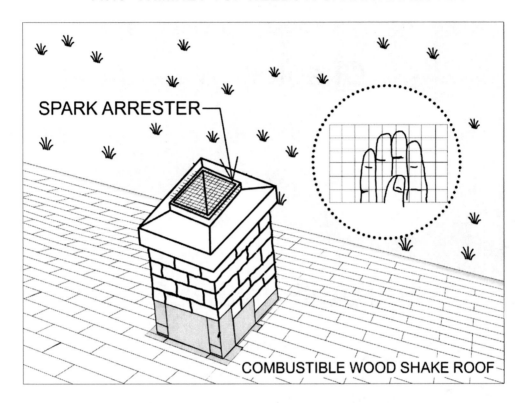

Fig. 11.15

      A chimney should be provided with a spark arrester atop it. A spark arrester is a screen cover usually made up of 12 guage wire mesh having openings not wider than 1/2 inch. They are especially important where there are rather combustible wood shake or wood shingle roofs.

Chapter **12**

GARAGE INSPECTION

The key to inspecting a garage is in the word 'observation.' You will find yourself looking for 'this problem' and 'that problem' and what the garage contains in order to determine its overall condition.

But don't be surprised when you realize that you spent more time inspecting the garage than you had originally anticipated. Many garages are filled and it's difficult getting around inside them. Just keep alert because stored items, later built-in cabinets and shelving can all be distracting and pose safety hazards.

12.1 TYPES OF GARAGE DOORS

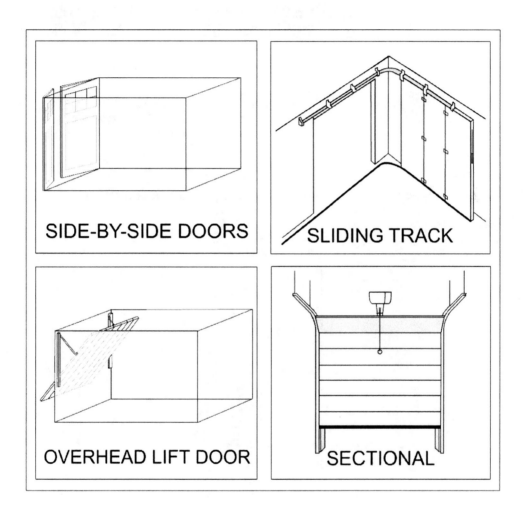

Fig. 12.1

Older side-by-side or track-type garage doors might work, but may do so with difficulty. Today, most homeowners desire the overhead lift or sectional variety of garage doors.

12.2 OVERHEAD GARAGE DOOR SPRINGS CAN BE DANGEROUS

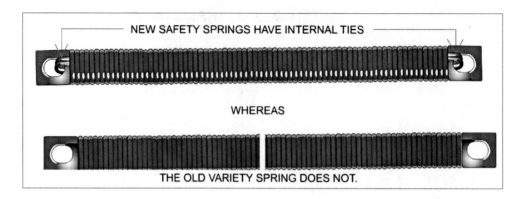

Fig. 12.2A

- When they are not of the new safety variety and they break;

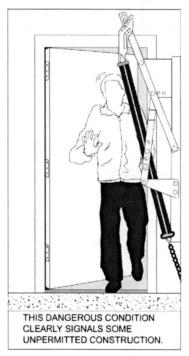

Fig. 12.2B

- or when they are in the way of a person's pathway and can

   inadvertently be walked into (whether the overhead door is either

   open or closed) .

12.3 BROKEN OVERHEAD GARAGE DOOR SPRING

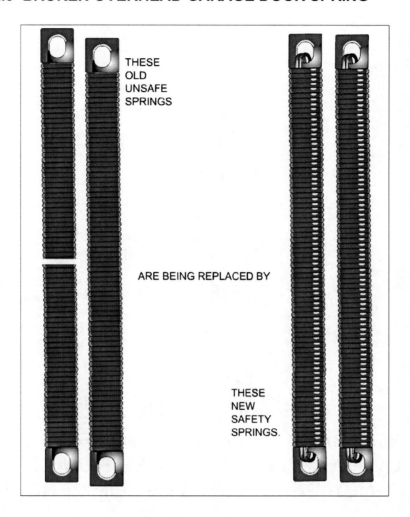

THESE
OLD
UNSAFE
SPRINGS

ARE BEING REPLACED BY

THESE
NEW
SAFETY
SPRINGS.

Fig. 12.3

Whenever only one overhead lift garage door spring breaks, consider the installation of new safety springs for both sides of the overhead door so that spring tension would be equalized.

12.4 GARAGE FLOOR AND PITCH

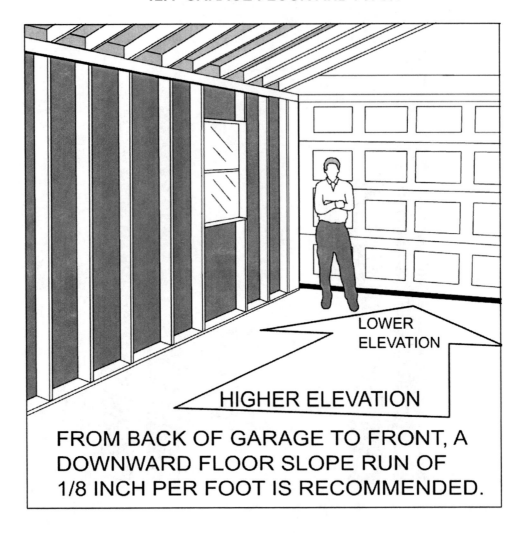

LOWER
ELEVATION

HIGHER ELEVATION

FROM BACK OF GARAGE TO FRONT, A
DOWNWARD FLOOR SLOPE RUN OF
1/8 INCH PER FOOT IS RECOMMENDED.

Fig. 12.4

Garage floors are required to be of non-combustible materials (such as of

concrete or asphalt pavement) and are normally pitched toward garage entries.

That way, during a rainstorm, water that drips from a wet car which has just

entered the garage can then exit it readily instead of forming puddles therein.

12.5 GARAGE SIZES

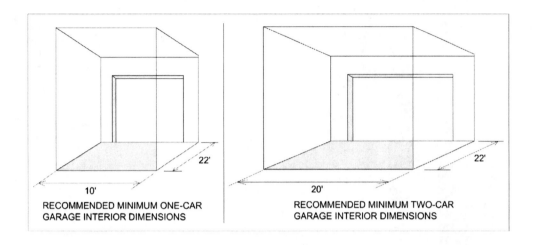

Fig. 12.5

Many would consider that single-car garages having inside dimensions of less than 10 feet by 22 feet and two-car garages having inside dimensions of less than 20 feet by 22 feet would be skimpy in their space. In addition to parking, garages are frequently used for storage.

12.6 POOR CONDITION OF GARAGE

Fig. 12.6

Some garages are in poor and marginally sound condition, perhaps partly resulting from the fashion of their construction. Since extensive work measures would be necessary for correction, the homebuyer should consider budgeting for repair and retrofitting costs. Some items of repair work, particularly those structural repairs, would have to be attended to immediately.

Chapter 13

GLAZING

Seek and you may find some cracked or broken glass panes around the house. Inspecting glazing further entails looking for the presence of safety tempered glazing, a much stronger glass, where this type of glass is needed. Normally you can identify tempered glazing by the small white stamp mark placed at the glass corner.

Check, too, how thick the glass panes are for safety reasons.

13.1 USE OF SAFETY GLAZING

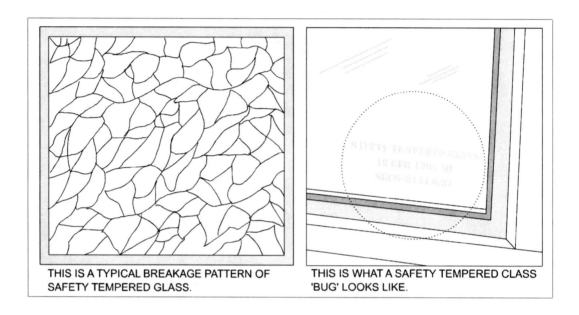

THIS IS A TYPICAL BREAKAGE PATTERN OF SAFETY TEMPERED GLASS.

THIS IS WHAT A SAFETY TEMPERED CLASS 'BUG' LOOKS LIKE.

Fig. 13.1

Check whether the glazing of sliding glass doors, all other exterior glass doors, transom windows, sidelights, stall shower doors and enclosures as well as the glazing of bathtub sliding doors is comprised of safety tempered glazing. Shards of fallen, broken glass can cut and kill! Your local building code probably requires this type of glazing in these windows, panels and doors in new home construction. A stamp or 'bug' marking should be present at the corner of each glass pane which identifies the glazing as that of the safety tempered variety.

13.2 LOW-TO-FLOOR WINDOWS ALSO NEED SAFETY GLAZING

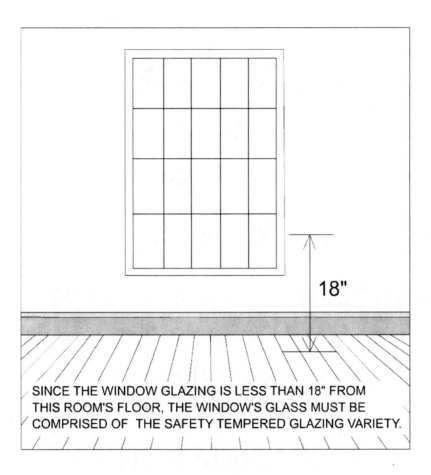

18"

SINCE THE WINDOW GLAZING IS LESS THAN 18" FROM
THIS ROOM'S FLOOR, THE WINDOW'S GLASS MUST BE
COMPRISED OF THE SAFETY TEMPERED GLAZING VARIETY.

Fig. 13.2

There are building codes today which also call for safety tempered glazing

at fixed windows should the bottom portion of the window be placed less than an

18 inch distance above the floor.

Chapter 14

HABITABLE ROOMS AND

VARIOUS ITEMS OF

CONFORMANCE

You might enter a room and sense that something is not quite right about that room's construction. You feel the room was built too narrow and that its entry passage was built too low, but weren't absolutely certain of this. It's just that your instinct tells you this.

Well, here you begin a chapter which outlines various items and dimensions of what is considered to be good construction practice in connection with rooms, stairways, doors, windows and even exterior wood siding. Learning the facts presented here will enable you to better identify often found construction errors which sometimes can be extremely expensive to correct.

14.1 MINIMUM CEILING HEIGHTS

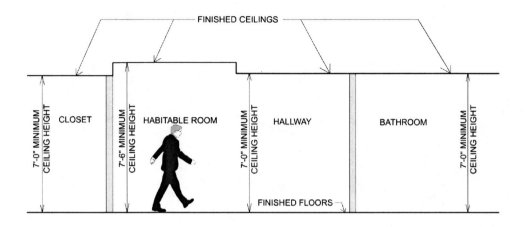

Fig. 14.1

A local building code might specify the heights in these illustrated locations as their required minimum clear ceiling heights. Notice that the 'habitable room' height is the tallest height which allows for the presence of a greater open feeling.

14.2 HABITABLE ROOM'S MINIMUM WIDTH

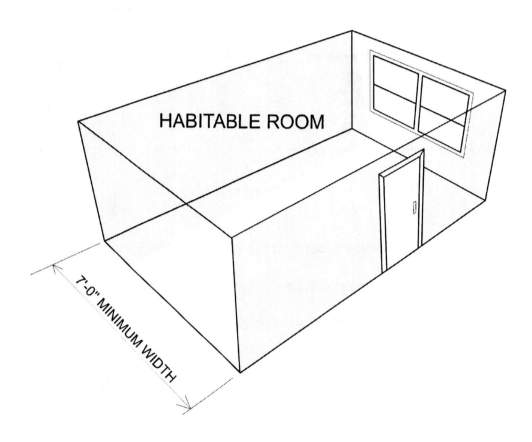

HABITABLE ROOM

7'-0" MINIMUM WIDTH

Fig.14.2

Except for kitchens, many building codes require that in order for a room to qualify as a 'habitable room,' it should measure at least 7'-0" along its width. Indeed, it would be difficult to freely move about in a furnished room narrower than this.

14.3 HABITABLE ROOM'S MINIMUM FLOOR AREA

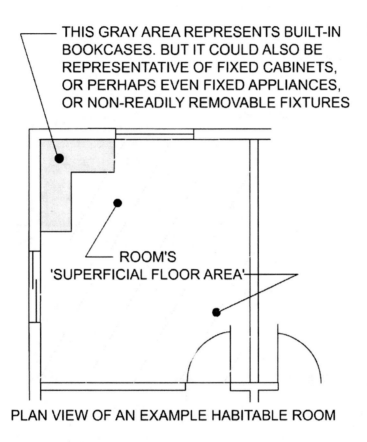

THIS GRAY AREA REPRESENTS BUILT-IN
BOOKCASES. BUT IT COULD ALSO BE
REPRESENTATIVE OF FIXED CABINETS,
OR PERHAPS EVEN FIXED APPLIANCES,
OR NON-READILY REMOVABLE FIXTURES

ROOM'S
'SUPERFICIAL FLOOR AREA'

PLAN VIEW OF AN EXAMPLE HABITABLE ROOM

Fig. 14.3

Building codes also specify the minimum area of habitable rooms.

For example, some codes define such a room as having a "superficial floor

area" not to be less than 90 square feet in size. The stripe-shaded area in the

illustration above shows that room's 'superficial' or clear floor area.

14.4 BATHROOM OPEN TO A KITCHEN

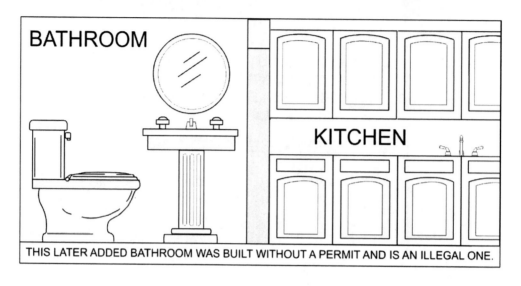

Fig. 14.4

Bathrooms which contain a toilet in them and which are open to kitchens are usually in violation of your local building code. In that case, what's acceptable instead would be the presence of two doorway openings between the kitchen and the bathroom.

14.5 WHAT LOOKS TO BE A BEDROOM MIGHT NOT BE A BEDROOM

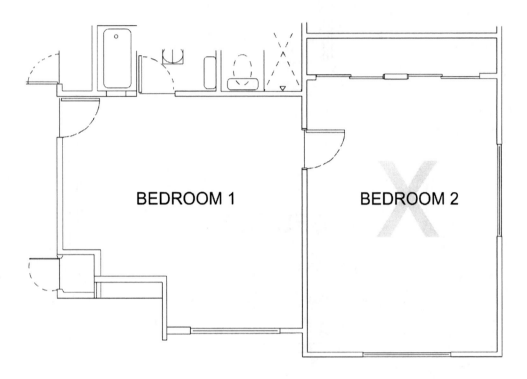

Fig. 14.5

Don't be deceived by someone else's count of the number of bedrooms that are in the house. You may be surprised to note that there are actually less bedrooms than that which have been represented. Here in the illustrated example, designated Bedroom '2' is located behind Bedroom '1.' Both are the same size of 150 square feet. By today's building codes this would be considered prohibited unless Bedroom '1' were to be called an 'anteroom' or a 'dressing room.' In theory, '1' could not be a bedroom inasmuch as it is used as a passageway. Note, however, that many may use '1' as a bedroom with '2' being its walk-in wardrobe closet.

14.6 BEDROOMS WITHOUT CLOSETS

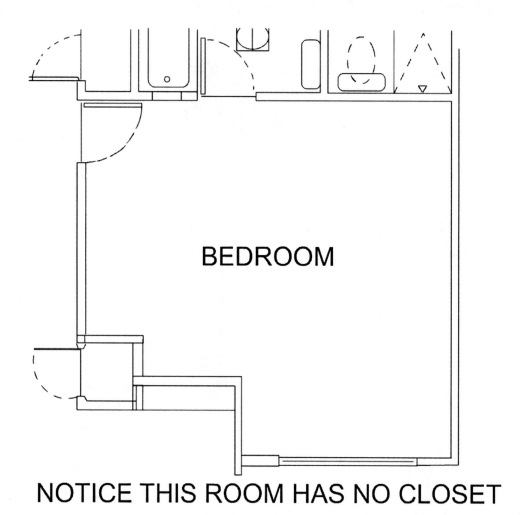

NOTICE THIS ROOM HAS NO CLOSET

Fig. 14.6

Bedrooms don't have to have closets, although many think that they are required to have them.

14.7 PROPER CLEARANCE IN UNDERFLOOR CRAWL SPACE

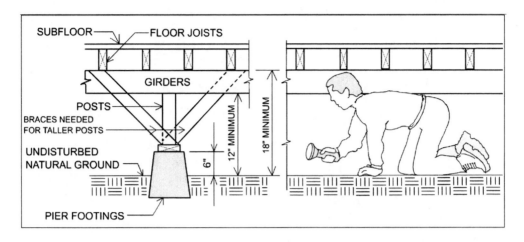

Fig. 14.7

For "raised foundation" houses (having an underfloor crawl space), the minimum distance that is usually built between the ground and the bottom of the building's floor joists is 18 inches. This distance allows one to gain access by crawling to various locations of the underfloor. Note that where there is less clearance found, and in numerous homes this turns out to be the case, crawling becomes difficult or impossible, prohibiting one to examine the crawl space in its entirety.

14.8 DOORWAY SIZES

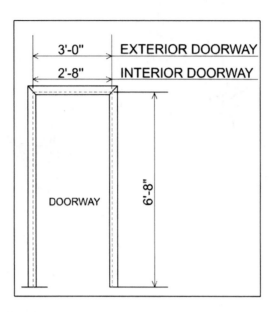

Fig. 14.8

Doorway passages are required to have certain minimum size dimensions. For example, see those minimum size dimensions in the above illustration as called for by one local building code. After all, they make sense since a rather tall person would have to duck through a doorway of a lesser height while an obese individual who enters through a narrower size doorway might find his or her efforts becoming a real squeeze.

14.9 HINGED SHOWER DOOR SHOULD OPEN OUTWARDLY

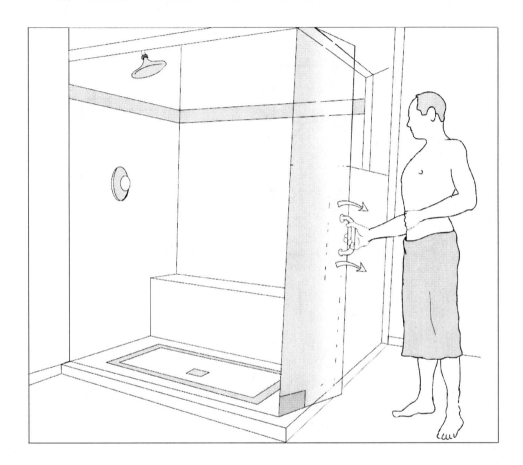

Fig. 14.9

Hinged doors of bathtub and shower enclosures are required to open outwardly, and not inwardly. We make mention of this because it would be quite difficult (and sometimes hazardous) for one to maneuver inside the shower stall with the enclosure door swung inside it.

14.10 GARAGE DOOR LEADS TO A BEDROOM

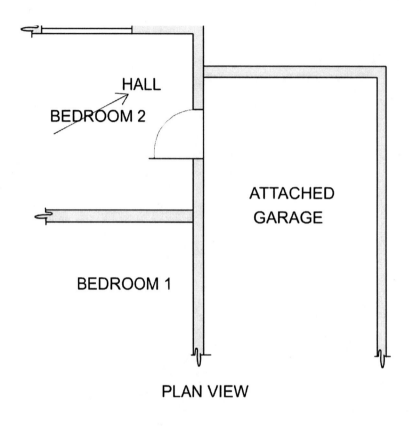

PLAN VIEW

Fig. 14.10

Although local building codes prohibit an attached garage's walk-in door from entering a bedroom, it is a commonly found hazardous improvement addition which many homeowners later do. First, for example, the door is often not a proper fire-rated door that's required between the garage and the house, and secondly, if the door were to be left open, emitting toxic car fumes could enter the so-called bedroom.

14.11 FIRE-RATED DOOR BETWEEN HOUSE AND GARAGE

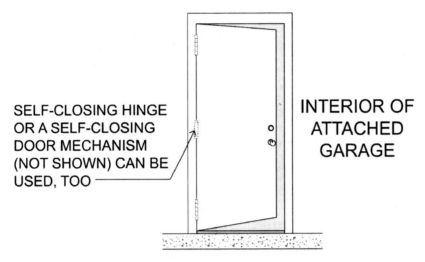

SELF-CLOSING HINGE OR A SELF-CLOSING DOOR MECHANISM (NOT SHOWN) CAN BE USED, TOO

INTERIOR OF ATTACHED GARAGE

FIRE-RATED DOOR BETWEEN HOUSE AND GARAGE

Fig. 14.11

In today's new homes, fire-rated doors are normally installed between the house and attached garage. They are usually 1 3/8 inch thick solid core doors which must self-close.

Many older houses, however, didn't even have such fire-rated doors when they were originally built. They were not called for back then. Fortunately, a number of these doors were later retrofitted with sheetmetal to serve as fire-barriers.

14.12 THE RISE, RUN AND WIDTH OF STAIRWAYS

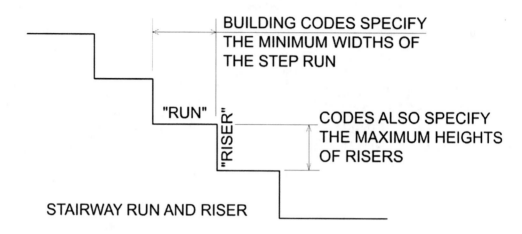

Fig. 14.12

Usual step 'runs' are not less than 10 inches wide while usual step 'risers' are built no more than 7 1/2 inches deep (although there are some occupancies which are required to have a 9 inch minimum run and an 8 inch maximum rise). Note that riser height is measured from the top of one tread to the top of the next, while the depth of a tread is measured from the face of one riser to the next riser face. Do not include the width of the nosing which overhangs the risers. As far as the minimum width of a stairway is concerned, many building codes specify that dimension as being as little as 30 inches.

14.13 VARIATION IN STEP RISERS

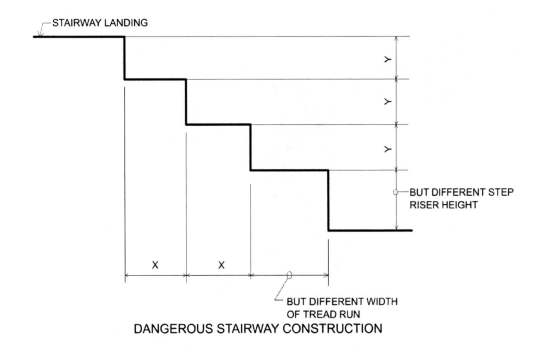

DANGEROUS STAIRWAY CONSTRUCTION

Fig. 14.13

Good construction practice dictates that the variation in step riser heights ought not to exceed 1/4" between steps. As such, greater differences in tolerance are just not expected, especially when one runs up or down the steps.

14.14 MINIMUM CLEARANCE HEIGHT ALONG STAIRWAYS

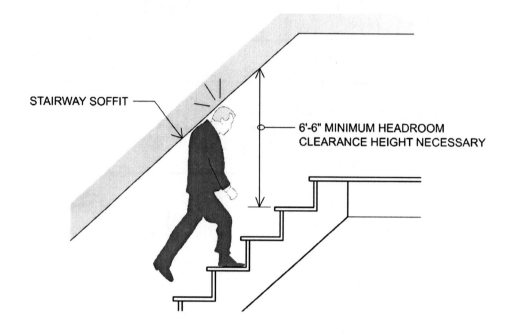

STAIRWAY SOFFIT

6'-6" MINIMUM HEADROOM
CLEARANCE HEIGHT NECESSARY

Fig. 14.14

To avoid taller people from bumping their heads along a stairway, stairways must offer an adequate headroom clearance for ascending and descending. For instance, building codes in general are known to specify this clearance to be at least 6 feet - 6 inches in height.

14.15 WHEN BANISTERS OR RAILINGS ARE NEEDED

THESE ARE DANGEROUS
STAIRS BECAUSE OF THEIR
ABSENCE OF A RAILING!

Fig. 14.15A

When there are four or more risers along a stairway, handrails are needed. They are also necessary at step, stoop or porch landings which are greater than 30 inches above floor or grade. Without them, a person can suffer severe harm from falling down steps or falling off a high landing.

Fig. 14.15B

As for those stairs which have fewer than four risers, banisters are generally not required.

FINISH FLOOR

SUBFLOOR

14.16 SPACING OF STAIRWAY BALUSTERS

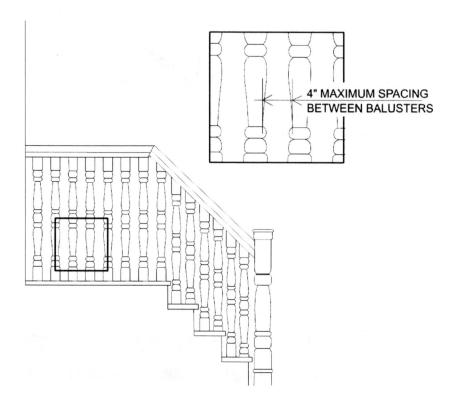

4" MAXIMUM SPACING
BETWEEN BALUSTERS

Fig. 14.16

Today, where handrail banisters are required, a 4 inch distance is the commonly recommended maximum space between immediate handrail balusters; so, too, is it for guardrail balusters. Formerly, there was 6 inch or wider spacing between immediate balusters used.

14.17 STAIR HANDRAIL'S WALL PROJECTION

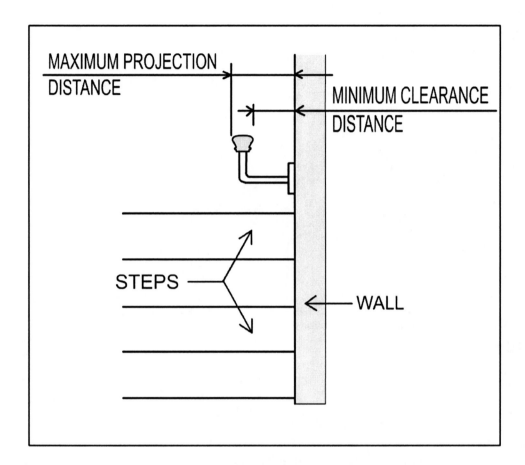

Fig. 14.17

To obtain a good grab of a handrail, there should be at least 1 1/2" distance between the rail bar and the stair wall. However, it is not recommended that handrails project more than 3 1/2" from the stairway wall into the width of the stairs.

14.18 HABITABLE ROOM'S MINIMUM WINDOW SIZE

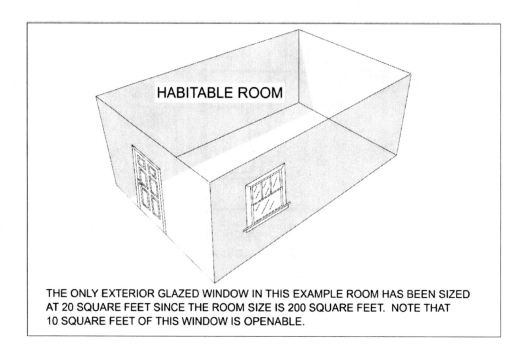

HABITABLE ROOM

THE ONLY EXTERIOR GLAZED WINDOW IN THIS EXAMPLE ROOM HAS BEEN SIZED
AT 20 SQUARE FEET SINCE THE ROOM SIZE IS 200 SQUARE FEET. NOTE THAT
10 SQUARE FEET OF THIS WINDOW IS OPENABLE.

Fig. 14.18

Window provision satisfies building code natural light and ventilation requirements for a habitable room of a house. The aggregate window area is normally dependent upon the size of the room. Specifically, there are building codes which define that size to be 1/10th of the room's superficial floor area, but with a minimum size of 10 square feet. Note that the same code calls for half of that required size to be openable. For bathrooms, laundry rooms, etc., that requirement is different.

14.19 MAXIMUM HEIGHT OF A WINDOW SILL

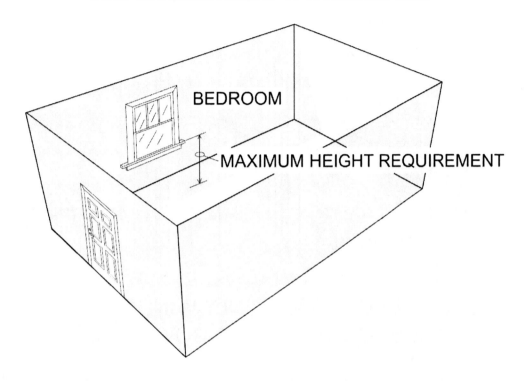

BEDROOM

MAXIMUM HEIGHT REQUIREMENT

Fig. 14.19

Inside a bedroom, the window sill height cannot be built too high above the bedroom floor. For those windows which are dependent upon ease of access in the event of an emergency, your local building code likely specifies 44 inches as that maximum common height allowed.

14.20 RELEASE FOR BEDROOM WINDOW SECURITY BARS

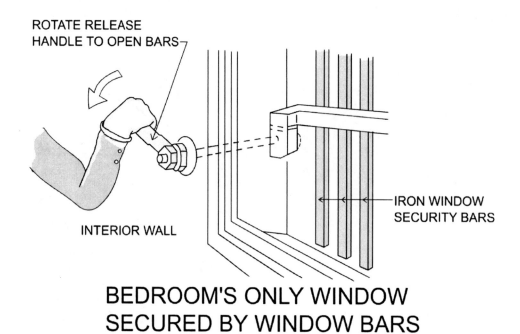

BEDROOM'S ONLY WINDOW
SECURED BY WINDOW BARS

Fig. 14.20

Check to see if an interior release handle has been equipped along at least one bedroom window that is secured by an iron bar grill so that one can escape through that window in the event of an emergency. Today, it would be a building code violation if there is not at least one window or door which is openable out to the exterior in each sleeping room.

14.21 FIRE-RATED SEPARATION BETWEEN HOUSE AND GARAGE

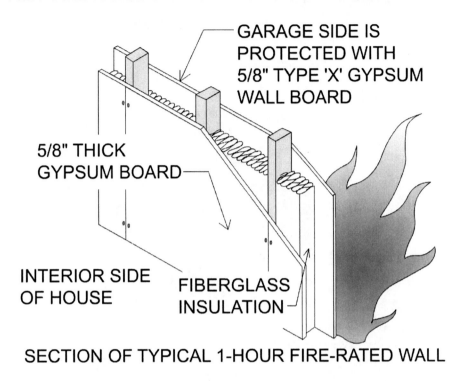

GARAGE SIDE IS
PROTECTED WITH
5/8" TYPE 'X' GYPSUM
WALL BOARD

5/8" THICK
GYPSUM BOARD

INTERIOR SIDE
OF HOUSE

FIBERGLASS
INSULATION

SECTION OF TYPICAL 1-HOUR FIRE-RATED WALL

Fig. 14.21

The wall which separates the house from an attached garage needs to
be one that is "fire-rated"; that is, of adequate fire resistive construction.
What's normally specified is 'one-hour' fire resistive construction. What this
means is that it would take about one hour for a fire to destroy a wall such that
the fire penetrates through the wall to its other side. Normally, other walls in
the garage do not have to be fire-rated and, consequently, don't receive
drywall. Their studs are left exposed. However, the ceiling separating a
garage from the house is typically required to be fire-rated, too.

14.22 ATTIC ACCESS

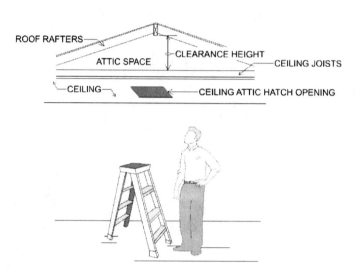

Fig. 14.22

Hatches are the normal means provided for one to gain access to the attic space. However, some homes have attics that lack a sufficient clearance height (for instance, 30 inches) and, in many of today's building codes, a scuttle hatch would not then be required.

The size of attic hatch openings usually depend upon whether a heating plant is located up in the attic space or not. Without the presence of one, hatches are normally sized to be 22" by 30"; and with a heating plant, a 30" by 30" minimum opening could be required.

14.23 LOW-TO-GRADE WOOD SIDING

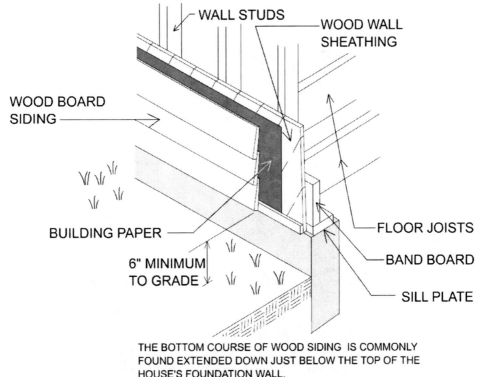

THE BOTTOM COURSE OF WOOD SIDING IS COMMONLY
FOUND EXTENDED DOWN JUST BELOW THE TOP OF THE
HOUSE'S FOUNDATION WALL.

Fig. 14.23

Although many building codes require a minimum 6" distance between outside grade and the top of the house's perimeter foundation wall, that requirement is not always adhered to. In fact, that distance often falls considerably short of the 6 inches. When this happens, the bottom course of wood siding becomes closer to grade. There is the condition, too, that the building's exterior wood siding alone starts too low-to-grade. Hence, watch out for low-to-grade woodwork since there is the possibility that termite damage or wood rotting action could have already taken place.

Chapter 15

HEATING AND AIR

CONDITIONING

Recognizing heating and air conditioning problems is the first step in making a safe and climate-comfortable home. You can learn some simple heating and air conditioning facts in the pages ahead and then apply this knowledge to check if climate control problems exist in the home that you are interested in purchasing. As such, when air temperatures rise and dip, you would want a reliably working heating and air conditioning system.

15.1 BIG HOUSE HAS SMALL AIR CONDITIONING SYSTEM

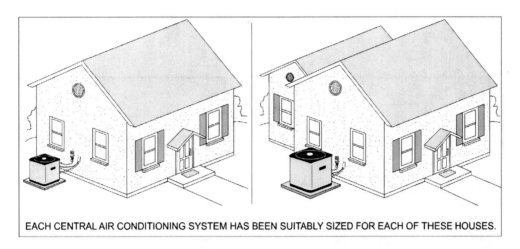

EACH CENTRAL AIR CONDITIONING SYSTEM HAS BEEN SUITABLY SIZED FOR EACH OF THESE HOUSES.

Fig. 15.1

Sometimes one finds that the tonnage of a house's central air conditioning system is on the small side considering the area of the house. That is, on some very hot summer days, the homeowner will find that the inside temperature does not sufficiently lower or remain low to the setting of the thermostat. Meanwhile, the air conditioning system virtually runs continuously. On those hot days, it's desirable to have the availability of more air conditioning tonnage. Figure that 1 ton capacity is needed for each 500 square feet of building area. That's a rough means to size up the capacity of the house's air conditioning tonnage needed.

15.2 WHERE'S THE HEAT?

SURPRISINGLY, THE ADDED MASTER BEDROOM LACKS DIRECT HEATING PROVISION AND, BECAUSE OF THIS, THE HOMEOWNER IN WINTER FEELS COLD.

Fig. 15.2

Realize that not every room of a house has to be directly heated. Generally, building codes still qualify a room in the absence of a direct source of heat as a 'habitable room' with some provision. For example, in Los Angeles, the room must be capable of reaching and keeping a minimum 70 degree Fahrenheit temperature three feet up from its floor for some time.

15.3 FUELED HEATING PLANTS LOCATED UNDER STAIRS

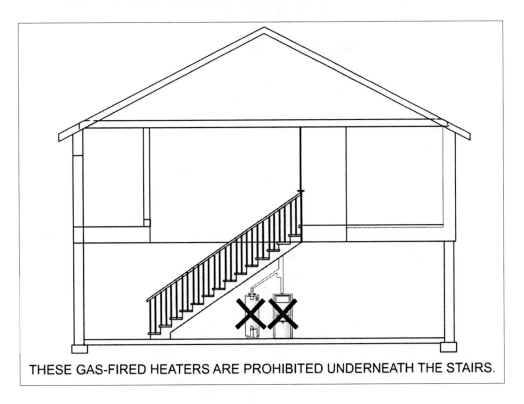

THESE GAS-FIRED HEATERS ARE PROHIBITED UNDERNEATH THE STAIRS.

Fig. 15.3

Gas or oil-fired furnaces and hot water heaters are not recommended to be located underneath stairway locations. In fact, there are mechanical codes which prohibit this. If a fire or an explosion caused by either of these heaters were to destroy the steps, there would be no easy access route for one to exit the dwelling from an upper level.

15.4 MORE LOCATIONS WHERE FUELED-FIRED FORCED WARM AIR FURNACES AND HOT WATER HEATERS ARE PROHIBITED

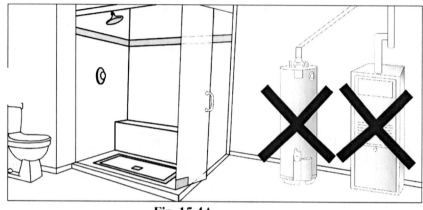

Fig. 15.4A

They are not allowed to be installed in a bathroom...

nor in a bedroom...

Fig. 15.4B

nor are they permitted to be located inside a closet that opens into a bedroom or a bathroom.

Fig. 15.4C

15.5 OLD GRAVITY HOT AIR FURNACE

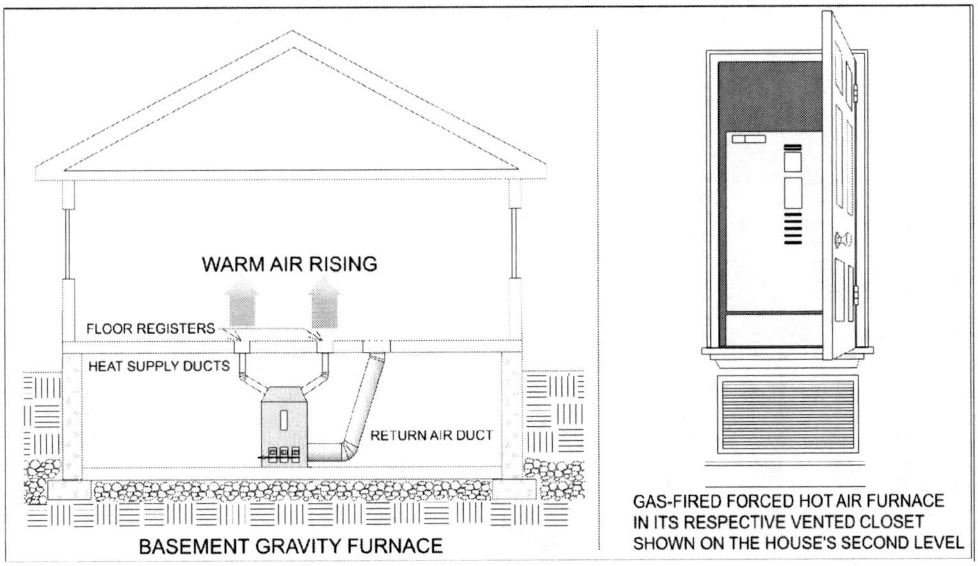

WARM AIR RISING

FLOOR REGISTERS

HEAT SUPPLY DUCTS

RETURN AIR DUCT

BASEMENT GRAVITY FURNACE

GAS-FIRED FORCED HOT AIR FURNACE
IN ITS RESPECTIVE VENTED CLOSET
SHOWN ON THE HOUSE'S SECOND LEVEL

Fig. 15.5

In older homes that have gravity furnaces, consider to realize their age. An old house might still have an old original unit running on borrowed time. If this is so, think to select a modern forced hot air furnace when it comes time for replacement. For one thing, the forced air furnace doesn't have to be located in the basement. It could be placed inside a vented closet or be located inside the attic. Forced air units are more energy efficient by re-heating returned warmed air whereas many gravity heating plants instead heat up cool air that comes in from the outside mixed in with the cooled off warm air that had settled back down to the basement. What's more about a forced air system is that it allows such advantages as electronic air cleaning, humidity control and, of course, air conditioning.

15.6 FACTS ABOUT CENTRAL STEAM AND HOT WATER OR AIR

HEATING SYSTEMS

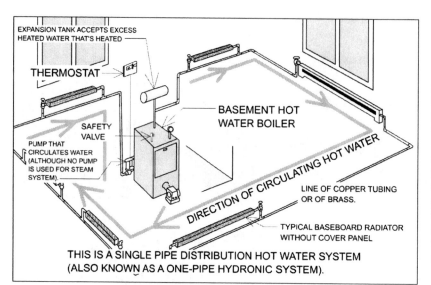

EXPANSION TANK ACCEPTS EXCESS
HEATED WATER THAT'S HEATED

THERMOSTAT

SAFETY
VALVE

PUMP THAT
CIRCULATES WATER
(ALTHOUGH NO PUMP
IS USED FOR STEAM
SYSTEM).

BASEMENT HOT
WATER BOILER

DIRECTION OF CIRCULATING HOT WATER

LINE OF COPPER TUBING
OR OF BRASS.

TYPICAL BASEBOARD RADIATOR
WITHOUT COVER PANEL

THIS IS A SINGLE PIPE DISTRIBUTION HOT WATER SYSTEM
(ALSO KNOWN AS A ONE-PIPE HYDRONIC SYSTEM).

Fig. 15.6A
Steam Heating System:
is either gas-fired or oil-
fired. The presence of a
water level glass outside
the heating plant
distinguishes a steam
boiler from that of a hot
water boiler. One
problem often found
with old boilers (and
furnaces) is that their
fireboxes (or heat
exchangers) crack.

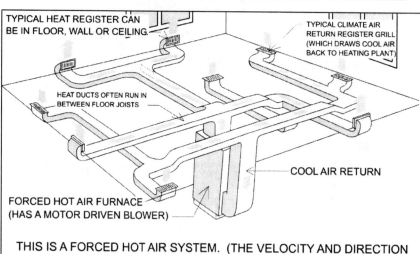

TYPICAL HEAT REGISTER CAN
BE IN FLOOR, WALL OR CEILING.

TYPICAL CLIMATE AIR
RETURN REGISTER GRILL
(WHICH DRAWS COOL AIR
BACK TO HEATING PLANT)

HEAT DUCTS OFTEN RUN IN
BETWEEN FLOOR JOISTS

COOL AIR RETURN

FORCED HOT AIR FURNACE
(HAS A MOTOR DRIVEN BLOWER)

THIS IS A FORCED HOT AIR SYSTEM. (THE VELOCITY AND DIRECTION
OF AIR FLOW ARE CONTROLLED BY VANES WITHIN THE DUCTS).

Fig. 15.6B
Forced Hot Air
Heating System: is
either gas-fired, or
oil-fired or even
electric. Typically,
however, gravity
warm air furnaces
are gas-fired units.

15.7 BIG HOUSE BUT SMALL FURNACE

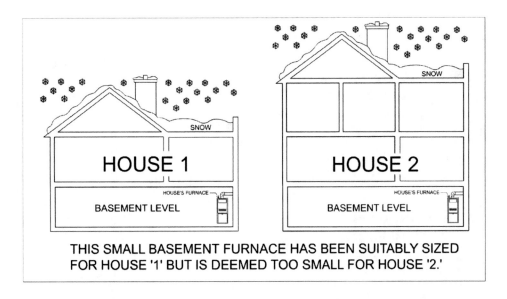

Fig. 15.7

A furnace having a low British thermal units per hour rating is a small size furnace for a large size house. When bitterly cold winter days come, the heating plant will continuously run and the temperature inside the house will either be incapable of reaching the temperature which the house was set for on the thermostat, or will have difficulty to maintain that temperature. If this is the case, adding another furnace system or replacing the existing one with more BTU's/hour rating would be recommended.

15.8 RESTRICTED FURNACE VENTILATION

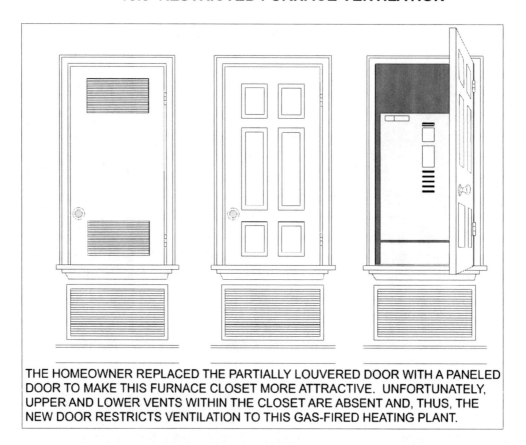

THE HOMEOWNER REPLACED THE PARTIALLY LOUVERED DOOR WITH A PANELED DOOR TO MAKE THIS FURNACE CLOSET MORE ATTRACTIVE. UNFORTUNATELY, UPPER AND LOWER VENTS WITHIN THE CLOSET ARE ABSENT AND, THUS, THE NEW DOOR RESTRICTS VENTILATION TO THIS GAS-FIRED HEATING PLANT.

Fig. 15.8

Some people don't like the sound of a gas-fired furnace firing up or the sound of the furnace blower running from a closet housing their furnace. Consequently, they close off their closet vents. This restricts furnace ventilation. A fueled heating plant (including a gas-fired hot water heater) must receive sufficient air for oxygen to sustain its process of combustion.

15.9 SEPARATED HEAT PLANT EXHAUST FLUES

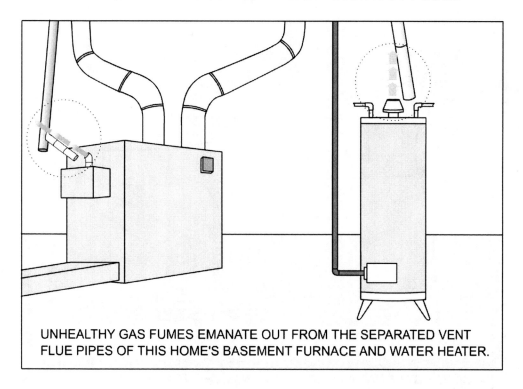

UNHEALTHY GAS FUMES EMANATE OUT FROM THE SEPARATED VENT
FLUE PIPES OF THIS HOME'S BASEMENT FURNACE AND WATER HEATER.

Fig. 15.9

Occasionally, exhaust flues are found to be partly separated from fuel-fired

furnaces and hot water heaters. Worse yet, they are sometimes found to be completely

detached from these heating plants. Either way, the flues need re-attachment. The

owner should know to have this condition corrected at once since exhaust fumes

contain carbon dioxide and carbon monoxide which mix in with the air stream that

circulates within the house. And that produces an unhealthy condition! Note that

electric hot water heaters and electric furnaces don't have exhaust vents.

15.10 LONG FLAT RUN OF FUEL-FIRED FURNACE[1]S EXHAUST DUCT

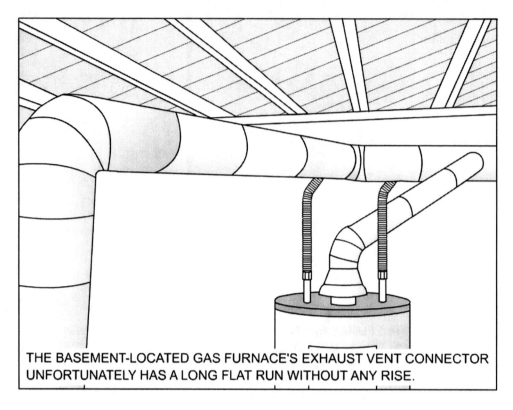

THE BASEMENT-LOCATED GAS FURNACE'S EXHAUST VENT CONNECTOR
UNFORTUNATELY HAS A LONG FLAT RUN WITHOUT ANY RISE.

Fig. 15.10

For basement or crawl space-located fuel-fired furnaces, the exhaust vent

connector should not run completely horizontal but, instead, have a rise or pitch.

Normally this is not less than 1/4 inch for each foot of run. Keep in mind that there is

also a maximum length of run permitted for a gravity vent connector. Short runs

aren't bad, but, of course, direct vertical exhaust venting is considered to be more

favorable.

15.11 DAMAGED DUCTING

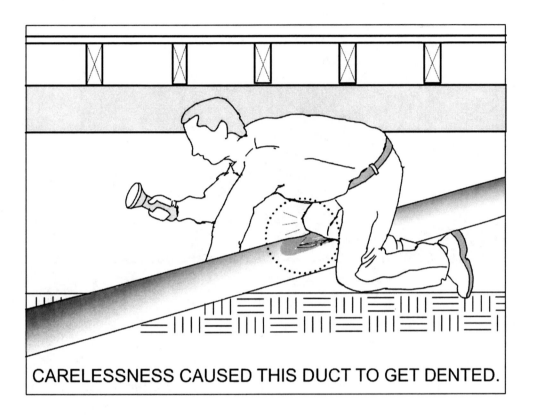

CARELESSNESS CAUSED THIS DUCT TO GET DENTED.

Fig. 15.11

Heating and air conditioning ducts in underfloor or attic spaces get dented from workers knocking into and crawling over them. Ducts develop holes and get separated, too. Be on the lookout for such damaged ducts.

15.12 NO HEAT COMES OUT FROM REGISTER

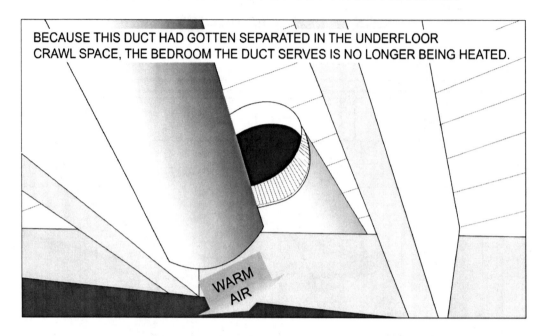

BECAUSE THIS DUCT HAD GOTTEN SEPARATED IN THE UNDERFLOOR
CRAWL SPACE, THE BEDROOM THE DUCT SERVES IS NO LONGER BEING HEATED.

WARM AIR

Fig. 15.12

Heat that fails to emanate from a supply register could be caused by a

separated duct. In that case, the underfloor or attic space is being heated, but not

the room.

15.13 WHAT STREAK MARKS OFF HEAT REGISTERS MEAN

TYPICAL STREAK MARKS
OFF HEAT REGISTER

Fig. 15.13

Black soot or what appear to be dirt streaks off heat supply registers of hot air systems could represent nothing more than dirty registers and grills or a dirty furnace blower filter, or even an accumulation of dirt inside the heat ducting. However, they could also reflect evidence of a cracked heat exchanger or firebox inside the furnace. When such a failure occurs, fumes that contain carbon dioxide and carbon monoxide flow out of the heating element and blend in with the warm air current that circulates throughout the house. Many would consider this dangerous condition as an indication of the beginning of the end of the furnace's life.

Chapter 16

HOT WATER HEATING

Most important while inspecting the hot water heating system involves checking some safety items about it. This includes making sure that the hot water heater has been installed in a safe place, that the hot water heating system has been equipped with a temperature/pressure relief valve and, if it is a fuel-fired unit, it has exhaust venting out to the exterior. Be certain that there is no gas leak at the heater, either. Seismic strapping or tank anchoring is a must feature to have in earthquake country.

Then, of course, it's smart to learn the tank size and rating (to realize that it can produce an adequate amount of hot water in the house relative to the number of the home's hot water outlets); its age and condition (especially if its old because it can leak); and the condition of the plumbing lines connected to it. Measure the hot water temperature (which should be somewhere between 110 degree F to 140 degree F). Check if the hot water is rusty in color. See, too, if it takes a lengthy time to get hot water. Do you hear 'sizzle' sounds from the tank which could very well reflect a leak? Read on to learn more.

16.1 GARAGE-LOCATED FUEL-FIRED HOT WATER HEATERS

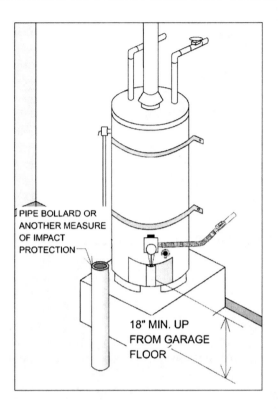

PIPE BOLLARD OR
ANOTHER MEASURE
OF IMPACT
PROTECTION

18" MIN. UP
FROM GARAGE
FLOOR

Fig. 16.1

Today, a fuel-fired water heater which is located inside a garage is required

to be elevated up from the garage floor such that its pilot light is a minimum height

of 18 inches up from the floor. This code requirement reduces the chances of

possible explosion from taking place from car fumes or vapors of stored flammable

products that could mix in with the water heater's pilot flame.

16.2 SMALL SIZE HOT WATER HEATER

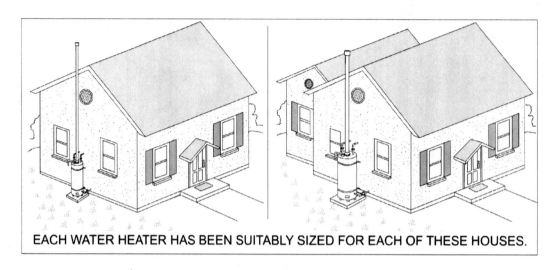

EACH WATER HEATER HAS BEEN SUITABLY SIZED FOR EACH OF THESE HOUSES.

Fig. 16.2

A hot water heater may be incorrectly sized for the house it is in. More often, the tanks are small when they are poorly-sized, producing an inadequate amount of hot water for normal family requirements in consideration of the number of hot water faucets available in the home. For families who are large consumers of hot water, a larger heater would be recommended to be installed. But some families wait until a new heater actually becomes needed. On the other hand, large tanks which produce ample or more than a sufficient amount of hot water can be big energy wasters.

16.3 DOES THE HOUSE HAVE AN ELECTRIC HOT WATER HEATER?

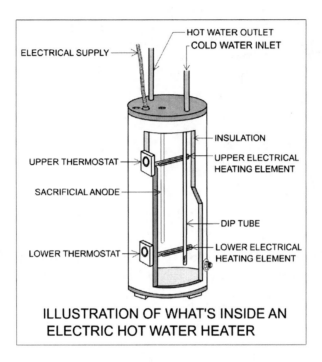

ILLUSTRATION OF WHAT'S INSIDE AN
ELECTRIC HOT WATER HEATER

Fig. 16.3

Generally speaking, electric hot water heaters are known to have lower recovery rates than oil or gas-fired water tanks. ("Recovery rate" is the term hot water heater manufacturers use to define the number of gallons of water their tanks would be capable of heating usually for a 100 degree Fahrenheit rise in temperature over its inlet temperature during the course of one hour). In fact, you can only expect recovery rates for electric water heaters to range from 18 gallons per hour to 22 gallons per hour. Indeed, when the hot water inside the tank is used up, there is some waiting time before there's more hot water...and that's not fun, especially when you're taking a shower. Thus, when a replacement tank becomes necessary, you can see why it is important to consider the proper tank size to suit your family's hot water needs.

16.4 WATER HEATER WORKS INEFFICIENTLY

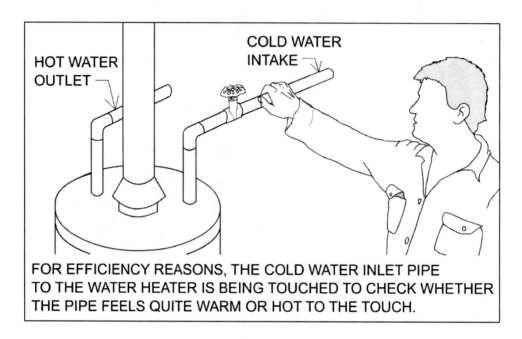

HOT WATER OUTLET

COLD WATER INTAKE

FOR EFFICIENCY REASONS, THE COLD WATER INLET PIPE TO THE WATER HEATER IS BEING TOUCHED TO CHECK WHETHER THE PIPE FEELS QUITE WARM OR HOT TO THE TOUCH.

Fig. 16.4

Sometimes the hot and cold water lines at a hot water heater are reversed, causing the tank to operate energy-wise in an uneconomical manner. That's because the cold water cools the tank's upper warm water when it comes in at the upper section of the tank. Instead, the cold water should go down the heater where there is other cold water inside the tank, which is at its bottom. You can check this out by feeling the pipes to see if the cold water pipe is actually quite warm to the touch just a few feet away from the heater.

Further, in order for a fuel-fired hot water tank to run efficiently, it must be periodically cleaned free of accumulated mineral sediment along its bottom. The sediment there serves to reduce the rising flow of heat that's generated from the low burner.

16.5 POPPING SOUNDS FROM WATER HEATER

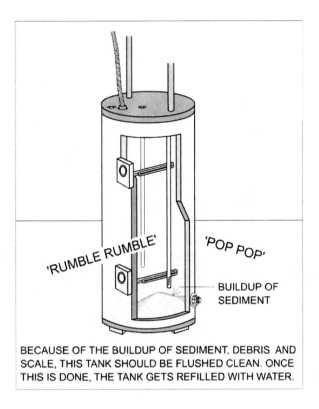

'RUMBLE RUMBLE'   'POP POP'

BUILDUP OF
SEDIMENT

BECAUSE OF THE BUILDUP OF SEDIMENT, DEBRIS AND
SCALE, THIS TANK SHOULD BE FLUSHED CLEAN. ONCE
THIS IS DONE, THE TANK GETS REFILLED WITH WATER.

Fig. 16.5

'Rumbling' and 'popping' sounds which are heard from a hot water

heater normally represent collected scale and sediment inside the tank. What

usually happens is that water gets under the sediment at the bottom and, when

heated, flashes into steam and makes that sound. The tank probably needs to

be drained and flushed clean.

16.6 DRIPPING HOT WATER HEATER'S CLEANOUT DRAIN

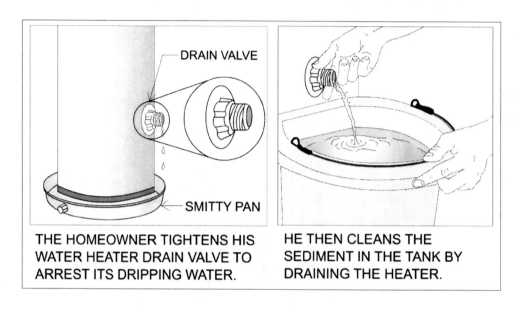

DRAIN VALVE

SMITTY PAN

THE HOMEOWNER TIGHTENS HIS
WATER HEATER DRAIN VALVE TO
ARREST ITS DRIPPING WATER.

HE THEN CLEANS THE
SEDIMENT IN THE TANK BY
DRAINING THE HEATER.

Fig. 16.6

Some water heater cleanout drains drip water. (A drain resembles a
hose bibb and has been provided so that a homeowner can use it to clean the tank of
collected sediment). Sometimes by simply tightening up the drain valve, the leakage
condition would be arrested. However, if this course of action fails to correct the
problem, engage the service of a plumber who would probably replace the valve.

16.7 EQUIP WATER HEATING SYSTEM WITH

TEMPERATURE/PRESSURE RELIEF VALVE

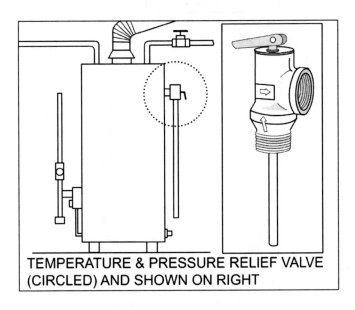

TEMPERATURE & PRESSURE RELIEF VALVE
(CIRCLED) AND SHOWN ON RIGHT

Fig. 16.7

A temperature & pressure relief valve should be installed for a home whose

plumbing system has been 'closed off,' not allowing water to flow back out into the water

main.   A home that is equipped with a water pressure regulator closes off the house

plumbing. Specifically, a pressure relief valve is a safety device that's supposed to work

when a hot water heater's thermostat doesn't. Indeed, the tank might heat up the water into

steam that could virtually destroy the tank. But the relief valve would safely permit the

built-up steam to escape. If no valve exists at the top of the tank, or there is none seen

outside the house, a plumber should be called in to make such a connection.

16.8 LEAKING PRESSURE RELIEF VALVE

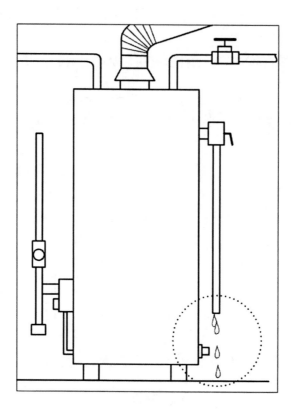

Fig. 16.8

A leaking pressure relief valve could mean that the hot water temperature is too high for this valve's setting. It could also reflect that too much pressure is building up in the hot water line, or that the valve is in need of replacement. Engage the services of a plumber to arrest a pressure relief valve that leaks frequently.

16.9 ANCHOR WATER HEATER IN EARTHQUAKE COUNTRY

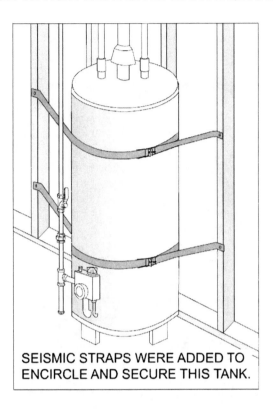

SEISMIC STRAPS WERE ADDED TO
ENCIRCLE AND SECURE THIS TANK.

Fig. 16.9

Anchoring a hot water heater tank or providing seismic straps around the water heater helps to prevent the tank from tumbling over or from too much horizontal or vertical displacement during some strong periods of earthquake activity.

Note that with gas-fired hot water heaters there is danger of gas leakage from semi-rigid aluminum tube gas supply connectors that can break with earthquake movement. And that is why many homeowners are replacing them with those of an approved corrugated metal connector variety.

Chapter **17**

INSULATION

When it is time for insulation inspection, there are several 'Is it?' questions to remember. They are:

Is it (the insulation) present (inside exterior walls, in the underfloor crawl space and in attic spaces)?

And, if so,

Is it acceptable? (For instance, 6 inches or thicker up in the attic)

Is it secure in place?

17.1 UNINSULATED ATTIC

Fig. 17.1

In old houses, if you do not find insulation in the attic - don't be surprised. Insulation was not typically provided years ago in neither attic spaces, nor in exterior walls. But you should consider at least insulating the attic so that you can conserve on your future heating and cooling costs. Remember that between 50 to 70 per cent of the average American house energy today is being utilized strictly for heating and cooling purposes.

17.2 MINIMAL INSULATION FOUND IN ATTIC

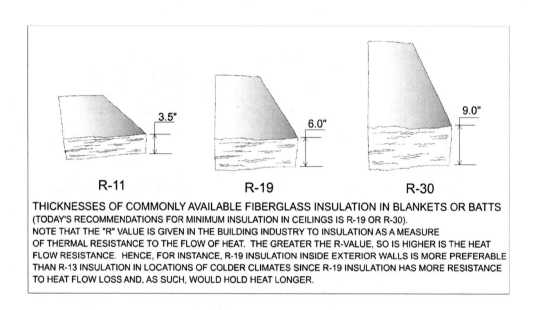

THICKNESSES OF COMMONLY AVAILABLE FIBERGLASS INSULATION IN BLANKETS OR BATTS
(TODAY'S RECOMMENDATIONS FOR MINIMUM INSULATION IN CEILINGS IS R-19 OR R-30).
NOTE THAT THE "R" VALUE IS GIVEN IN THE BUILDING INDUSTRY TO INSULATION AS A MEASURE
OF THERMAL RESISTANCE TO THE FLOW OF HEAT. THE GREATER THE R-VALUE, SO IS HIGHER IS THE HEAT
FLOW RESISTANCE. HENCE, FOR INSTANCE, R-19 INSULATION INSIDE EXTERIOR WALLS IS MORE PREFERABLE
THAN R-13 INSULATION IN LOCATIONS OF COLDER CLIMATES SINCE R-19 INSULATION HAS MORE RESISTANCE
TO HEAT FLOW LOSS AND, AS SUCH, WOULD HOLD HEAT LONGER.

Fig. 17.2

In general, the insulation that has been originally provided in older houses is

minimal in comparison to the insulation that is used today. Consider installing

new insulation or, at least, adding more insulation in attic and underfloor crawl

space locations for reason of conserving on heat.

17.3 RE-LAY ATTIC INSULATION

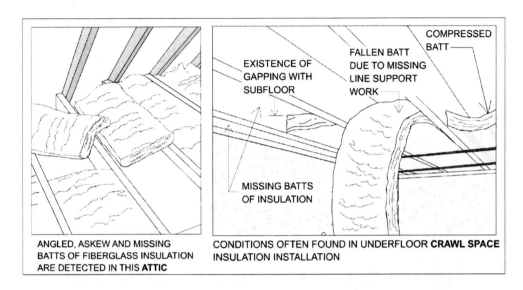

Fig. 17.3

Attic insulation which has fallen, that is found angled, dangled or askew needs to be re-laid with better workmanship.

Chapter 18

IRRIGATION SPRINKLERS

This chapter points out several frequently found irrigation sprinkler problems. You might note that because plumbing permits aren't always issued at the time of a sprinkler system's installation, there is no one to check how correct has been the installer's work and, consequently, errors could exist in the system.

Demonstrate the sprinklers while you are checking out the exterior improvements. Moreover, be sure to determine whether all pertaining ground areas are sprinkled.

18.1 IRRIGATION SPRINKLER VALVES

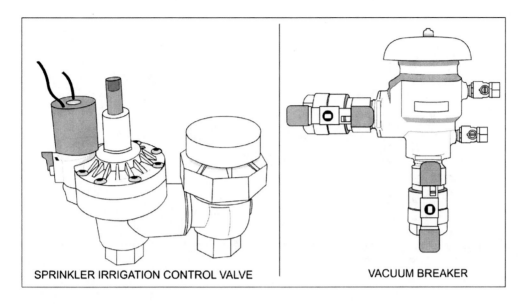

SPRINKLER IRRIGATION CONTROL VALVE   VACUUM BREAKER

Fig. 18.1

Today, the control valves of lawn sprinkler irrigation systems are supposed to be provided with anti-syphon valves. Normally they are installed at least 6" above grade. The home's sprinkler system otherwise, instead, may be equipped with a "vacuum breaker." But either of these devices should help deter sprinkler water from backflowing into the house's domestic water supply. That's relevant since sprinkler water can be contaminated with pesticides and fertilizers. Note that control valves at many older sprinkler systems are found to be barely above soil grade and don't even have anti-syphon valves.

18.2 DIVERT SPRINKLER SPRAY WATER AWAY PROM HOUSE

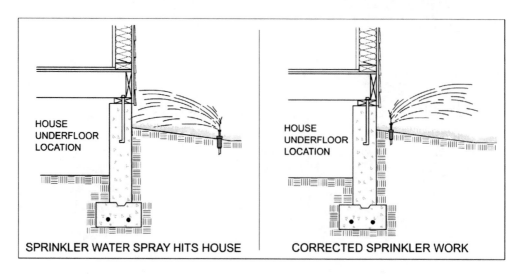

Fig. 18.2

All water that emanates from underground lawn sprinkler heads which are located just adjacent to the house's exterior wall sections and which are directed toward the house should be diverted away from the building structure. That's because it's possible that water could enter the underfloor as a result of the spray action. Sprayed water could also cause permanent stain damage along lower lengths of outside walls.

Chapter 19

MAINTENANCE, REPAIR AND

ITEMS TO CORRECT

Problems develop or conditions worsen when maintenance has been neglected. The following pages identify some key building areas where maintenance should not be omitted.

19.1 TRIM VEGETATION

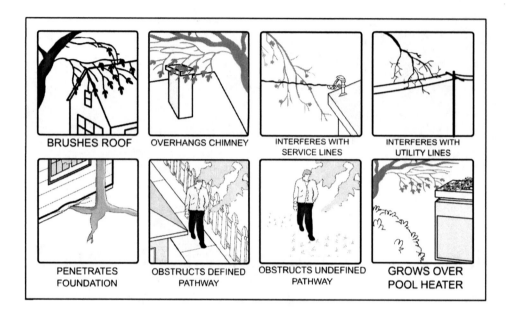

Fig. 19.1

    Maintaining trim vegetative growth provides for a good margin of fire safety. Trees that closely brush and overhang the house, the house chimney, the electrical service lines and outside heating plants (such as a pool/spa heater or a hot water heater) should be accordingly either trimmed back or cropped; so should the vegetative growth that's found to be in the way of defined and undefined pathways so that no one hurts themselves from that growth. Hopefully the vegetation did not already cause significant damage to the structure (and that is one reason why it is recommended that all underfloor areas be viewed). Check if the local municipality would attend to trim back vegetation which obstructs a sidewalk. You can possibly also get some help from the utility company with the trimming of vegetation that can adversely affect their utility lines and equipment.

19.2 MAINTAIN OUTSIDE DRAINS CLEAN

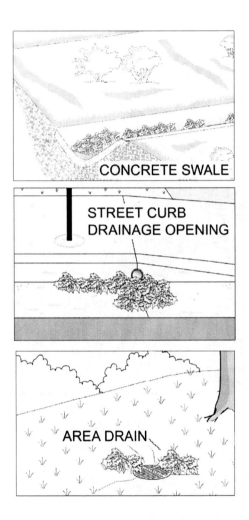

CONCRETE SWALE

STREET CURB
DRAINAGE OPENING

AREA DRAIN

Fig. 19.2

It's necessary to maintain all exterior drainage devices free of leaves, gravel, snow, ice, dirt and debris. If this is not done, area flooding or water backup could take place. This includes clearing and maintaining clear the illustrated examples above.

19.3 CLEAN LEADERS AND GUTTERS

Fig. 19.3

Don't underestimate how significant it is to keep the leaders and rain gutters on the house and garage free of leaves, gravel and debris. Indeed, under certain circumstances when roof drainage systems become clogged, water could back up beneath the eaves of some houses and penetrate down into exterior walls. And this is the risk one faces regarding this work if it is gone unattended.

19.4 CLEAN ROOFS

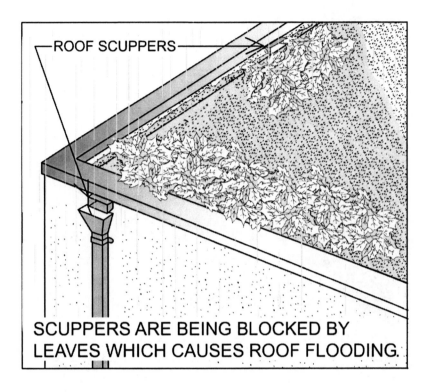

ROOF SCUPPERS

SCUPPERS ARE BEING BLOCKED BY LEAVES WHICH CAUSES ROOF FLOODING.

Fig. 19.4

Roof areas should be freed of leaves and debris. A clean and properly pitched roof helps to prevent water backup and consequent roof leakage. It can also help reduce the chance of structural failure occurrences often caused by the weight of standing water which collects upon relatively flat roofs.

19.5 REPAVE UPROOTED PATHWAY LOCATION

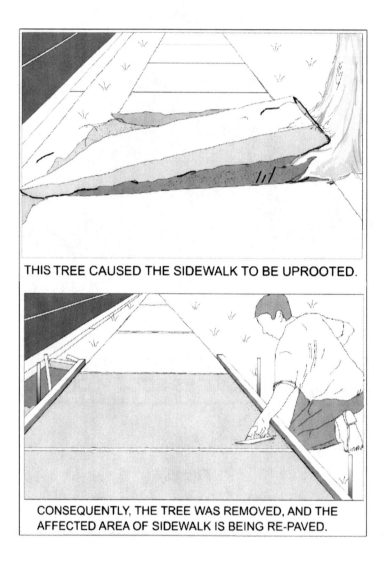

THIS TREE CAUSED THE SIDEWALK TO BE UPROOTED.

CONSEQUENTLY, THE TREE WAS REMOVED, AND THE AFFECTED AREA OF SIDEWALK IS BEING RE-PAVED.

Fig. 19.5

Trees uproot walkways and cause potential tripping hazards. Someone who trips and becomes injured on account of a lifted edge of a pathway could elect to sue.

19.6 CAULK AND SEAL

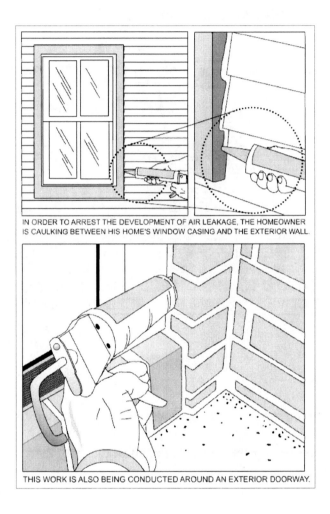

IN ORDER TO ARREST THE DEVELOPMENT OF AIR LEAKAGE, THE HOMEOWNER IS CAULKING BETWEEN HIS HOME'S WINDOW CASING AND THE EXTERIOR WALL.

THIS WORK IS ALSO BEING CONDUCTED AROUND AN EXTERIOR DOORWAY.

Fig. 19.6

To protect the house against the elements, caulking and sealing work should accordingly be periodically done. This includes sealing off exterior areas of the house open to weather and insect exposure.

19.7 REPLACE CRAWL SPACE ACCESS COVER

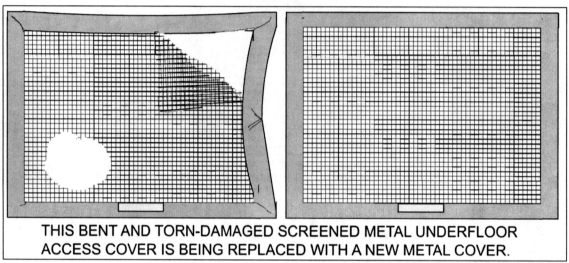

THIS BENT AND TORN-DAMAGED SCREENED METAL UNDERFLOOR ACCESS COVER IS BEING REPLACED WITH A NEW METAL COVER.

Fig. 19.7

Should the screened hatchway covers for underfloor crawl space access wall openings be badly damaged or missing, then it's time to replace them with new covers. Today, crawl space access openings are normally sized 18" by 24", but are sometimes smaller in old houses.

19.8 RE-SCREEN UNDERFLOOR SCREENED VENTILATION WALL OPENINGS

THESE TORN-DAMAGED SCREENED UNDERFLOOR WALL
VENT OPENINGS ARE SCHEDULED TO BE RE-SCREENED.

Fig. 19.8

Torn or otherwise damaged underfloor screened ventilation wall

openings should be re-screened to bar the entry of small animals. Typically,

1/4 inch square corrosion-resistant metal mesh is used for this purpose.

19.9 RE-SCREEN DAMAGED ATTIC PORT VENTS

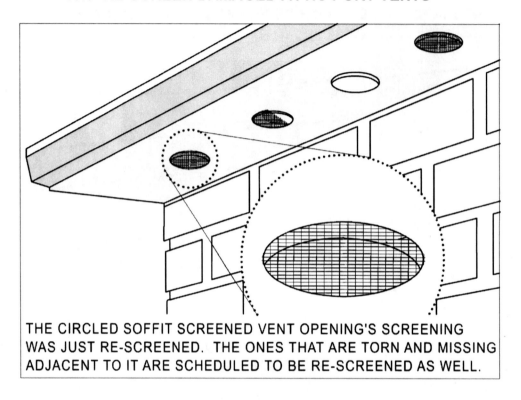

THE CIRCLED SOFFIT SCREENED VENT OPENING'S SCREENING
WAS JUST RE-SCREENED. THE ONES THAT ARE TORN AND MISSING
ADJACENT TO IT ARE SCHEDULED TO BE RE-SCREENED AS WELL.

Fig. 19.9

Attic port vent openings or roof eave soffit openings which are torn or

missing ought to be re-screened, too. Note that if this condition is left

unattended, bees and other insects might use the attic for a nesting area.

19.10 REPLACE DAMPROTTED WOOD

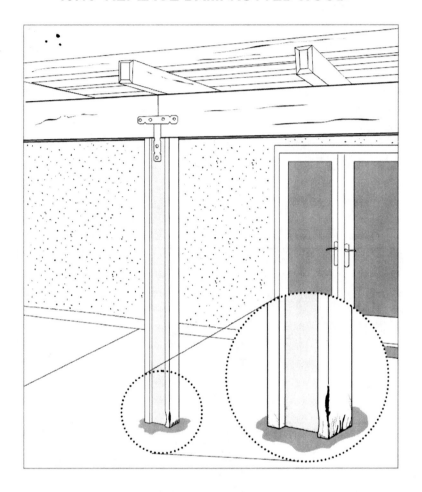

Fig. 19.10

Unprotected exterior woodwork in constant contact with soil and water could rapidly damprot. For example, the base of the illustrated wooden patio overhang post was found to be badly damprotted. The homeowner realized that there was not much choice about remedying the problem except for member replacement.

19.11 PATCH AND PARGE STUCCO FASCIA

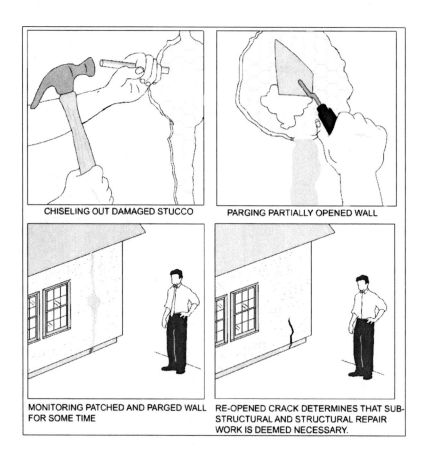

CHISELING OUT DAMAGED STUCCO

PARGING PARTIALLY OPENED WALL

MONITORING PATCHED AND PARGED WALL FOR SOME TIME

RE-OPENED CRACK DETERMINES THAT SUB-STRUCTURAL AND STRUCTURAL REPAIR WORK IS DEEMED NECESSARY.

Fig. 19.11

Fallen and missing stucco finish wall surfacing on a house can be re-coated or "parged" and then, if desired, painted.

Stucco cracks need patching to help stop them from becoming larger cracks. Additionally, patching prevents the possibility of insect entry or water entry through them. The more severe cracks might require periodic inspections after the patchwork to determine whether they reappear or not.

19.12 PERFORM CORRECTIVE WOOD SIDING WORK

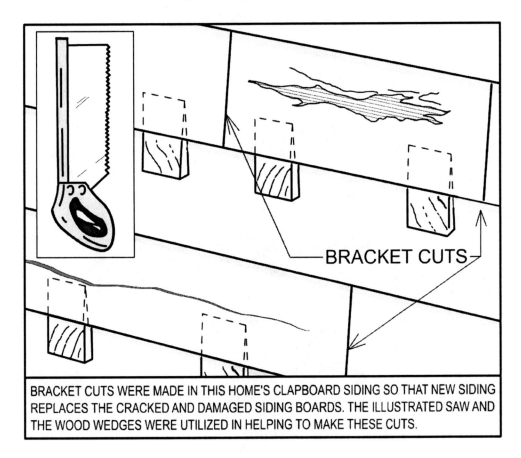

BRACKET CUTS WERE MADE IN THIS HOME'S CLAPBOARD SIDING SO THAT NEW SIDING REPLACES THE CRACKED AND DAMAGED SIDING BOARDS. THE ILLUSTRATED SAW AND THE WOOD WEDGES WERE UTILIZED IN HELPING TO MAKE THESE CUTS.

Fig. 19.12

To further help keep the house weather-tight, it's necessary to secure all loose wood siding members and replace those siding members which are significantly damaged.

19.13 RE-POINT MASONRY

Fig. 19.13

When masonry looses some of its mortar, it is time to "re-point."
Masons 're-point' when they fill in the small cracks and holes which occur
between masonry blocks and their mortar with new mortar. They also replace
all missing masonry. In the illustration, the stone wall is being re-pointed.

19.14 REPLACE CRACKED GLAZING

THIS CRACKED WINDOW PANE IS BEING REPLACED.

Fig. 19.14

19.15 REPUTTY WINDOW PANES

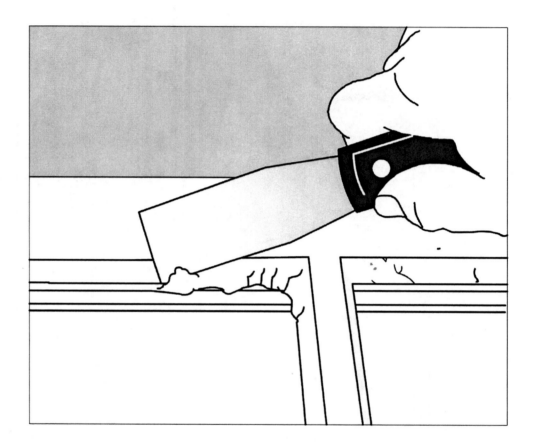

Fig. 19.15

Re-puttying around panes of window glazing should be attended to when there is fallen glazing compound. Do the same at windows that have loosened or even cracked glazing compound. That way, the window joints are kept both airtight and watertight.

19.16 THE NEED TO PAINT

SANDING WORK PREPARES THIS CLAPBOARD
SIDING FOR PRIMING AND PAINTING

Fig. 19.16

There is a need to paint:

--   exterior wood trim that is subject to dryrot, especially at locations
where considerable areas of raw wood have been exposed if it is not
painted. Paint helps to protect the wood and is, of course,
decorative, too;

-- the exterior of the house, perhaps merely for aesthetic reasons;

− the exterior metal trim where paint has peeled, exposing the metalwork to
continued rusting if it is not painted;

− and some exterior improvements, such as steps where paint markings aid in
making the existence of elevation differentials obvious so as to prevent you
and your guests from accidental injury.

19.17 MAINTAIN ROOF FLASHINGS

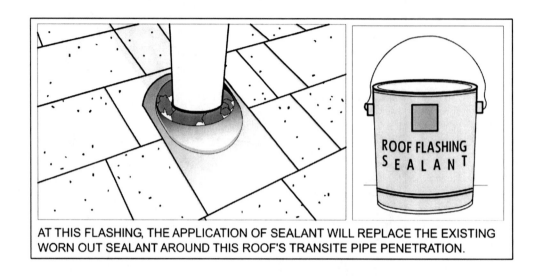

AT THIS FLASHING, THE APPLICATION OF SEALANT WILL REPLACE THE EXISTING WORN OUT SEALANT AROUND THIS ROOF'S TRANSITE PIPE PENETRATION.

Fig. 19.17

Roof flashing is installed along roof intersections to prevent leakages from taking place. For instance, flashing is used around chimneys, around roof dormers, at wall intersections as well as along roof valleys of intersecting roof planes, etc.. Sheets of galvanized iron is commonly used as the material for it, but flashing could also be of another metal.

Because there is movement of buildings in response to volume changes and to structural loading, gaps can develop at the flashings which would allow water to penetrate through the roof. That's why it is so important to repair flashings, or to seal them occasionally with roofing cement. Remember, most common roof leaks are those type through flashings which leak.

19.18 REPAIR LEAKS

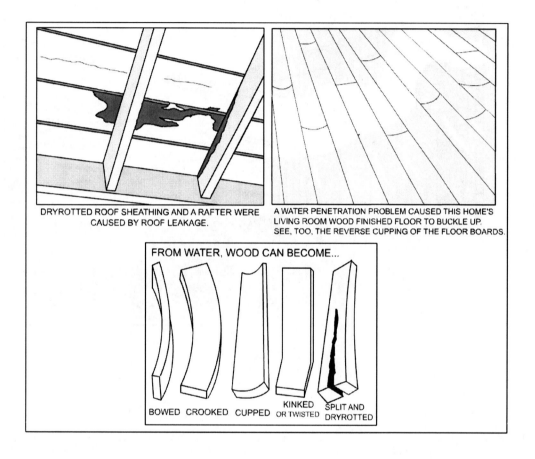

DRYROTTED ROOF SHEATHING AND A RAFTER WERE
CAUSED BY ROOF LEAKAGE.

A WATER PENETRATION PROBLEM CAUSED THIS HOME'S
LIVING ROOM WOOD FINISHED FLOOR TO BUCKLE UP.
SEE, TOO, THE REVERSE CUPPING OF THE FLOOR BOARDS.

FROM WATER, WOOD CAN BECOME...

BOWED   CROOKED   CUPPED   KINKED OR TWISTED   SPLIT AND DRYROTTED

Fig. 19.18

Catch and arrest water penetration problems since they can cause serious damages to a house. Just to name several damages resulting to wood members alone from water penetration that frequently occur include wood warpage and loosened framing members as well as dryrot inside ceilings, walls and floors... And if such damages go unattended, they could worsen and even further damage could occur at many locations in a home.

19.19 MAINTAIN A CLEAN UNDERFLOOR CRAWL SPACE

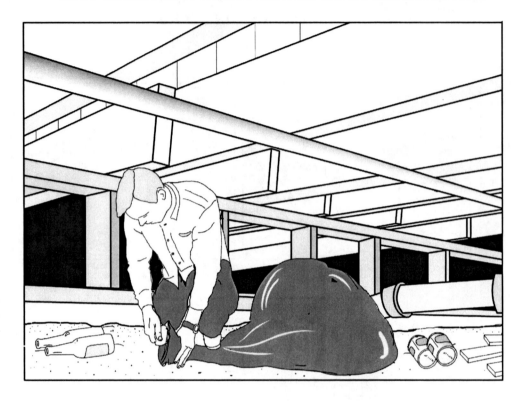

Fig. 19.19

It is a good practice to clear out the crawl spaces free of all loose wood and debris. For one thing, this helps to prevent termite damage to the house. For another, there is less chance for you or your workmen who occasionally might traverse the underfloor location from accidentally getting hurt there.

19.20 IF YOU SHOULD DETECT PESTS

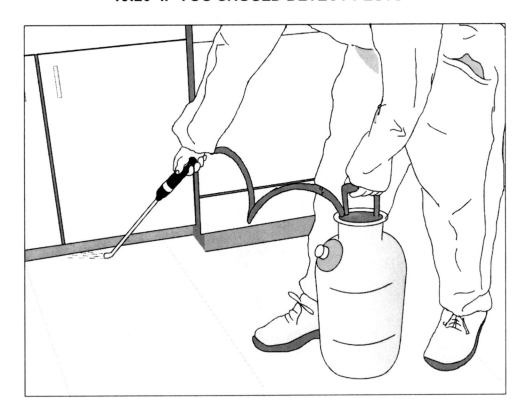

Fig. 19.20

If you should see pests (including a significant number of bees or wasps which hover about the site), or should you see their nests, consider budgeting for an exterminator to rid the premise of their presence.

Moreover, should you notice the presence of rodent traps, rodent droppings, trails of ants, cockroaches or other unwanted pests, you may be faced with the prospect of having a monthly service with a licensed pest control contractor for some period of time after you move in.

19.21 CORRECT FIRE HAZARDS

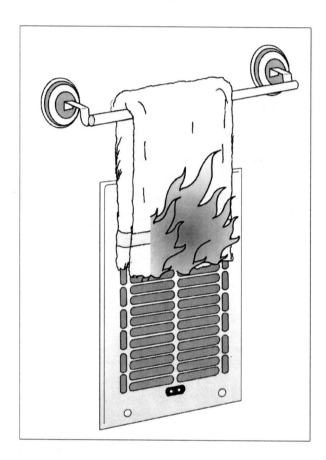

Fig. 19.21

Correct all potential fire hazards. A towel rod placed directly over a bathroom's electric space heater is one example of a potential fire hazard. Realize that it is better to relocate the rod than to deal with a towel having gotten caught on fire from the hot heater

19.22 ATTEND TO WEAK STEPS

THE CRACKED STRINGER, STEP RISER, STEP TREAD AND KICK PLATE WERE ALL SISTER-REINFORCED TO STRENGTHEN THIS STAIRWAY.

Fig. 19.22

Wood steps which are weaker than normal either require reinforcement or entire replacement.

19.23 SECURE SHAKY RAILINGS

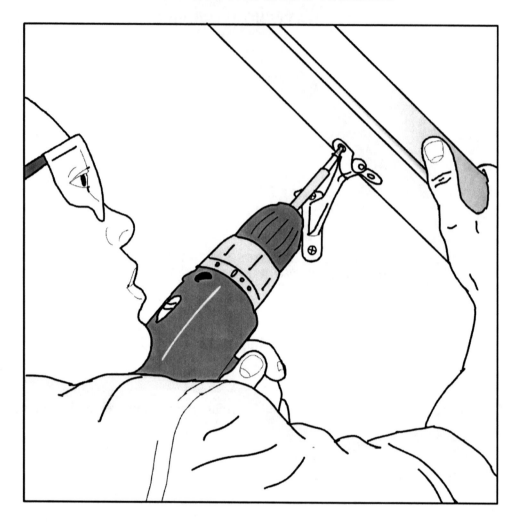

Fig. 19.23

For safety reasons, lengths of loose or shaky railings need to be resecured.

19.24 ATTEND TO NOISY FANS

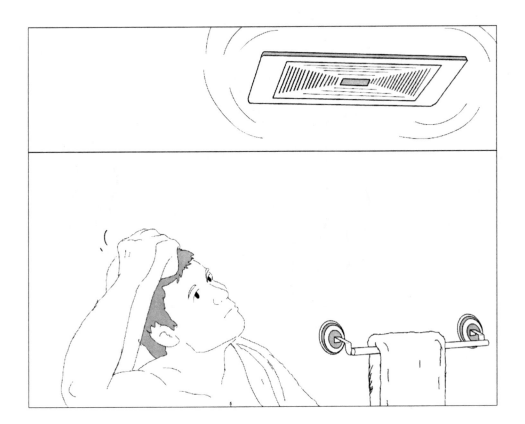

Fig. 19.24

Be cautious of noisy exhaust fans. Some may be in need of cleaning or repair. That reduces the chances of a fire hazard. Enough grease or dirt can restrict a sufficient amount of air flow to cause fan motors to overheat.

19.25 MAINTAIN UNCLUTTERED UTILITY CLOSETS

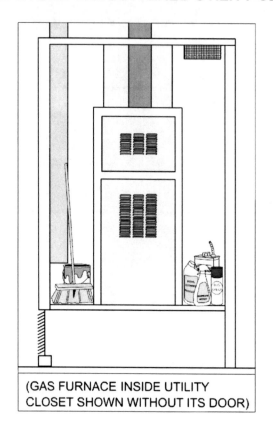

(GAS FURNACE INSIDE UTILITY
CLOSET SHOWN WITHOUT ITS DOOR)

Fig. 19.25

All stored material that is located inside fuel-fired heating plant closets should be removed from these closets for fire safety reasons. This includes flammable products such as varnish, cleaning products, insecticides, solvents, spray paints and gasoline.

19.26 MAINTAIN HEATING PLANT

Fig. 19.26

Periodic servicing of heating plants ensures their safe and efficient operation. It helps them to meet and sometimes exceed their rated life expectancy as well. This work includes servicing oil burners, cleaning the inside of gas burner compartments of built-in vented wall furnaces to prevent lint built-up, securing in place as necessary access panels of forced hot air furnaces to help avoid the risk of carbon monoxide poisoning, periodically replacing filters in forced air furnaces, checking the color of the gas flame so as to also avoid the risk of carbon monoxide poisoning, and adjusting combustion parts as deemed necessary.

19.27 REGROUT SINK AND OTHER BASINS

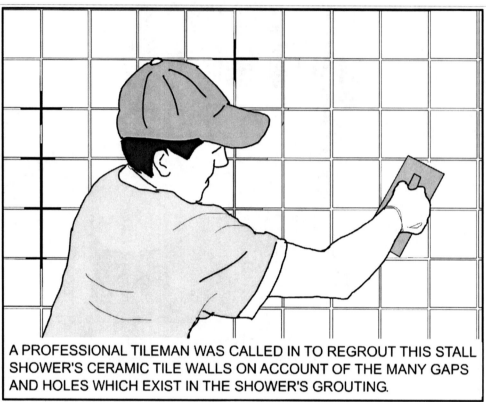

A PROFESSIONAL TILEMAN WAS CALLED IN TO REGROUT THIS STALL SHOWER'S CERAMIC TILE WALLS ON ACCOUNT OF THE MANY GAPS AND HOLES WHICH EXIST IN THE SHOWER'S GROUTING.

Fig. 19.27

Because water could seep through holes and gaps in old groutings around sinks, bathtubs and stall showers and cause the wood below and in back of these plumbing fixtures to eventually rot, regrouting work is required to be performed periodically.

Chapter 20

OLD ITEMS, MISSING

ITEMS AND TELLTALE

SIGNS

In this chapter, there is 'something old', 'something missing' and some

'telltale signs' presented to you. Refer to these pages and make use of the

information in them for comparison with the home that you're inspecting.

20.1 OLD MECHANICAL EQUIPMENT IN THE HOUSE

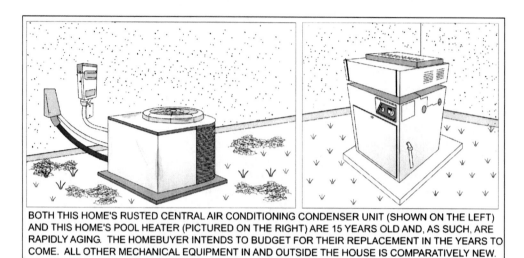

BOTH THIS HOME'S RUSTED CENTRAL AIR CONDITIONING CONDENSER UNIT (SHOWN ON THE LEFT) AND THIS HOME'S POOL HEATER (PICTURED ON THE RIGHT) ARE 15 YEARS OLD AND, AS SUCH, ARE RAPIDLY AGING. THE HOMEBUYER INTENDS TO BUDGET FOR THEIR REPLACEMENT IN THE YEARS TO COME. ALL OTHER MECHANICAL EQUIPMENT IN AND OUTSIDE THE HOUSE IS COMPARATIVELY NEW.

Fig. 20.1

Here's a guide to some mechanical equipment in the house that is considered to be old equipment, or equipment that is approaching their trouble-free life expectancy:

IN CENTRAL AIR CONDITIONING SYSTEMS:

Electric Air Conditioning Units: Compressors are rated for 5 to 10 years. Homeowners tend to generally replace the entire condenser unit which includes the compressor.

Gas Air Conditioning Units: Tend to have 8 to 12 year life expectancy.

IN HEATING SYSTEMS:

Cast Iron Boilers for Steam Heating or for a Circulating Hot Water Heating System: Could last 40 years or longer. Check the firebox condition to see if it is cracking and crumbling.

Steel Boilers for a Circulating Hot Water Heating System: Has a rated life expectancy of about 20 years.

Hot Air Furnaces: 20 year rated life expectancy, although gravity furnaces have been known to last a lot longer.

Oil Burners: Tend to last 10 to 15 years.

Oil Tanks: Those tanks which have been located inside the house tend to last 15 to 20 years, while those which are buried in the ground get rusted out and manage to last only 10 to 15 years.

HOT WATER HEATERS: Water heaters have an 8 to 10 year rated life expectancy. Although they may be found rusted or dented on their exterior, these tanks do not usually get replaced until the time of which they leak (perhaps through small holes they develop normally caused by internal corrosion).

SWIMMING POOL "SUPPORT" EQUIPMENT:

Pool Heaters: Are expected to last between 10 to15 years. Normally what

happens is that the expensive heat exchanger fails and causes water to

leak from the heater.

Pool Filters: Have a rated life expectancy varying between 10 to15 years.

They get replaced because of tank (crack) leakage that's often

difficult to repair.

Pool Motors: Are expected to last more than 5 years. The motor might

burn out or get a short.

Pool Pumps: Can last up to 20 years. Its housing might get crack-damaged.

WATER WELL EQUIPMENT:

Well Pumps: Can last between 8 to 15 years.

Well Water Storage Tanks: Have a rated life between 8 to 12 years.

20.2 NO DOORBELL

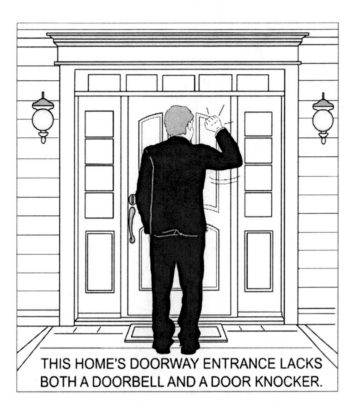

THIS HOME'S DOORWAY ENTRANCE LACKS
BOTH A DOORBELL AND A DOOR KNOCKER.

Fig. 20.2

Electric or mechanical doorbells are convenient to visitors; so are door knockers. But there are numerous homes which are not equipped with either of them. When doorbells do exist, however, many are found to be inoperative. Further, in colder climates, some doorbells have been incorrectly placed inside storm doors rather than having been located outside them. Homeowners lock their storm doors and leave no access available to the doorbells.

20.3   BALCONY OR PATIO LACKS LIGHT, HOSE BIBB AND ELECTRICAL OUTLET

LANTERN LIGHT FIXTURES, A HOSE BIBB AND AN ELECTRICAL CONVENIENCE OUTLET ARE ABSENT AT THIS HOME'S BACK PATIO.

Fig. 20.3

Not all builders provide hose bibbs, lights or electrical outlets at balconies or patios, although homeowners find them both helpful and desirable. Of course, they can be later added. Note that when electrical convenience outlets do get added, it is recommended that they be of the ground fault interrupter variety for electrical safety reasons.

20.4 MORE COMMONLY MISSING ITEMS

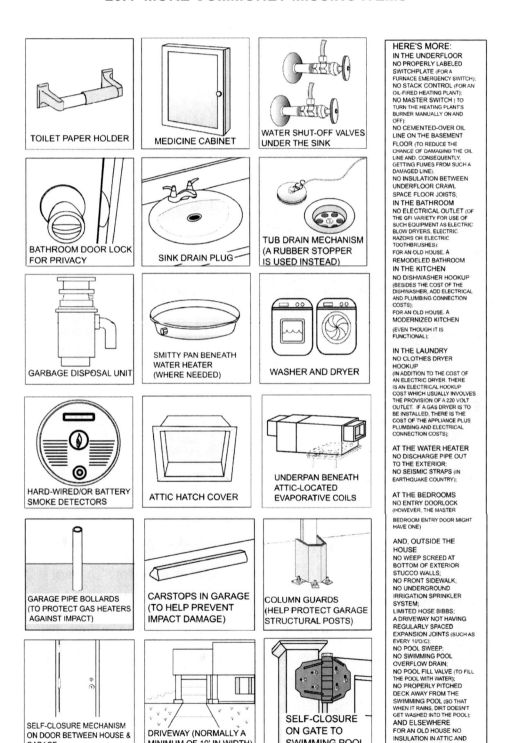

TOILET PAPER HOLDER

MEDICINE CABINET

WATER SHUT-OFF VALVES UNDER THE SINK

BATHROOM DOOR LOCK FOR PRIVACY

SINK DRAIN PLUG

TUB DRAIN MECHANISM (A RUBBER STOPPER IS USED INSTEAD)

GARBAGE DISPOSAL UNIT

SMITTY PAN BENEATH WATER HEATER (WHERE NEEDED)

WASHER AND DRYER

HARD-WIRED/OR BATTERY SMOKE DETECTORS

ATTIC HATCH COVER

UNDERPAN BENEATH ATTIC-LOCATED EVAPORATIVE COILS

GARAGE PIPE BOLLARDS (TO PROTECT GAS HEATERS AGAINST IMPACT)

CARSTOPS IN GARAGE (TO HELP PREVENT IMPACT DAMAGE)

COLUMN GUARDS (HELP PROTECT GARAGE STRUCTURAL POSTS)

SELF-CLOSURE MECHANISM ON DOOR BETWEEN HOUSE & GARAGE

DRIVEWAY (NORMALLY A MINIMUM OF 10' IN WIDTH)

SELF-CLOSURE ON GATE TO SWIMMING POOL

HERE'S MORE:
IN THE UNDERFLOOR
NO PROPERLY LABELED SWITCHPLATE (FOR A FURNACE EMERGENCY SWITCH);
NO STACK CONTROL (FOR AN OIL-FIRED HEATING PLANT);
NO MASTER SWITCH (TO TURN THE HEATING PLANT'S BURNER MANUALLY ON AND OFF);
NO CEMENTED-OVER OIL LINE ON THE BASEMENT FLOOR (TO REDUCE THE CHANCE OF DAMAGING THE OIL LINE AND, CONSEQUENTLY, GETTING FUMES FROM SUCH A DAMAGED LINE);
NO INSULATION BETWEEN UNDERFLOOR CRAWL SPACE FLOOR JOISTS;
IN THE BATHROOM
NO ELECTRICAL OUTLET (OF THE GFI VARIETY FOR USE OF SUCH EQUIPMENT AS ELECTRIC BLOW DRYERS, ELECTRIC RAZORS OR ELECTRIC TOOTHBRUSHES);
FOR AN OLD HOUSE, A REMODELED BATHROOM
IN THE KITCHEN
NO DISHWASHER HOOKUP (BESIDES THE COST OF THE DISHWASHER, ADD ELECTRICAL AND PLUMBING CONNECTION COSTS);
FOR AN OLD HOUSE, A MODERNIZED KITCHEN (EVEN THOUGH IT IS FUNCTIONAL);

IN THE LAUNDRY
NO CLOTHES DRYER HOOKUP
(IN ADDITION TO THE COST OF AN ELECTRIC DRYER, THERE IS AN ELECTRICAL HOOKUP COST WHICH USUALLY INVOLVES THE PROVISION OF A 220 VOLT OUTLET. IF A GAS DRYER IS TO BE INSTALLED, THERE IS THE COST OF THE APPLIANCE PLUS PLUMBING AND ELECTRICAL CONNECTION COSTS);

AT THE WATER HEATER
NO DISCHARGE PIPE OUT TO THE EXTERIOR;
NO SEISMIC STRAPS (IN EARTHQUAKE COUNTRY);

AT THE BEDROOMS
NO ENTRY DOORLOCK (HOWEVER, THE MASTER BEDROOM ENTRY DOOR MIGHT HAVE ONE)

AND, OUTSIDE THE HOUSE
NO WEEP SCREED AT BOTTOM OF EXTERIOR STUCCO WALLS;
NO FRONT SIDEWALK;
NO UNDERGROUND IRRIGATION SPRINKLER SYSTEM;
LIMITED HOSE BIBBS;
A DRIVEWAY NOT HAVING REGULARLY SPACED EXPANSION JOINTS (SUCH AS EVERY 10'0/C);
NO POOL SWEEP;
NO SWIMMING POOL OVERFLOW DRAIN;
NO POOL FILL VALVE (TO FILL THE POOL WITH WATER);
NO PROPERLY PITCHED DECK AWAY FROM THE SWIMMING POOL (SO THAT WHEN IT RAINS, DIRT DOESN'T GET WASHED INTO THE POOL);
AND ELSEWHERE
FOR AN OLD HOUSE NO INSULATION IN ATTIC AND EXTERIOR WALLS.

Fig. 20.4

20.5 WHAT PEELED PAINT ON AN INSIDE WALL MEANS

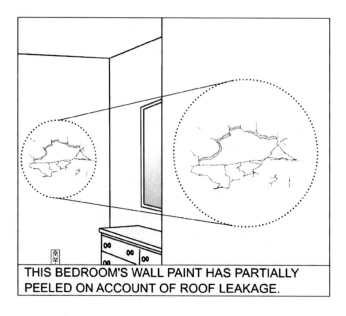

THIS BEDROOM'S WALL PAINT HAS PARTIALLY
PEELED ON ACCOUNT OF ROOF LEAKAGE.

Fig. 20.5

Peeled paint could simply be the result of poor bonding between the base primer paint and the surface finish paint. There is also the possibility that peeled paint represents a moisture or water problem in the wall such as from roof leakage.

Note that water leakages inside walls or above ceilings at areas of peeling paint or water staining can cause mold / or wood rot. To learn if the mold/ or rot condition does exist (which might be costly to repair), one might have to open up the wall to divulge the condition. This can be done just before the next paint job. However, in the meanwhile, you could be faced with this risk.

20.6 BLISTERED INTERIOR WALL REFLECTS MOISTURE

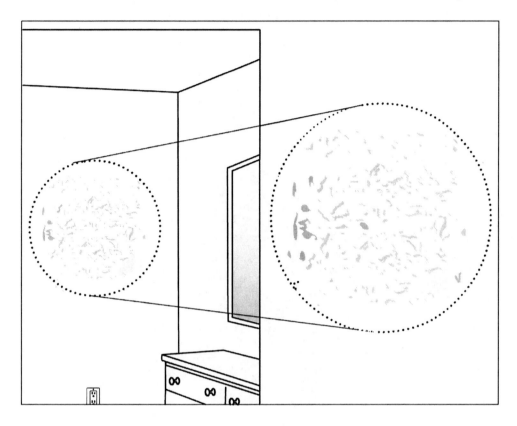

Fig. 20.6

Water or moisture penetration can also cause an interior wall to blister. The illustrated blistered bedroom's plaster wall example points up the necessity to ensure that all exterior walls are weathersealed, /or patch-repaired, and that all roof and roof flashing be appropriately maintained.

20.7 MILDEW CAUSES

Fig. 20.7

If mildew is found on interior walls and ceilings of the house, the air inside the house is most likely too moist. Basically, besides heat, good ventilation helps to stop mildew. Where applicable, try removing the mildew with chlorine bleach and trisodium phosphate.

20.8 COMMONLY OBSERVED WATER STAINS

AS A RESULT OF WATER SPRINKLER ACTION HAVING SPRAYED AGAINST THE HOUSE FOR AN EXTENDED PERIOD OF TIME, WATER STAINS, STREAK MARKS AND DISCOLORATION NOW MARK THIS HOME'S BOTTOM EXTERIOR WALL.

Fig. 20.8

Along lower lengths of exterior walls can result from:

-snow;

-irrigation sprinkler water spray action;

-or from drainage run-off water or flood water.

Along underfloor foundation walls and wood members probably caused by:

-plumbing leakage or water penetration problems.

On a basement floor:

-flood occurrences due to washing machine backup, hot water heater leakage, basement water seepage, sewer backup, other plumbing leaks;

-moderate water seepage;

-watering down the floor.

Along interior floors result from:

> -radiator valve water leak;
>
> -watering plants;
>
> -sink, toilet or other plumbing fixture leaks;
>
> -mopping.

Along lengths of interior walls result from:

> -mopping;
>
> -rain water entry though a doorway;
>
> -rain water entry through a window ;
>
> -washing action;
>
> -plumbing leakage;
>
> -flooding;
>
> -burst or leaking hot water heater;
>
> -the placement of a wet mop up against the wall.

Along ceilings result from:

> -bathtub overflow;
>
> -washing action;
>
> -leak from hot water heater above;
>
> -plumbing fixture leak;
>
> -leakage during repair of a plumbing fixture
>   above;
>
> -plumbing leak from above;
>
> -radiator leak from above;
>
> -condensation dripping from a pipe above;
>
> -roof leakage;
>
> -leakage caused by clogging of the roof drainage system.

But some dry stains may:

-be quite old and presently inactive because their causing

conditions have already been corrected;

-antedate a new roof or roofing repair.

Ask the owner about all stains and try obtaining any

guarantees which pertain to the remedial work.

20.9 COMMON REASONS FOR PATCHWORK

THIS CEILING WAS JUST PATCHED AS A RESULT OF A
FORMER LEAK THAT HAD DEVELOPED ABOVE THIS AREA.

Fig. 20.9

Patches arise from the following frequently found example conditions:

-leakages;

-plumbing repairs;

-impact damages;

-removal (for instance, of a lighting fixture in the area of the patch);

-structural cracks;

-revision work, including installations and

closures.

Question the seller about the patchwork and acquire any pertaining guarantees, too.

Chapter 21

PLUMBING

Here's one part of the inspection where you can't be shy if you want to catch plumbing problems which could involve expensive repair costs. This means to say that you should ask the seller some key questions concerning the home's plumbing, including learning the age of the house's waste drainage system, what it actually consists of, and learning the kind of pipes that's equipped in the house.

Go through the motions like flushing and shaking toilets, running water in the plumbing fixtures, and searching for leaks. It's better to know of seriously low water pressure problems before the purchase. Indeed, don't be overly surprised when you learn that the seller has left a host of plumbing problems to have gone unattended to date.

21.1 STANDING WATER INSIDE WATER METER PIT

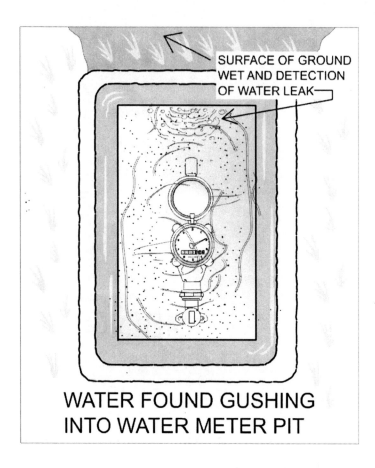

SURFACE OF GROUND
WET AND DETECTION
OF WATER LEAK

WATER FOUND GUSHING
INTO WATER METER PIT

Fig. 21.1

If the water meter is located in an outside pit, be sure to examine the meter and pit for there could be standing water inside the pit. If this turns out to be the case, ask the seller to call the local water company to free the pit of water, view the meter itself and inspect for possible leakage. The standing water might have simply resulted from rain water entry or perhaps from irrigation sprinkler spray action. However, valve or meter leakage could have developed there. If it is determined with certainty that there is leakage from the water main, the cost of a new water main can be expensive.

21.2 WET AREA CAUSED BY DAMAGED PIPING

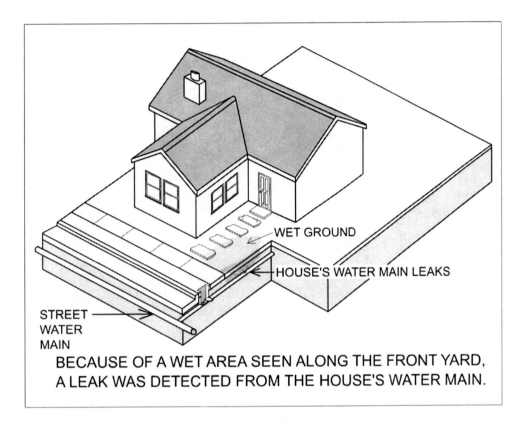

BECAUSE OF A WET AREA SEEN ALONG THE FRONT YARD, A LEAK WAS DETECTED FROM THE HOUSE'S WATER MAIN.

Fig. 21.2

You might find a ground area outside the house that's wet while elsewhere on the site, the soil is dry. It could be that someone had just watered the yard in that area before the inspection. Request verification of the fact that the wet area does not represent existing evidence of a damaged or broken underground water main or sprinkler line which could have to be replaced. Request a viewing of that area again before closing.

21.3 GAS LEAK AT GAS METER

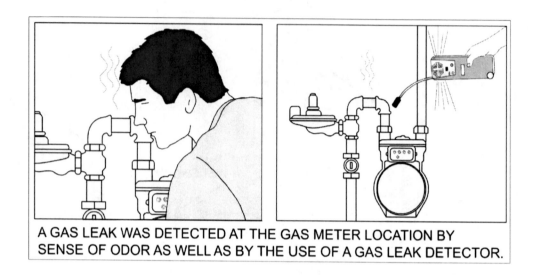

A GAS LEAK WAS DETECTED AT THE GAS METER LOCATION BY
SENSE OF ODOR AS WELL AS BY THE USE OF A GAS LEAK DETECTOR.

Fig. 21.3

At times, gas leaks develop at gas meter locations. Your nose can be a good

indicator of gassy odors. So can be the smear of soapy water onto the gas meter, its

piping and unions as could be the use of a gas leak detector. Thus, be certain the

meter is checked for the possibility of any such leakage. The local gas company

should be immediately notified if a gas odor does exist at the meter so that their

personnel could take care of the repair at once.

21.4 KNOW YOUR PLUMBING SHUT-OFF VALVES

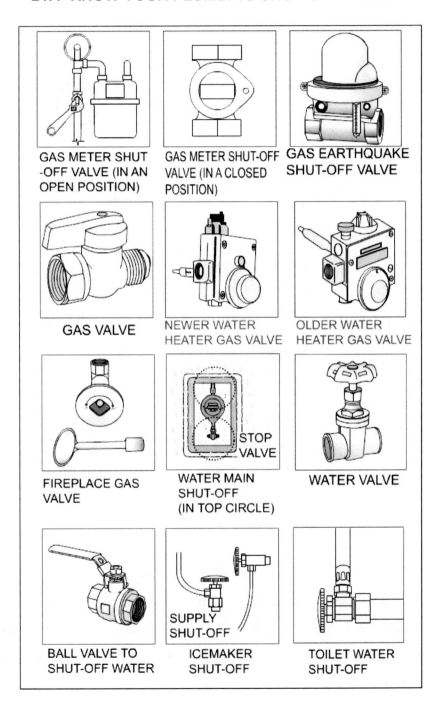

Fig. 21.4

21.5 HIGH WATER PRESSURE

WATER PRESSURE
REDUCING VALVE

WATER PRESSURE
TEST GAUGE

Fig. 21.5

Faucets which spray water fiercely out of their spouts could mean that the water pressure is way too high. Knowing this, you probably would want to engage the services of a plumber to install a pressure reducing valve. This valve (or "pressure regulator") will lower the pressure without recognizably diminishing the amount of water that is taken into the house. Usually it is located where the water main protrudes up from grade to enter the house. 50 to 60 psi is normal, workable pressure for the interior of a home. Indeed, some building codes require the installation of this device when the water pressure that's delivered to the building exceeds 80 psi.

21.6 LOW WATER PRESSURE

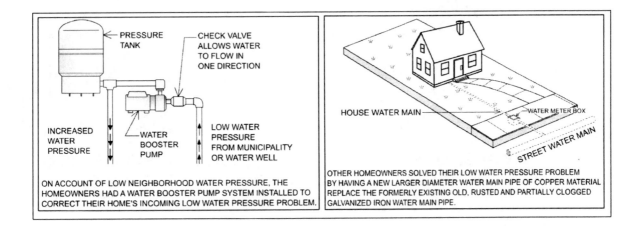

Fig. 21.6

Low or diminished water pressure is not unusual in older homes for it might represent the need for a new or greater-sized water main. (Old mains such as those of galvanized iron material sometimes clog by mineral deposits in hard water and/or may become corroded or rusted). There is also the possibility that low water flow may be due to low neighborhood pressure. Learn if the entire neighborhood has been complaining of this problem, especially during hot summer months. Water pressure varies in a number of communities during the daytime, too.

Note that if the low water pressure condition is an individual one which so happens to pertain only to your prospective home, consider selecting the installation of a tank and booster pump system to increase the house's water pressure.

21.7 LOW WATER PRESSURE AT FAUCET

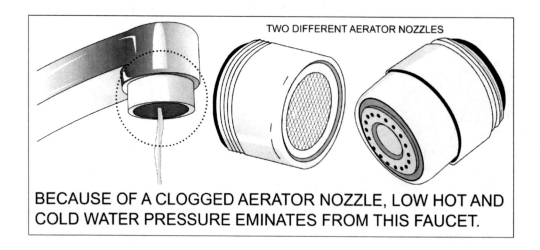

TWO DIFFERENT AERATOR NOZZLES

BECAUSE OF A CLOGGED AERATOR NOZZLE, LOW HOT AND COLD WATER PRESSURE EMINATES FROM THIS FAUCET.

Fig. 21.7

Low hot and cold water pressure at individual faucets could merely be the result of restrictions caused by clogged faucet aerator nozzles. If you should find in the inspection that this is a concern to you, check the cleanliness of the aerators out first before calling in a plumber. Generally, clogged aerator problems do not justify the services of a plumber for aerators are easy to remove and clean.

21.8 LOW HOT OR COLD WATER PRESSURE AT FAUCETS

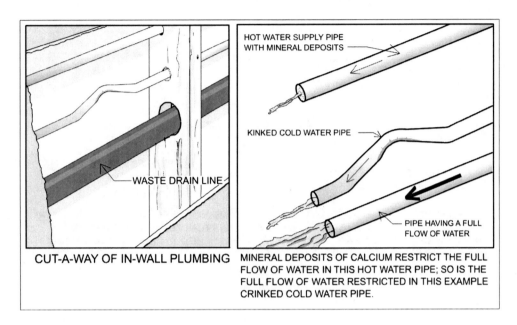

CUT-A-WAY OF IN-WALL PLUMBING

HOT WATER SUPPLY PIPE
WITH MINERAL DEPOSITS

KINKED COLD WATER PIPE

PIPE HAVING A FULL
FLOW OF WATER

WASTE DRAIN LINE

MINERAL DEPOSITS OF CALCIUM RESTRICT THE FULL
FLOW OF WATER IN THIS HOT WATER PIPE; SO IS THE
FULL FLOW OF WATER RESTRICTED IN THIS EXAMPLE
CRINKED COLD WATER PIPE.

Fig. 21.8

In older houses you might find that the water pressure is lower than

what might normally be expected at some faucets throughout the house.

There may be constrictions (such as possibly of mineral deposits or of kinks)

in those lines.

21.9 OLD GALVANIZED IRON PLUMBING

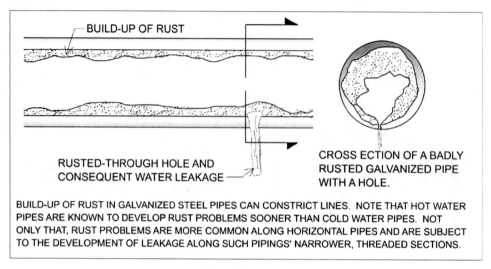

BUILD-UP OF RUST

RUSTED-THROUGH HOLE AND
CONSEQUENT WATER LEAKAGE

CROSS ECTION OF A BADLY
RUSTED GALVANIZED PIPE
WITH A HOLE.

BUILD-UP OF RUST IN GALVANIZED STEEL PIPES CAN CONSTRICT LINES. NOTE THAT HOT WATER
PIPES ARE KNOWN TO DEVELOP RUST PROBLEMS SOONER THAN COLD WATER PIPES. NOT
ONLY THAT, RUST PROBLEMS ARE MORE COMMON ALONG HORIZONTAL PIPES AND ARE SUBJECT
TO THE DEVELOPMENT OF LEAKAGE ALONG SUCH PIPINGS' NARROWER, THREADED SECTIONS.

Fig. 21.9

Old galvanized iron water plumbing pipes often are a source of problems in older homes because of their interior rusting. Sometime following the occurrence of interior rusting, the water pressure diminishes and the water turns to rust in its color. At that time, many homeowners change some or all their water pipes with new pipes. Try running water at several plumbing fixture cold water taps simultaneously. A home's plumbing system that's in good condition should not experience significant pressure drop. Afterwards, do the same with several of the hot water faucets.

21.10 ELECTROLYTIC ACTION

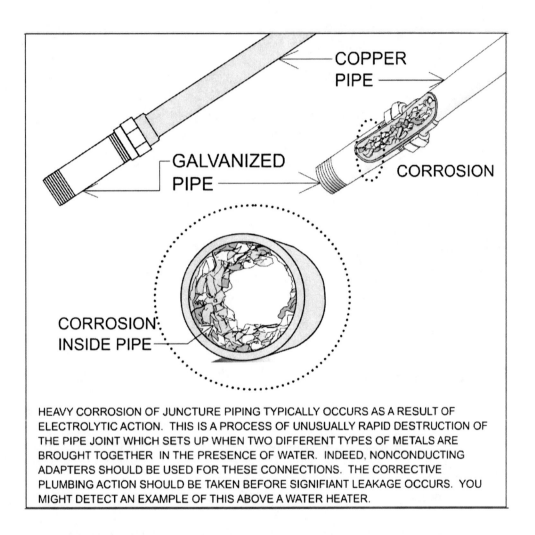

COPPER PIPE

COPPER PIPE

GALVANIZED PIPE

CORROSION

CORROSION INSIDE PIPE

HEAVY CORROSION OF JUNCTURE PIPING TYPICALLY OCCURS AS A RESULT OF
ELECTROLYTIC ACTION. THIS IS A PROCESS OF UNUSUALLY RAPID DESTRUCTION OF
THE PIPE JOINT WHICH SETS UP WHEN TWO DIFFERENT TYPES OF METALS ARE
BROUGHT TOGETHER IN THE PRESENCE OF WATER. INDEED, NONCONDUCTING
ADAPTERS SHOULD BE USED FOR THESE CONNECTIONS. THE CORRECTIVE
PLUMBING ACTION SHOULD BE TAKEN BEFORE SIGNIFIANT LEAKAGE OCCURS. YOU
MIGHT DETECT AN EXAMPLE OF THIS ABOVE A WATER HEATER.

Fig. 21.10

21.11 CORROSION OF PLUMBING PIPES

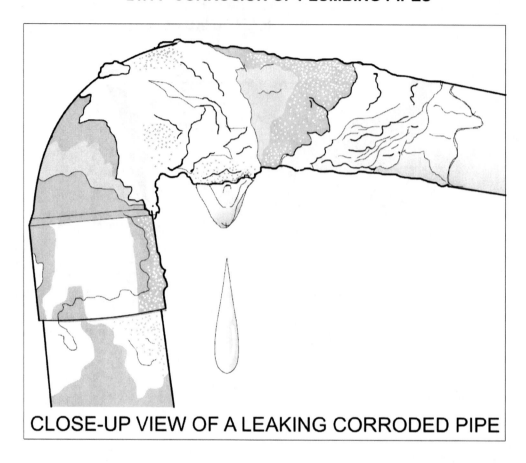

CLOSE-UP VIEW OF A LEAKING CORRODED PIPE

Fig. 21.11

When plumbing pipes show corrosion, they could be so deeply pitted and so weak that they require immediate replacement. The corrective action should be attended to before leakage occurs.

21.12 UNSUPPORTED PIPES

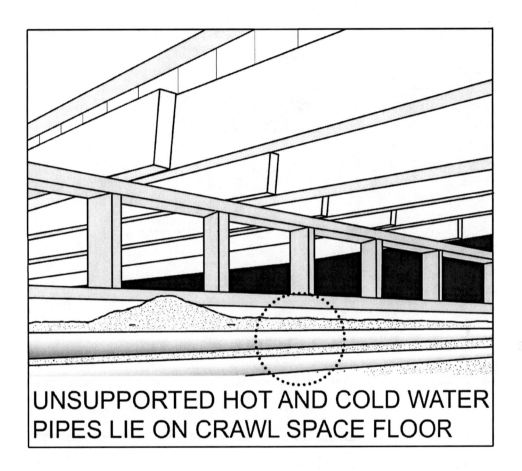

UNSUPPORTED HOT AND COLD WATER
PIPES LIE ON CRAWL SPACE FLOOR

Fig. 21.12

Search for plumbing supply pipes which are not supported at all or which are inadequately supported. Look for this especially in the crawl space where some pipes just rest upon the ground. Indeed, inadequately secured water pipes to the house's framework often shudder when a valve is being closed. (Water hammer is not the only cause that contributes to banging and thumping noises one hears when a faucet is being shut off) .

21.13 BANGING 'WATER HAMMER' NOISES

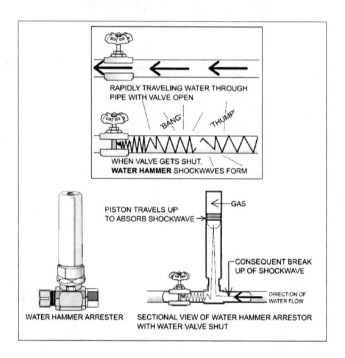

Fig. 21.13

Noises of pipe "banging" or "thumping" which are heard when a water faucet is being shut off could be sounds resulting from a "water hammer" condition. What happens is that when rapidly moving water suddenly gets stopped, there are shock waves formed along a run of the pipe. Those shock waves create the "bang" or "thump" sounds.

Water hammer could come about from the lack of air cushions at individual fixtures in old houses whereby, in that case, the installation of air chambers would likely be the recommended remedy. It could also be caused by the loss of air cushion, necessitating the need to drain the pipes. Note that if the condition causing water hammer is left unattended for awhile, leaks might develop in the plumbing system.

21.14 CHATTERING NOISES WHEN A FAUCET IS TURNED ON

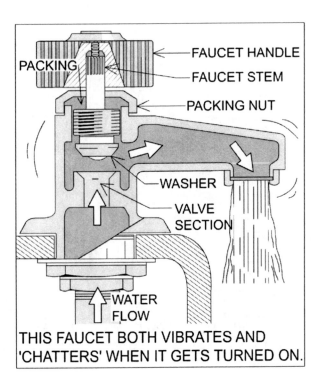

FAUCET HANDLE
FAUCET STEM
PACKING
PACKING NUT
WASHER
VALVE
SECTION
WATER
FLOW
THIS FAUCET BOTH VIBRATES AND
'CHATTERS' WHEN IT GETS TURNED ON.

Fig. 21.14

Listen for chattering vibrational noises when you turn on a water faucet. This may simply be due to a wrong size washer, a worn faucet washer, or perhaps to looseness of an inside part. Indeed, the washer may not be held securely to its stem. Repair might include replacing the washer or merely tightening the loose part. Note that the noise may occur from another cause as well. For instance, it could be that the washer seat became closed with residue and the water flow that's restricted causes the chattering noise. The seat then would need to cleaned.

21.15 WASTE BACKUP

THE OVERFLOWING TOILET AND THE WASTE BACKUP ARE
CAUSED BY THIS HOME'S DAMAGED DRAIN LINE.

Fig. 21.15

Toilets which overflow when flushed or sinks that don't drain could

indicate that there's a constriction in the main plumbing waste line. But

backup problems can also represent the existence of a badly cracked or

damaged drain line which could have to be replaced. That's why it is

recommended to test all the plumbing fixtures in the house and be satisfied

that all are in working order. Search, too, for stained or wetted drain pipes

since the cost of such possible plumbing replacement work can be expensive.

21.16 OLD SEWER LINES

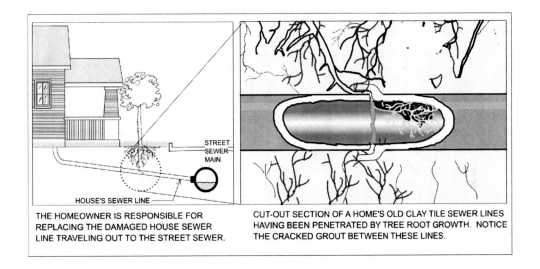

THE HOMEOWNER IS RESPONSIBLE FOR REPLACING THE DAMAGED HOUSE SEWER LINE TRAVELING OUT TO THE STREET SEWER.

CUT-OUT SECTION OF A HOME'S OLD CLAY TILE SEWER LINES HAVING BEEN PENETRATED BY TREE ROOT GROWTH. NOTICE THE CRACKED GROUT BETWEEN THESE LINES.

Fig. 21.16

Many older houses still have their original sewer lines (the plumbing waste lines between the house and the street's municipal sewer line) that are at or even beyond their rated life expectancy. These lines will likely need replacement in the years ahead. They get old, punctured by tree roots and break. Sewer lines which are more than 40 years old are considered to be getting old.

21.17 FACTS ABOUT A HOME'S INDEPENDENT WASTE DISPOSAL SYSTEM

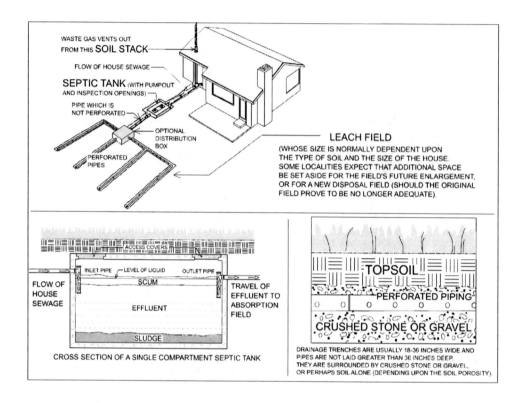

Fig. 21.17

Today's sanitary codes do not usually allow the construction of

cesspools. Cesspools are not as safe as modern septic systems. Here's how a

septic system works:

Sewage exits the house through a waste pipe into a septic tank. The sewage separates into 4 parts. These are:

Scum & Sludge - which get trapped inside the septic tank;

Gas - which travels back through the waste pipe back into the house and then exhausts out the roof's "soil stack" (the vertical waste vent pipe)

& Effluent - (the liquid portion of the sewage) which travels out to the drainage disposal field via an outlet pipe.

The disposal field or "leach field" usually having rows of 4 inch diameter perforated pipes lying in a trench of gravel is where the effluent seeps down into the ground neutralizing its impurities. A "seepage pit" might be utilized instead of a leach field should there be unfavorable soil absorption or perhaps if little room actually exists for a leach field.

Note that some municipalities allow a home to be equipped with a sink garbage disposal unit, while the building department in other communities doesn't permit this. Building departments generally disallow water that is collected from roof drainage systems to enter a private waste disposal system, either.

To help avoid those untimely backups, and to help keep the system working, the tank should be periodically pumped clean to remove the scum and sludge. Preferably, this should be done every 2 to 3 years.

21.18 BEDROOMS WERE LATER ADDED, BUT THE PRIVATE WASTE WASN'T INCREASED YET

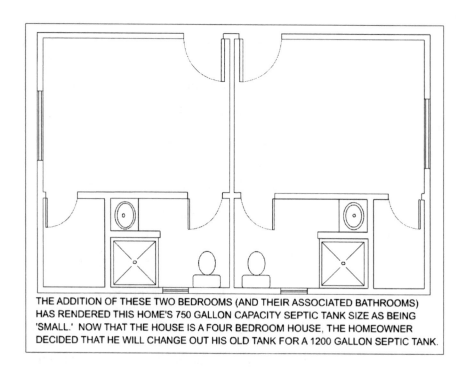

THE ADDITION OF THESE TWO BEDROOMS (AND THEIR ASSOCIATED BATHROOMS) HAS RENDERED THIS HOME'S 750 GALLON CAPACITY SEPTIC TANK SIZE AS BEING 'SMALL.' NOW THAT THE HOUSE IS A FOUR BEDROOM HOUSE, THE HOMEOWNER DECIDED THAT HE WILL CHANGE OUT HIS OLD TANK FOR A 1200 GALLON SEPTIC TANK.

Fig. 21.18

Normally a septic tank is sized to the number of bedrooms that are in the house and not determined by the number of people who dwell in it. With the addition of new bedrooms, the septic system could theoretically be considered too small. Indeed, if it is determined with certainty that it is too small, another tank should then be accordingly connected onto either the inlet or outlet side of the existing tank, or the existing tank can be replaced with that of a larger size capacity.

21.19 OLD SEPTIC SYSTEM

THE OCCURRENCE OF SOME FAILURE OF A HOME'S LEACH FIELD.

Fig. 21.19

When septic systems reach 50 years of age, they are considered to be quite old. In reality, however, they are intended to work in an efficient manner for only about 20 years. In fact, often their trouble-free rated life expectancy comes even earlier than that due to neglecting the system and/or of their excessive use. Trees planted in a leach field or adjacent to the tank can hurt the system. Further, periodic cleanouts should be done before the backup trouble begins, for if scum builds up enough to get into the leach field, it will seal the leach field walls and cause the field to fail.

21.20 AIR GAP IS MISSING

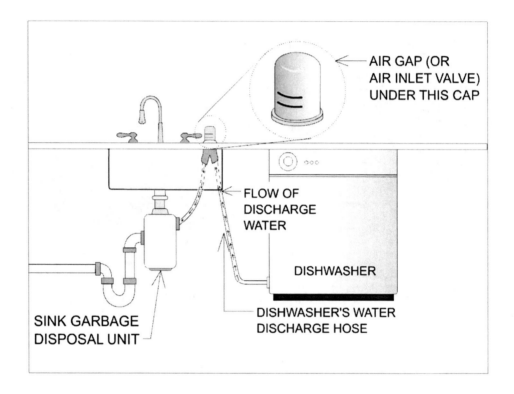

AIR GAP (OR
AIR INLET VALVE)
UNDER THIS CAP

FLOW OF
DISCHARGE
WATER

DISHWASHER

SINK GARBAGE
DISPOSAL UNIT

DISHWASHER'S WATER
DISCHARGE HOSE

Fig. 21.20

Frequently, "air gap" or "vacuum breaker" fittings are missing at kitchen sink locations for dishwasher drains. The purpose of this device that you would normally see set on top of a kitchen sink or in the wall behind the sink whenever a dishwasher is present is to prevent a vacuum in the waste line that could cause siphoning of waste water back into the dishwasher. A plumber can be engaged to make this connection.

21.21 WATER EMPTIES OUT THROUGH AIR GAP

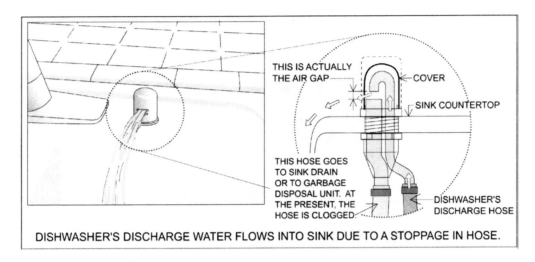

DISHWASHER'S DISCHARGE WATER FLOWS INTO SINK DUE TO A STOPPAGE IN HOSE.

Fig. 21.21

While a dishwasher is in operation, you might see water emptying out through the air gap vent connection rather than directly into the drain. Likely, there is some stoppage in the drain line. And that's another purpose of an air gap connection for if the drain hose does become clogged, the dishwasher can still pump out its water by flowing out of the air gap into the sink.

21.22 FAUCETS DRIP WATER

Fig. 21.22

Water faucets which constantly drip water just might need repacking and new washers to arrest the problem.

21.23 FAUCETS ARE REVERSED

Fig. 21.23

This sink's left and right faucets are reversed. The hot water for plumbing

fixtures are normally found on the left, but instead it is located on the right.

21.24 CLOCKWISE TURNING FAUCETS

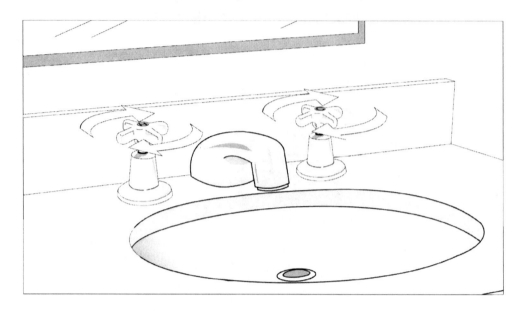

Fig. 21.24

You might find that some water faucets in the house turn in a

clockwise motion. Usually, the direction of turning a plumbing fixture's

water faucet handle is counterclockwise.

21.25 WATER IS SLOW TO DRAIN

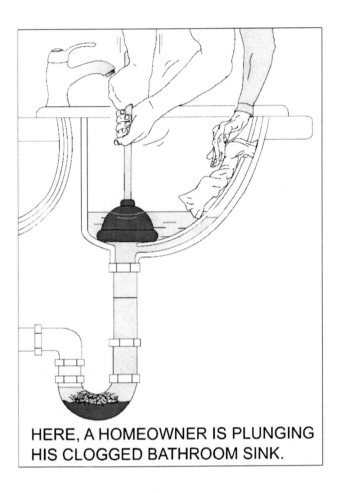

HERE, A HOMEOWNER IS PLUNGING
HIS CLOGGED BATHROOM SINK.

Fig. 21.25

A constriction which exists in the drain line usually causes a sink

or a bathtub to drain slowly. Employing mechanical means is a sure way

to open up a clogged drain.

21.26 POP-UP SINK DRAIN PLUG DOESN'T HOLD BASIN WATER

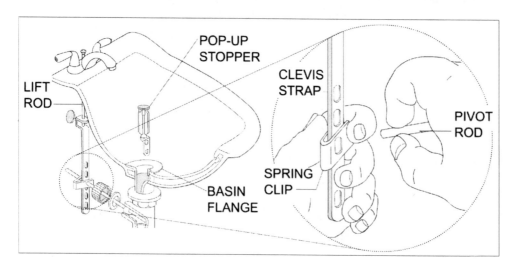

Fig. 21.26

The sink's pop-up drain plug, when in a closed position, fails to hold this basin's contained water. Perhaps an adjustment of the pivot rod to the clevis underneath the sink is all that is necessary. If not, more costly drain repair costs of making a watertight seal could become necessary.

21.27 TAPED ELBOW DRAIN PIPES

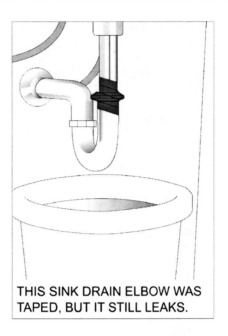

THIS SINK DRAIN ELBOW WAS
TAPED, BUT IT STILL LEAKS.

Fig. 21.27

When taped elbows are detected under a sink, a more permanent repair

is recommended.

21.28 LEAKS BENEATH SINKS

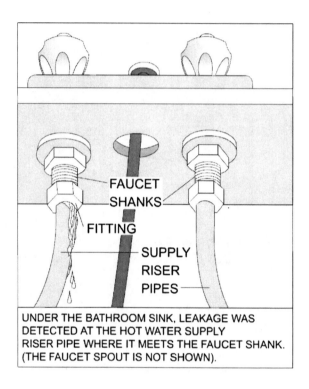

FAUCET
SHANKS

FITTING

SUPPLY
RISER
PIPES

UNDER THE BATHROOM SINK, LEAKAGE WAS
DETECTED AT THE HOT WATER SUPPLY
RISER PIPE WHERE IT MEETS THE FAUCET SHANK.
(THE FAUCET SPOUT IS NOT SHOWN).

Fig. 21.28

Leakage is often detected under sinks while tap water is left to run. It could come about from either leaky water supply valves, a cracked, loose or damaged drain elbow pipe, through gaps around the sink basin, or perhaps even from a damaged sink basin itself. But whatever the source of the leak may be, you 've got to look for the possibility of leaks. A pail that is found placed beneath the sink (especially when it is partly full of water) is normally a telltale sign of leakage.

21.29 SMALL SIZE STALL SHOWER

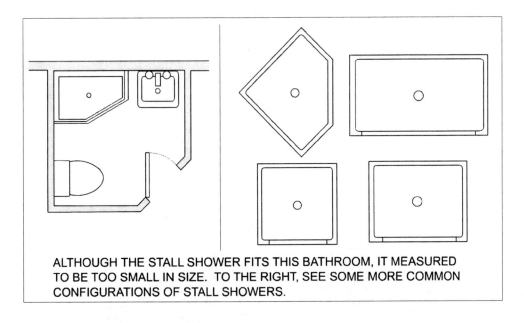

ALTHOUGH THE STALL SHOWER FITS THIS BATHROOM, IT MEASURED TO BE TOO SMALL IN SIZE. TO THE RIGHT, SEE SOME MORE COMMON CONFIGURATIONS OF STALL SHOWERS.

Fig. 21.29

Comfortable sized stall showers should not measure less than 36" x 36" so that one doesn't bump their elbows so much while showering and feel too confined. In fact, your local building code probably doesn't allow shower stalls to have an interior dimension having less than 30 inches, nor have a floor area smaller than 900 square inches in size.

21.30 STALL SHOWER LEAKS

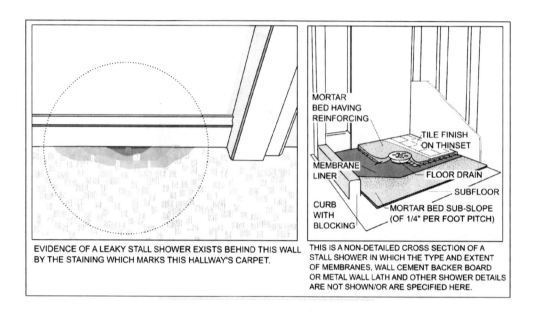

EVIDENCE OF A LEAKY STALL SHOWER EXISTS BEHIND THIS WALL BY THE STAINING WHICH MARKS THIS HALLWAY'S CARPET.

MORTAR BED HAVING REINFORCING

TILE FINISH ON THINSET

MEMBRANE LINER

FLOOR DRAIN

SUBFLOOR

CURB WITH BLOCKING

MORTAR BED SUB-SLOPE (OF 1/4" PER FOOT PITCH)

THIS IS A NON-DETAILED CROSS SECTION OF A STALL SHOWER IN WHICH THE TYPE AND EXTENT OF MEMBRANES, WALL CEMENT BACKER BOARD OR METAL WALL LATH AND OTHER SHOWER DETAILS ARE NOT SHOWN/OR ARE SPECIFIED HERE.

Fig. 21.30

A stall shower can leak from a pan that's cracked and damaged underneath it. However, just by merely running the stall shower water during your inspection doesn't mean that leakage will occur. Someone, now and then, just might have to bathe in the stall shower to render active any cracks and institute leakage. So look for evidences beneath, behind and outside stall showers because repair costs are quite costly and you just might be taking a risk in this regard.

If you suspect any leakage such as by evidences of stains or blisters, consider guarding yourself against this risk. Ask that possible repair cost money be held in an escrow account until sometime after you move in. At that time, if a new shower pan is needed, then the funds would be ready for repair; and, if not, you can return the money to the selling party.

21.31 WRONG FINISHES OF SHOWER AREAS

UNFORTUNATELY, THIS STALL SHOWER'S
WALLS WERE NOT TILED, BUT WERE
PAINTED INSTEAD.

Fig. 21.31

Whether in a stall shower or in a bathtub where a shower head is present, the floors

of these shower areas need to have a surface finish that uses a hard material that is both smooth

and non-absorbent. For instance, ceramic tile can be used. The surface material is

recommended to extend up to a height of at least 72 inches above the plumbing fixture's floor

so that spray and splash water doesn't penetrate and cause rot inside the walls. Watch out,

however, for a slippery floor!

21.32 LEAKAGE AT BATHTUB'S DIVERTER VALVE

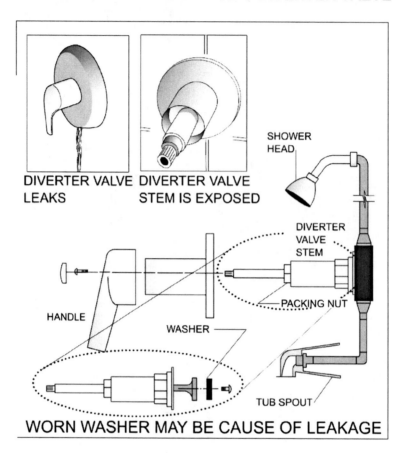

Fig. 21.32

Be on the lookout for water leakage that has developed at the tub-shower diverter valve. It may be possible to see this while running the bathtub water. If you do notice such leakage the remedial repair should be immediately instituted since water can cause rot inside the bathroom wall. Because it's costly to repair damprot inside walls, you might be taking a risk in this matter. Attempt to disclose the wall condition if it's possible.

21.33 BACK WATER SIPHONAGE AT OLD BATHTUB

BACK WATER SIPHONAGE IS TAKING PLACE AT THIS BATHTUB.

Fig. 21.33

Many bathtubs and sinks found in old homes still have their faucet spouts situated inside their basins rather than having been relocated outside them. When the sink or tub water line reaches to fill the basin above the spout orifice, there is a possibility that dirty water inside the tub would be vacuum-sucked back into the potable water supply lines. This action is known as "back water siphonage." Remember, pollutants which contaminate a home's potable water could cause serious illness or could even be fatal.

21.34 TUB DRAIN MECHANISM DOESN'T WORK

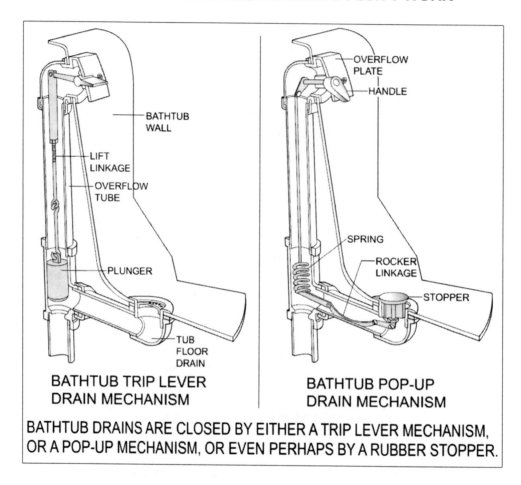

BATHTUB TRIP LEVER
DRAIN MECHANISM

BATHTUB POP-UP
DRAIN MECHANISM

BATHTUB DRAINS ARE CLOSED BY EITHER A TRIP LEVER MECHANISM,
OR A POP-UP MECHANISM, OR EVEN PERHAPS BY A RUBBER STOPPER.

Fig. 21.34

Drain mechanisms are notorious for not working. Since many people

don't quite know how to execute costly drain mechanism repairs, they simply

use rubber stoppers at the drains instead.

21.35   NO TUB PLUMBING ACCESS

THIS PLUMBER IS PREPARING THE WALL BEHIND THE
BATHTUB FOR A TUB PLUMBING ACCESS DOOR.

Fig. 21.35

Most often a minimum 12 inch by 12 inch access door is located on the
wall behind bathroom spigots as a hatchway for the bathtub's water and waste
connections. These connections can be accessible and exposed without the
provision of an access door. Still, the door is very useful if plumbing repairs
have to be made at the bathtub without the necessity of having to break open
the wall.

21.36 DON'T FEEL CRAMPED AT THE TOILET

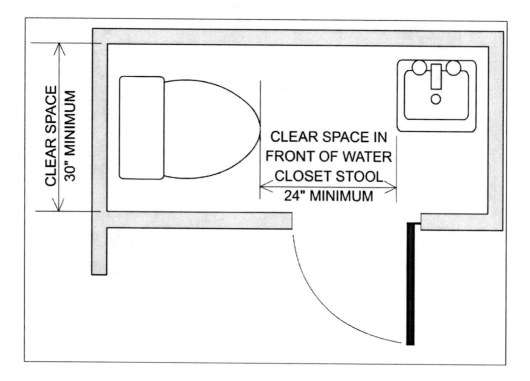

CLEAR SPACE
30" MINIMUM

CLEAR SPACE IN
FRONT OF WATER
CLOSET STOOL
24" MINIMUM

Fig. 21.36

Your local building code might figure the same minimum clearances as indicated in the sketch above which offer the least sufficient room for feeling comfortable while one uses the toilet.

21.37 TOILET LEAKS AT ITS BASE

DETECTION OF LEAKAGE
AT THE TOILET BASE

INSTALLATION OF NEW WAX RING

CROSS SECTION OF TOILET DRAIN

Fig. 21.37

If you should find water leaking out from under the toilet bowl, there

is a possibility that the large wax ring which is used to seal the joint between

the bowl and its drain has deteriorated so that it requires replacement. To do

this chore, the toilet bowl must be taken up from the floor.

21.38 TOILET MOVES

Fig. 21.38

Toilets that can easily be moved need to be secured in place. Just try to shake the toilets to see if they are loose.

21.39 TOILET 'RUNS'

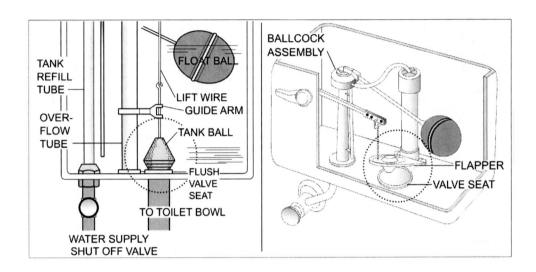

Fig. 21.39

Toilets often continue to "run" for considerably lengthy times after they are flushed, or allow water to continuously trickle into their bowls. The trickling could be the result of a tank ball or flapper not seating properly, or perhaps be from a leaky ballcock. The condition could be representative of other problems as well.

21.40 TO FLUSH, HOLD TOILET LEVER

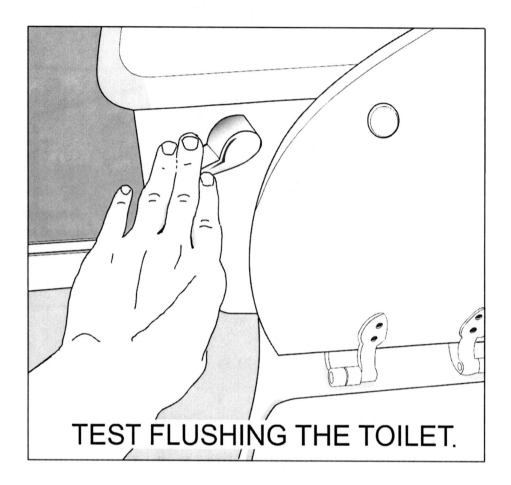

TEST FLUSHING THE TOILET.

Fig. 21.40

In order to flush some problem toilets, their trip-lever handles
must be held down continuously. So when the house is being inspected,
don't be shy to flush all the toilets in the dwelling to determine if this
condition exists.

21.41 TOILET FLUSHES WEAKLY

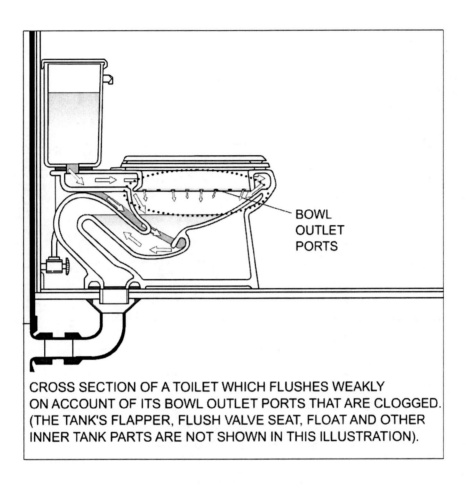

BOWL
OUTLET
PORTS

CROSS SECTION OF A TOILET WHICH FLUSHES WEAKLY
ON ACCOUNT OF ITS BOWL OUTLET PORTS THAT ARE CLOGGED.
(THE TANK'S FLAPPER, FLUSH VALVE SEAT, FLOAT AND OTHER
INNER TANK PARTS ARE NOT SHOWN IN THIS ILLUSTRATION).

Fig. 21.41

You might find that the toilets in the house flush weakly. This condition could be caused by low water levels inside the tanks or possibly from the tank balls or flappers seating too soon. It could also be representative of clogged bowl outlet ports around the underside of the rims or even trouble in the drain. Indeed, when toilets can't not be flushed a second time without waiting rather lengthy time periods, there could be low water pressure in the house.

21.42 BROKEN TOILET TANK LIDS

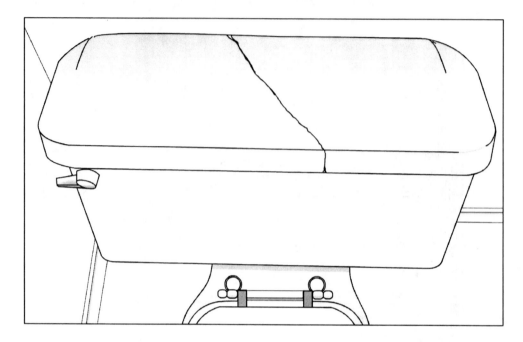

Fig. 21.42

Toilet tank lids break when mishandling them, but replacement lids can be searched for at used plumbing supply stores.

21.43 CRACKED PLUMBING FIXTURES

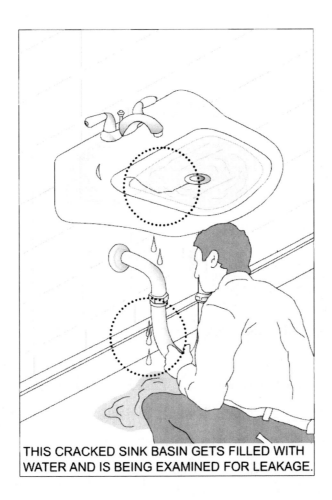

THIS CRACKED SINK BASIN GETS FILLED WITH
WATER AND IS BEING EXAMINED FOR LEAKAGE.

Fig. 21.43

Fine cracks are frequently found in sinks and toilets. Indeed, some

cracked plumbing fixtures even leak. As such, replacement sinks or toilets

will likely be needed in the future.

Chapter 22

ROOF

A big replacement cost item can be the roof.   Hence, it must be evaluated properly.

Following the examination of the home's exterior improvements, consider inspecting the roof. It would be daylight and you will need to view the roof from different perspectives.

First cite a pitched roof from a distance and analyze it structurally. Are there deflecting or sagging rafter members? And, is the ridge line level?

After that, while up on a ladder, either climb the roof or view it close up. At that time, the type and condition of the roofing cover could be examined as could be its drainage provision and flashing.

Then, sometime later on in the inspection, at the time the attic is entered into, the underside of the roof should be viewed and there should be a search made for existing leaks, leakage stain evidences and for any holes or daylight that can be seen through the roof. Indeed, if possible, examine the underside of the roof and room ceilings on a rainy day.

22.1 ROOFING COVER MATERIALS DEPEND ON ROOF PITCH

Permissible roofing cover materials vary with the roof pitch:

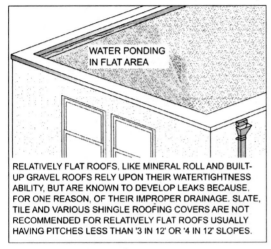

RELATIVELY FLAT ROOFS, LIKE MINERAL ROLL AND BUILT-UP GRAVEL ROOFS RELY UPON THEIR WATERTIGHTNESS ABILITY, BUT ARE KNOWN TO DEVELOP LEAKS BECAUSE, FOR ONE REASON, OF THEIR IMPROPER DRAINAGE. SLATE, TILE AND VARIOUS SHINGLE ROOFING COVERS ARE NOT RECOMMENDED FOR RELATIVELY FLAT ROOFS USUALLY HAVING PITCHES LESS THAN '3 IN 12' OR '4 IN 12' SLOPES.

Fig. 22.1A

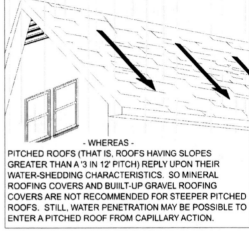

- WHEREAS -
PITCHED ROOFS (THAT IS, ROOFS HAVING SLOPES GREATER THAN A '3 IN 12' PITCH) REPLY UPON THEIR WATER-SHEDDING CHARACTERISTICS. SO MINERAL ROOFING COVERS AND BUIILT-UP GRAVEL ROOFING COVERS ARE NOT RECOMMENDED FOR STEEPER PITCHED ROOFS. STILL, WATER PENETRATION MAY BE POSSIBLE TO ENTER A PITCHED ROOF FROM CAPILLARY ACTION.

Fig. 22.1B

Here are a few inspection hints: Be on the lookout for different varieties of roofing covers along the various sections of the house roof of the same or like pitch. Sometimes they're actually different! Lastly, pitched shingle roofs, in addition to the underlayment of tile roofs, tend to have a 20 to 25 year rated life expectancy. During that time, shingles and tiles tend to lift, crack, split, shift, get worn and accordingly tear. Flashing problems cause the development of leaks in both types of roofs.

22.2 SOME FACTS AND PROBLEMS WITH FLAT ROOFS

Two popular relatively flat roofs utilize 'mineral roll roofing' and 'built-up gravel membrane roofing' as their covers. The mineral roll roof has a rated life of about 10 to 12 years, while the built-up gravel roof's life expectancy is somewhere between 15 to 20 years. The built-up roof is comprised of alternate layers of asphalt and asphalt-saturated roofing felt. Slag, gravel or stone chips are embedded on the top layer of asphalt.

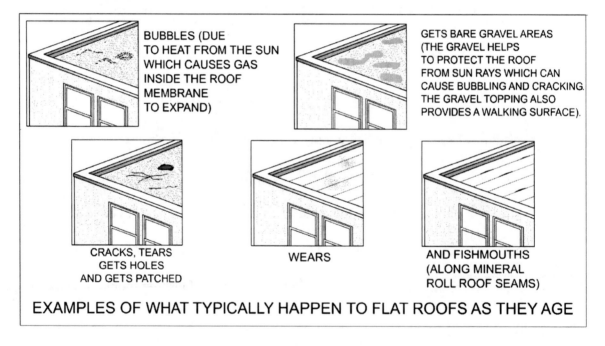

BUBBLES (DUE TO HEAT FROM THE SUN WHICH CAUSES GAS INSIDE THE ROOF MEMBRANE TO EXPAND)

GETS BARE GRAVEL AREAS (THE GRAVEL HELPS TO PROTECT THE ROOF FROM SUN RAYS WHICH CAN CAUSE BUBBLING AND CRACKING. THE GRAVEL TOPPING ALSO PROVIDES A WALKING SURFACE).

CRACKS, TEARS GETS HOLES AND GETS PATCHED

WEARS

AND FISHMOUTHS (ALONG MINERAL ROLL ROOF SEAMS)

EXAMPLES OF WHAT TYPICALLY HAPPEN TO FLAT ROOFS AS THEY AGE

Fig. 22.2

Relatively flat roofs built with poor pitches should be corrected to avoid excessive ponding.

22.3 SEARCH FOR ROOF LEAKAGE

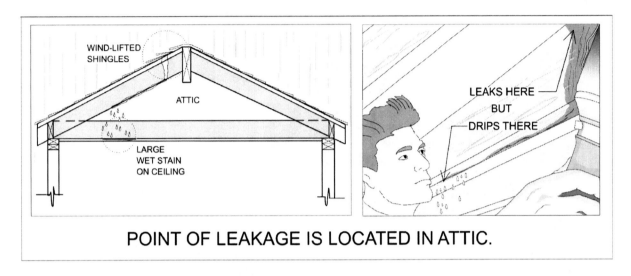

Fig. 22.3

Roof leakage is best detected on rainy days for you could actually see wet ceiling and wall areas. You could feel damp areas, too. During dry weather, past roof leakage is evident by water stains which mark roof sheathing, roof rafters and ceiling joists up in the attic space and, additionally, by stains which mark ceiling and wall areas. Indeed, paint might be observed to peel along a ceiling or wall and there may be areas of bubbling or surface-formed drywall or plaster blisters being found in a granular state.

Note, however, that the stainings where rain water drips may not represent the actual points of location of where leakage took place since, many times, water will go for long distances before it falls.

Chapter 23

SCREENING

Screens are frequently overlooked in many home inspections. So be sure to be on the lookout for their presence. Check if the screens are new or old, consistently the same type and in good condition.

23.1 COMMON SCREENING CONDITIONS

SOME COMMON SCREENING CONDITIONS INCLUDE:

ENTRY DOORS AND SLIDING GLASS DOORS WHICH
OFTENTIME LACK THE USE OF ASSOCIATED SCREEN DOORS;

HOMES HAVING WINDOW SCREENS WHICH ARE TORN,
RIPPED OR POOR FITTING AS SHOWN HERE;

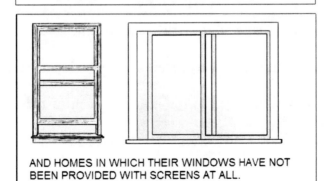

AND HOMES IN WHICH THEIR WINDOWS HAVE NOT
BEEN PROVIDED WITH SCREENS AT ALL.

Fig. 23.1

23.2 ATTIC VENTS LACK SCREENS

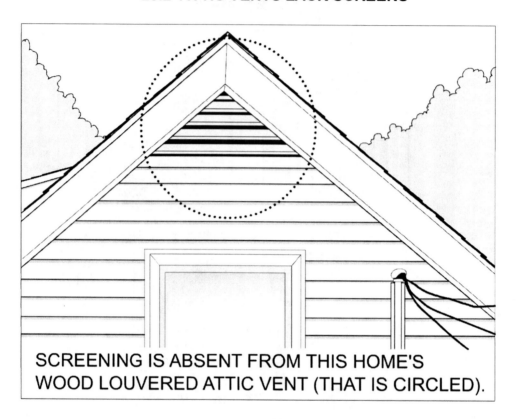

SCREENING IS ABSENT FROM THIS HOME'S
WOOD LOUVERED ATTIC VENT (THAT IS CIRCLED).

Fig. 23.2

It's not uncommon to find attic vents lacking screens. Thus, remember to examine the attic vents. Where there is none, window screening would be recommended to be attached to the inside of each of the attic's louver vent frames. If this is not done, wasps, bees, hornets and other insects may make use of the attic space for a nesting area.

Chapter 24

SITE DRAINAGE AND WATER

SEEPAGE

A house is supposed to be built watertight but, unfortunately, many homes are not. Because the costs of attempting to arrest serious drainage and water seepage problems are high, it is best to inspect for the possibility of the existence of such problems prior to purchase.

This chapter introduces you to some straightforward facts about drainage and to what you ought to know about water seepage problems.

24.1 NO LEADERS AND RAIN GUTTERS ON THE HOUSE

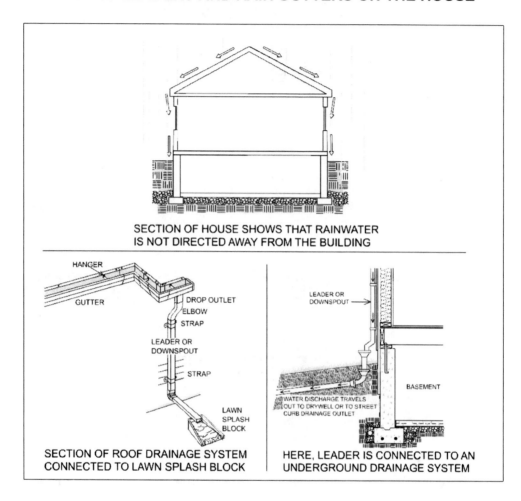

Fig. 24.1

Numerous houses lack the use of a roof drainage system. A roof drainage system consists of leaders (downspouts) and rain gutters. It serves to manage the direction of water from a roof. Primarily, leaders and rain gutters are recommended to be installed on houses, including particularly ones with short roof eaves, to help prevent damage to the foundations and exterior walls caused by water action. Providing precast concrete lawn splash blocks that are placed beneath the downspout sections so that water can be carried away from the house is possible at a nominal cost; however, underground drainpipes to which the ends of the downspouts could connect onto would generally be better.

24.2 ADD EXTENSION LEADERS

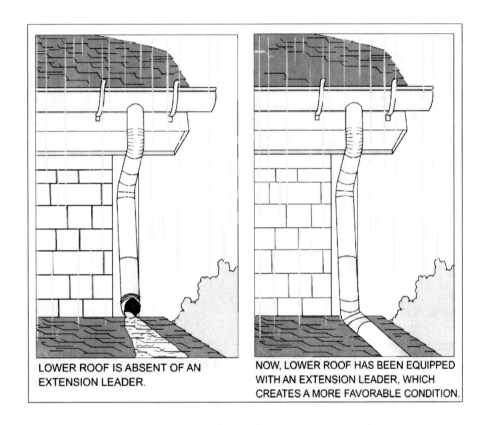

LOWER ROOF IS ABSENT OF AN EXTENSION LEADER.

NOW, LOWER ROOF HAS BEEN EQUIPPED WITH AN EXTENSION LEADER, WHICH CREATES A MORE FAVORABLE CONDITION.

Fig. 24.2

One condition often encountered about houses which have been equipped with a roof drainage system is their missing extension leaders where they are really needed. Many extension leaders should have been added to existing upper downspout sections, but were not. Instead, in their absence, water from the downspouts is permitted to drain directly onto lower roof areas below them.

24.3 POOR PITCH OF RAIN GUTTERS

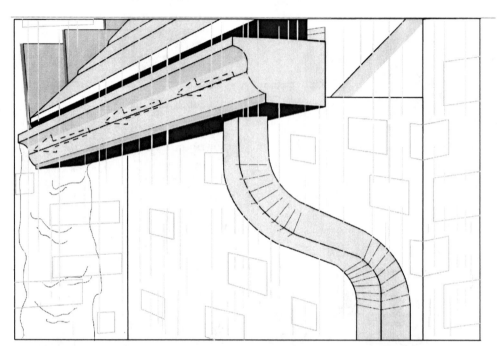

RAINWATER WASHES DOWN EXTERIOR WALL OF HOUSE DUE TO INCORRECT GUTTER PITCH.

Fig. 24.3

Oftentimes, rain gutters have been incorrectly pitched away from their respective downspouts, rather than sloping towards them. Adjustments are then necessary.

24.4 AGING LEADERS AND RAIN GUTTERS

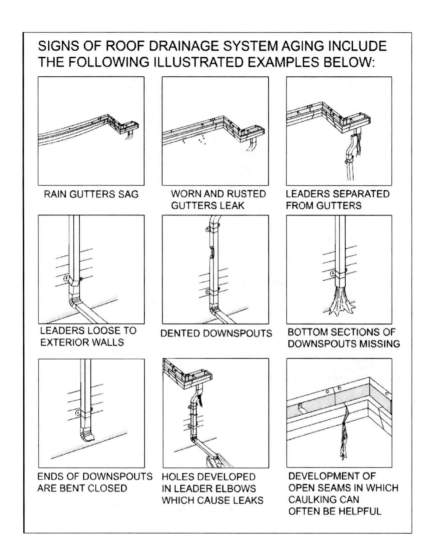

SIGNS OF ROOF DRAINAGE SYSTEM AGING INCLUDE THE FOLLOWING ILLUSTRATED EXAMPLES BELOW:

RAIN GUTTERS SAG

WORN AND RUSTED GUTTERS LEAK

LEADERS SEPARATED FROM GUTTERS

LEADERS LOOSE TO EXTERIOR WALLS

DENTED DOWNSPOUTS

BOTTOM SECTIONS OF DOWNSPOUTS MISSING

ENDS OF DOWNSPOUTS ARE BENT CLOSED

HOLES DEVELOPED IN LEADER ELBOWS WHICH CAUSE LEAKS

DEVELOPMENT OF OPEN SEAMS IN WHICH CAULKING CAN OFTEN BE HELPFUL

Fig. 24.4

Lots of old homes still have their original leaders and gutters on them. It's easy to tell this for they show evidences of their age. A new roof drainage system may be then in order right away. Or, perhaps, if the system is not so bad, consider budgeting for ultimate leader and gutter replacement in the years ahead.

24.5 POOR YARD DRAINAGE

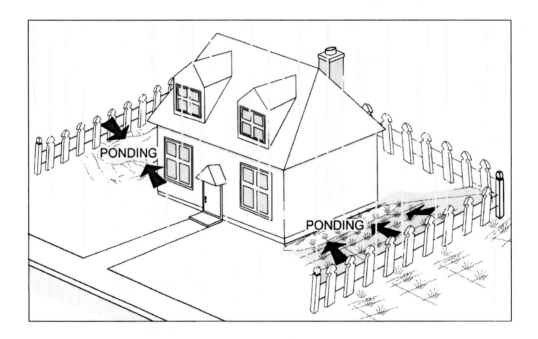

Fig. 24.5

Because of improper gradework, water will tend to accumulate along some yard areas. In the above example illustration, rain and sprinkler water tend to puddle in the bumpily-graded left side yard and stand next to the house in the right side yard. This is easy to see in the picture. But certain ground areas actually require heavy precipitation to be more easily evaluated for detection of possible puddling. Should poor or inadequate yard drainage ultimately be a problem to you, what would be helpful in remedying poor drainage conditions would be to accordingly regrade areas and / or add drainage devices like area drains and swales.

24.6 DRIVEWAY SLOPES TOWARD THE HOUSE

DRIVEWAY HAS BEEN EQUIPPED WITH A LINEAR DRAIN TO HELP PREVENT WATER FROM ENTERING THIS HOME'S GARAGE.

Fig. 24.6

Not all homes whose driveways slope toward their garages have been provided with proper drainage provision. An area drain or a linear drain at the foot of a garage might be a good recommendation to help control flooding in that area. It can also be used to intercept water from actually entering a garage.

24.7 UNFAVORABLE GRADING

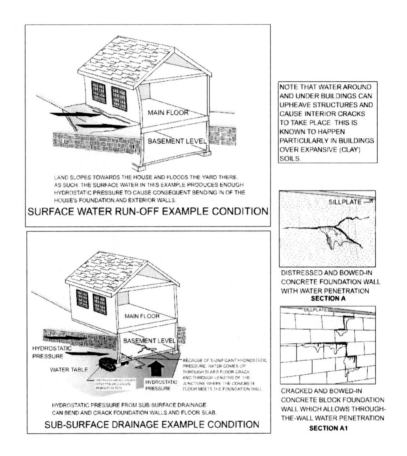

Fig. 24.7

Unfavorable grading of the land might mean that the land slopes toward the house instead of sloping away from it. With such a grading condition, the hydraulic pressure on the building can be increased. Further, it can lead to water seepage problems (from both ground surface water run-off and subsurface drainage).

24.8 WATER SEEPAGE PROBLEMS

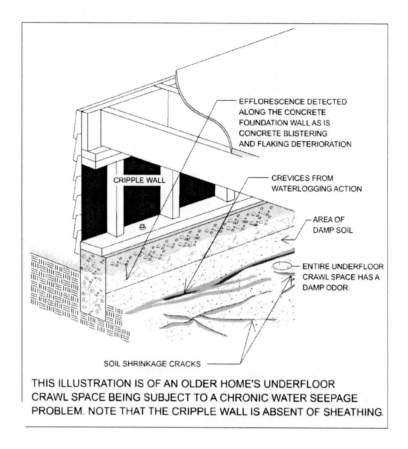

EFFLORESCENCE DETECTED ALONG THE CONCRETE FOUNDATION WALL AS IS CONCRETE BLISTERING AND FLAKING DETERIORATION

CREVICES FROM WATERLOGGING ACTION

AREA OF DAMP SOIL

CRIPPLE WALL

ENTIRE UNDERFLOOR CRAWL SPACE HAS A DAMP ODOR

SOIL SHRINKAGE CRACKS

THIS ILLUSTRATION IS OF AN OLDER HOME'S UNDERFLOOR CRAWL SPACE BEING SUBJECT TO A CHRONIC WATER SEEPAGE PROBLEM. NOTE THAT THE CRIPPLE WALL IS ABSENT OF SHEATHING.

Fig. 24.8

Basements, underfloor crawl spaces as well as at- and below-grade levels of homes are subject to the possibility of through-the-wall and through-the-floor water seepage. The problem might be a severe and chronic one (with flooding conditions, possible waterlogging action taking place, or even structural undermining); perhaps a moderate problem (that could very well blister and stain below-grade finished walls); or it could merely be a minor seepage problem of limited extent.

If you do not detect water actually penetrate your prospective home's lower level, you should still examine for the following typical evidences one finds with water penetration problems because it is common to so many homes:

-Efflorescence along or flaking deposits of concrete and masonry walls. "Efflorescence" is a deposit of water soluble salts seen on concrete and masonry surfaces when water affects them;

-deterioration of concrete and masonry foundation walls or areas thereof. Usually the deterioration is thin at the efflorescence and, most times, doesn't seriously adversely affect their structural integrity;

-mud or wet soil in the crawl space;

-soil shrinkage cracks within the crawl space;

-rust staining on the bottom of furnace and hot water heater legs;

-dry water stains on the bottom of some wood posts or other woodwork in contact with the floor;

-damp or musty odors in the basement;

-an area of floor slab bubbling caused by a substructural hydraulic pressure that has been exerted on the slab.

-cupped wood finish floor boards on the level above the underfloor level or on the slab-on-ground;

-and cracking of the building from some saturated soil upheaval - soil shrinkage settlement action.

An initial inspection with these signs seen might not quite reveal the exact source and character of the problem. Note that poor site drainage, with land sloping toward the house, could invite underfloor water seepages.

With any of these evidences observed, it would be wise not to place or leave valuables placed in these locations for a considerable length of time. That time could be a year or longer until more is learned of the water penetration. Should water seep or penetrate the underfloor during this time period of evaluation, you could be faced with expensive corrective drainage/possible regrading/waterproofing costs.

Note that one method to waterproof basement walls involves digging the soil away from around the house down to the footings, covering the basement walls with a few thin layers of a cementous plaster material and a few coats of an asphalt waterproofing compound. In more serious cases, asphalt-saturated building felt is placed between the layers of asphalt compound. Note, too, that a sump pump would remove basement water, but it doesn't stop the act of water penetration.

Lastly, the work of waterproofing a concrete slab might consist of placing polyethylene sheeting on top of the floor slab and then pouring a two inch thick concrete slab on top of the existing slab. Unfortunately, a whole lot of minimum doorway and ceiling heights become altered smaller that way.

Chapter **25**

STRUCTURE

This is the most serious part of the inspection because you'll want to be sure the home of interest: is a "fundamentally sound" home, or even better yet, a "structurally sound" home. The home that you initially think is structurally integral could instead be less favorably rated... as being in only "marginally sound" condition, or worse yet, "potentially sound" or "unsound" altogether.

A structural inspection consists of examining both the building's foundation and superstructure. Be sure both are examined well. As a structural analyst, there will be citing of walls to do (especially to see that they are plumb); walking of floors to do (while using your cerebellum or a level instrument to determine how level they are); jumping upon floors to do (to feel how well the floor system can take a dynamic load); and even banging against some walls to do. You might even need to crawl cramped underfloor and attic areas. But that's all a part of structural testing and analysis.

25.1 STRUCTURAL DAMAGE FROM TERMITES

**CLOSE-UP VIEWING OF HOUSE'S
INTERIOR WOODEN MAIN BEAM**

Fig. 25.1

Serious structural damage can occur to a house because of a termite infestation problem. Do not be surprised to learn that extensive damage has gone unattended to date. In fact, the seller should be advised at once of the resultant damage.   Entire replacement of affected wood members could be in order.

25.2 ADDITIONAL SOURCES OF STRUCTURAL DAMAGE

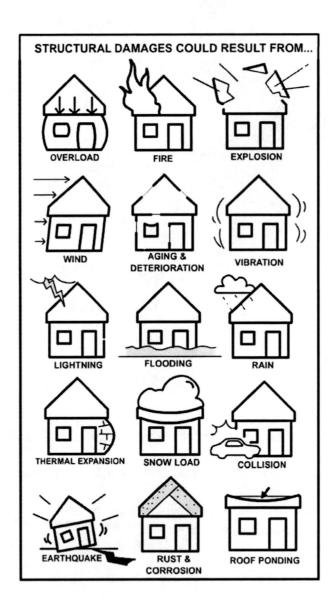

Fig. 25.2

25.3 TEMPORARY OR MAKESHIFT CONSTRUCTION UNDER THE HOUSE

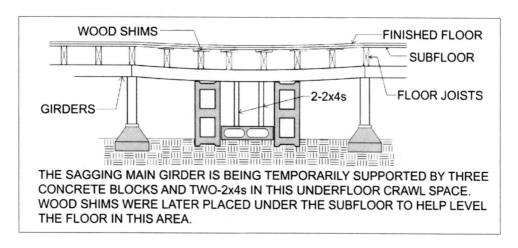

Fig. 25.3

Later added support work may be encountered in some underfloor locations. Oftentimes, however, the type of 'shoring' work that is used is that which is found in only temporary construction. The removal of the support work could lead to floor deflection.   But proper permanent structural support work should replace all temporary or makeshift construction. Keep in mind that there would be no approvals or certificates in order (or that which could be forthcoming) for such structural changes that are not in compliance with local code.

25.4 OFF- CENTER POST LOADING

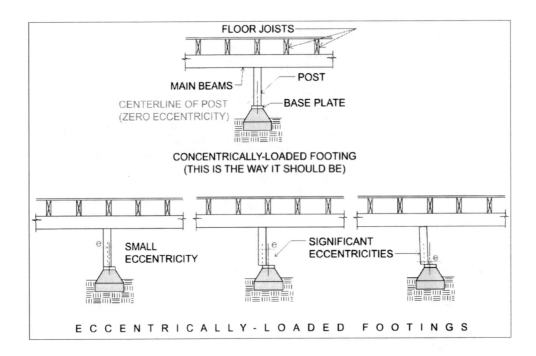

Fig. 25.4

Many times structural wood posts are off-center to (or 'eccentrically loaded' on) their respective pier/footing supports. Small eccentricities are deemed to be structurally insignificant. However, structural failure could much more easily occur from 'loss of support' where the eccentricities are large.

25.5 MORE COMMON FOOTING- RELATED PROBLEMS

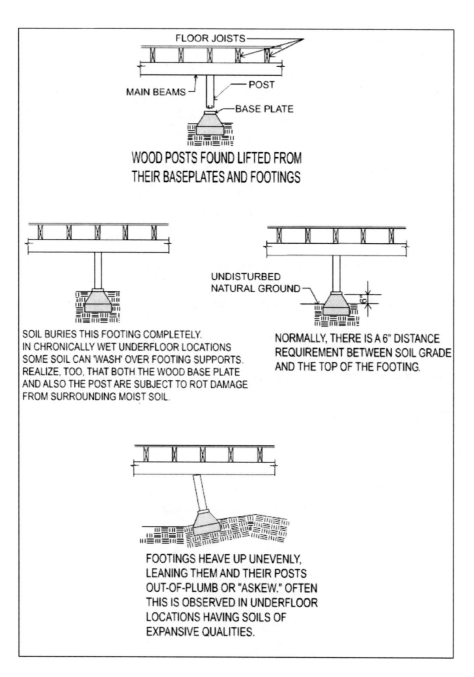

FLOOR JOISTS

MAIN BEAMS — POST

BASE PLATE

WOOD POSTS FOUND LIFTED FROM
THEIR BASEPLATES AND FOOTINGS

SOIL BURIES THIS FOOTING COMPLETELY.
IN CHRONICALLY WET UNDERFLOOR LOCATIONS
SOME SOIL CAN 'WASH' OVER FOOTING SUPPORTS.
REALIZE, TOO, THAT BOTH THE WOOD BASE PLATE
AND ALSO THE POST ARE SUBJECT TO ROT DAMAGE
FROM SURROUNDING MOIST SOIL.

UNDISTURBED
NATURAL GROUND

NORMALLY, THERE IS A 6" DISTANCE
REQUIREMENT BETWEEN SOIL GRADE
AND THE TOP OF THE FOOTING.

FOOTINGS HEAVE UP UNEVENLY,
LEANING THEM AND THEIR POSTS
OUT-OF-PLUMB OR "ASKEW." OFTEN
THIS IS OBSERVED IN UNDERFLOOR
LOCATIONS HAVING SOILS OF
EXPANSIVE QUALITIES.

Fig. 25.5

25.6   MAIN BEAMS ARE IN POOR CONDITION

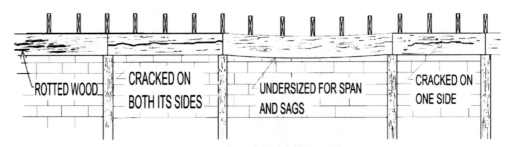

ROTTED WOOD | CRACKED ON BOTH ITS SIDES | UNDERSIZED FOR SPAN AND SAGS | CRACKED ON ONE SIDE

BASEMENT'S WOOD POSTS, GIRDERS AND JOISTS

Fig. 25.6

Be sure to examine the condition of the main beams or "girders" of a house. These structural members are used to carry the 'dead and live' loads to the posts and footings. Those main beams which are observed to be in poor condition should be replaced immediately. However, instead, supporting posts (with proper footings) are oftentimes placed beneath those finely cracked and sagging girders to give them additional support. Reinforcement of some damaged beams could be helpful as well.

25.7 FOUNDATION CRACKS

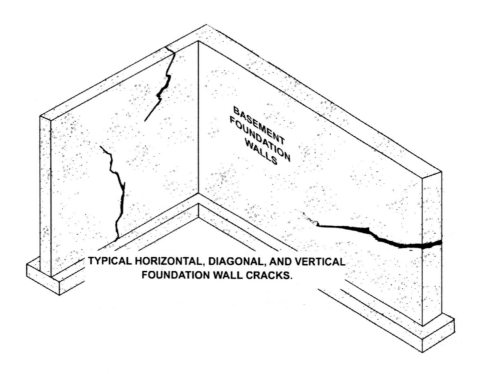

BASEMENT FOUNDATION WALLS

TYPICAL HORIZONTAL, DIAGONAL, AND VERTICAL FOUNDATION WALL CRACKS.

Fig. 25.7

Numerous foundation wall cracks can be pointed and patched in their entirety. An epoxy or lean cement would be satisfactory for this purpose. Those distresses that are significant should be periodically inspected following the patchwork to see if the cracking recurs. Should significant cracking reappear sometime following the patchwork, expensive sub-structural "underpinning" work (which supports the foundation) may then be in order.

25.8 DETERIORATED FOUNDATION WALLS

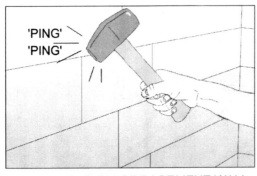 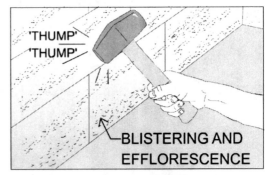

UPPER PORTION OF BASEMENT WALL   BOTTOM PORTION OF BASEMENT WALL

Fig. 25.8

Chronic underfloor water seepage problems can eventually deteriorate concrete, concrete block and other masonry foundation walls. In fact, some foundation walls could have become weakened so that their concrete or masonry block, once grabbed, easily crumbles in one's hands. Telltale signs of water seepage that you may cite could be blisters in the concrete and efflorescence. Hence, it's a good idea to test hammer-hit the concrete or masonry and carefully listen for a healthy 'ping' sound to advise you that the concrete or masonry material is still structural integral in this regard. (Hammer-hitting a weak wall makes a dull, 'thump' sound instead). Note that the cost of rebuilding weakened foundation walls is quite high.

25.9 HOUSE FRAMING NOT SECURED TO ITS FOUNDATION

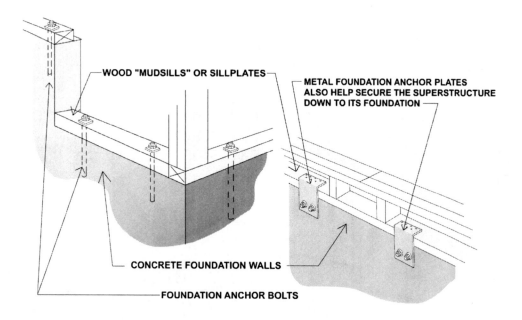

Fig. 25.9

Tying the house down to its foundation has been required for both today's homes and homes that were built years and years ago. However, there are many such old houses which have not been tie-down secured. The tying is normally done by utilizing anchor bolts. Look for their existence. They are helpful to prevent wood building frames (called the "superstructure") from shifting or even sliding off their respective foundation walls during an earthquake event, or, perhaps help to withstand other potential damages from taking place such as possibly during some seismic activities. Specifically, the mudsills or sillplates are typically bolted down to the foundation walls by using 1/2" diameter by 10" long bolts embedded 7" into the foundation walls. They are supposed to be regularly spaced every 4 or 6 feet on center. The anchor bolts should not be located more than 12 inches from the end of a sill corner.

25.10 CRACKS IN CONCRETE SLAB-ON-GROUND

NOTE THAT SLAB-ON-GROUND
CRACK EXTENDS TO
EXTERIOR WALL

Fig. 25.10

Cracks are expected to develop in concrete floor slabs of slab-on-grade houses. In fact, most distresses are not deemed to be structurally significant at all for typical house slabs basically serve as earth covers. Slab cracks which develop at exterior walls and at other footing locations are of concern, however.

25.11 BOUNCY FLOOR

Fig. 25.11

Test jump all raised floors in the house. They could be a bit bouncier than what might be normally expected. If they are, the floor joists might be undersized for their long span. Or, perhaps, the condition could be the result of the use of an improper grade and species of wood. Additional bracing or additional support work is usually helpful in remedying a bouncy floor. If possible, compare with the structural drawing plans to see if the floor was intentionally designed in the fashion in which it was constructed.

25.12 FLOOR SLOPES

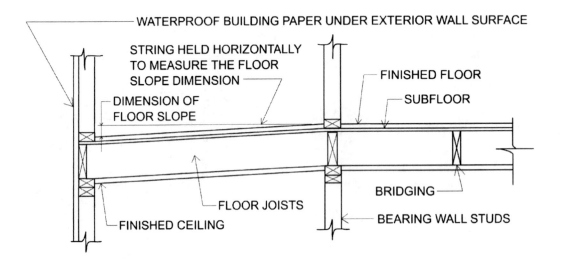

Fig. 25.12

Sloping floors could be caused by the fashion in which they were built. The same is true for floors having humps in them. Many consider a gradual 1/2 inch slope in 12 feet of floor run as being the acceptable tolerance for wood framing. Nonetheless, if possible, obtain access directly below the floor area in question to see if there are any obvious structural support problems. All that may be necessary is to measure and re-inspect the floor periodically to note if the sloping condition worsens. Note that only a 1/4 inch slope for a 12 feet run is considered by many as the acceptable tolerance along concrete floors.

25.13 CREAKS

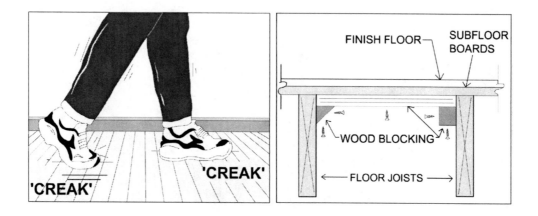

Fig. 25.13

Creaking sounds heard while walking a raised wood floor is likely due to the loosening of the nails which hold the subfloor down to the floor joists. The sound could also be created when one floor board is rubbed against another while weight is being applied and then removed. Most creaks are deemed to be structurally insignificant. One common means of resolution to eliminate them would be to drive new nails through the subfloor into the wooden floor joists; another means is illustrated above.

25.14 OUT-OF-PLUMB WALLS

Fig. 25.14

Just like one must see the forest from the trees, you've got to cite the house from a distance in order to more easily observe possible leaning, bowed-out or bulging exterior walls. One good place to do this would be to stand across the street from the building. Following this, go cite other walls of the home in the other direction to detect if they are plumb as well. This process, of course, includes viewing all the interior walls in addition to examining all foundation and underfloor walls (for the latter of which could relate to the cause of possible main and upper level wall leaning or bulging).

25.15 CRACK IN EXTERIOR WALL AT LINE OF NEW ADDITION

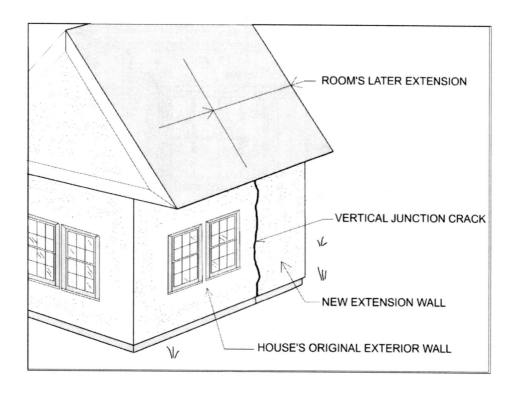

ROOM'S LATER EXTENSION

VERTICAL JUNCTION CRACK

NEW EXTENSION WALL

HOUSE'S ORIGINAL EXTERIOR WALL

Fig. 25.15

Vertical cracks in exterior walls that have developed at the juncture of the house's new wall construction with that of the existing wall section are usually typical distresses which are the result of differential settlement.

25.16 CRACKS WHICH RADIATE OUT OVER WINDOWS AND DOORS

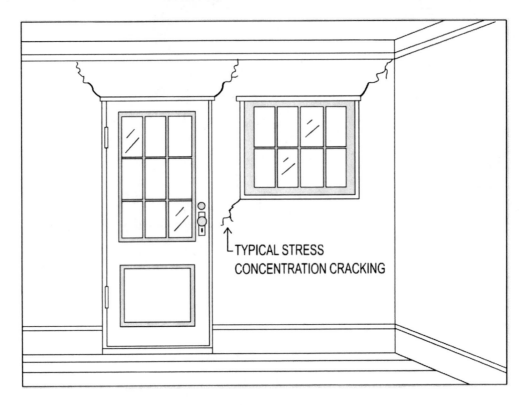

TYPICAL STRESS
CONCENTRATION CRACKING

Fig. 25.16

Cracks which radiate out from over window and doorway corners are usually typical "stress concentration cracks." They are the result of stress transfer. Concentrations of tensile stress have to be resisted at square openings - like those of doorway passages. Normally, homeowners merely have the cracks patched and painted.

25.17 INTERIOR CRACKS AT CEILING AND WALL JUNCTURES

CRACK SEPARATIONS NOTED
ALONG WALL RETURN AND CEILING

Fig. 25.17

In some newer homes, interior cracks which are found at wall corners or along wall junctures with ceilings could have developed from wood shrinkage as a part of the wood framing's drying process. The cracks usually do eventually stop. At that time, it's a good time to do drywall patch repair.

Other interior cracks could be caused by impact or settlement of support. This is particularly so of the latter condition if the soil beneath the building were to have been poorly compacted, or oftentimes when wet expansive soil dries and shrinks. What's more is that cracks additionally develop on account of sagging or deflecting structural members. An example of the latter is a line crack that is often noted along a ceiling.

25.18 HAVE THE BALCONIES TESTED FOR STRENGTH

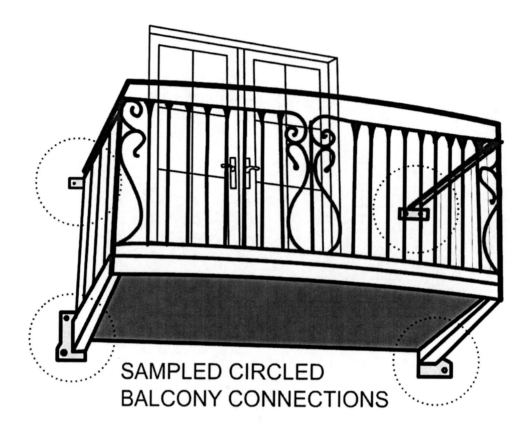

SAMPLED CIRCLED
BALCONY CONNECTIONS

Fig. 25.18

Because balconies weaken, have them tested for strength, particularly at their connections. Don't be surprised to learn that structural connection repair would be in order. Until this is done, no one should be permitted to use weakened balconies where structural fatigue or other supportive failure is possible.

25.19 LATERAL RIGIDITY NEEDS INCREASING

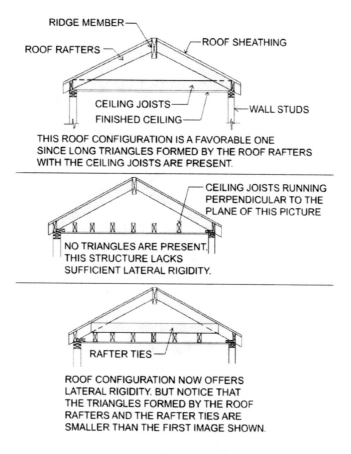

Fig. 25.19

The triangles formed by roof rafters and the ceiling joists help to make the house roof structure laterally rigid since, in structural analysis, a triangle constitutes a structurally rigid configuration. Where ceiling joists don't run parallel to the rafters (but instead run perpendicular), regularly spaced "rafter ties" (as shown above in the third figure) are needed to help stiffen or make up a laterally rigid structure. So while the attic is being inspected, be sure these structural members are present as needed.

25.20 STRUCTURAL FAILURE AT CONNECTIONS

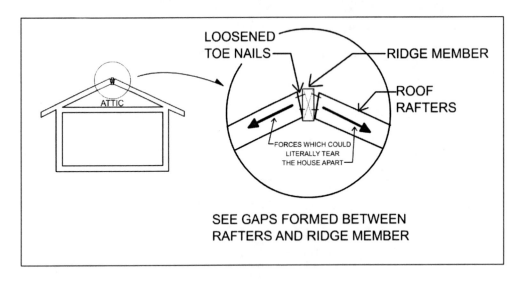

Fig. 25.20

Problems with structural connections are leaders in the cause of

structural failure. One big connection problem pertains to loose or loosened

structural connections. Look, for example, for roof rafters which have

loosened up from or have become separated from their ridge member up in the

attic. Note that houses are commonly built with some loose connections. But

even so, remember that most structural failures occur because of poor or

faulty connections.

25.21 ROOF SAGGING

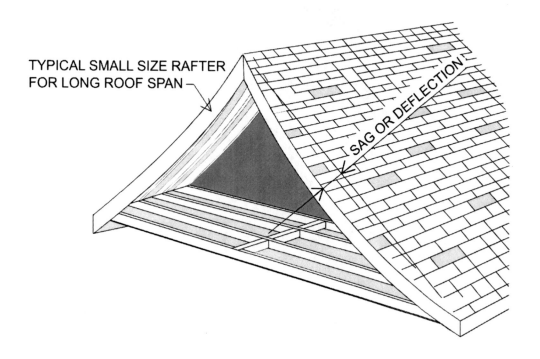

TYPICAL SMALL SIZE RAFTER
FOR LONG ROOF SPAN

SAG OR DEFLECTION

Fig. 25.21

Roof sagging (or "roof deflection") is often due to the long span of

undersized roof rafters. When this is determined with certainty to be the case

at significantly sagging roofs, either bracing the roof rafters, adding more

rafter members or increasing their size becomes necessary.

Chapter 26

VENTILATION

In a structural sense, all underfloor crawl spaces and attic spaces require ventilation for fresh air. Therefore, outside the house look for the presence of vent openings. Be aware that some building improvements might have either blocked or covered them up.

Inside and outside, inspect for the provision of exhaust ventilation.

26.1 UNDERFLOOR LOCATIONS NEED ADEQUATE VENTILATION

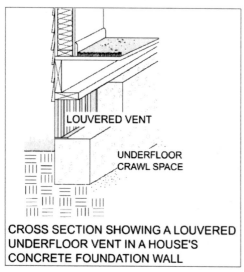

CROSS SECTION SHOWING A LOUVERED
UNDERFLOOR VENT IN A HOUSE'S
CONCRETE FOUNDATION WALL

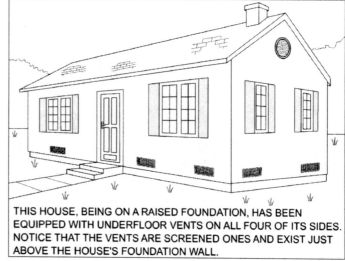

THIS HOUSE, BEING ON A RAISED FOUNDATION, HAS BEEN
EQUIPPED WITH UNDERFLOOR VENTS ON ALL FOUR OF ITS SIDES.
NOTICE THAT THE VENTS ARE SCREENED ONES AND EXIST JUST
ABOVE THE HOUSE'S FOUNDATION WALL.

Fig. 26.1

Houses which have crawl spaces beneath them need their underfloor

locations to be adequately vented. Your municipality might consider

screened/or louvered openings on 3 sides of a 4-sided house as being adequate

to reduce condensation and consequent rot damage from taking place to a

home's underfloor wooden framing members.

26.2 VENTILATION REQUIREMENTS OF BATHROOMS OR TOILET COMPARTMENTS

BATHROOM WITH A WINDOW   BATHROOM WITHOUT A WINDOW (BUT WITH AN EXHAUST FAN)

Fig. 26.2

If a bathroom or a toilet compartment in a house doesn't have an openable window, it can be provided with mechanical ventilation instead. Likely, your local code building states this and calls for the aggregate openable window size to have an area of not less than 1/20th of the floor area of the bathroom or toilet compartment (but with 1 1/2 square feet minimum size). For a bathroom or a toilet compartment of a new house, your local building code probably also requires a bathroom exhaust fan to activate when the light switch gets turned on.

26.3 VENTING THE GARAGE

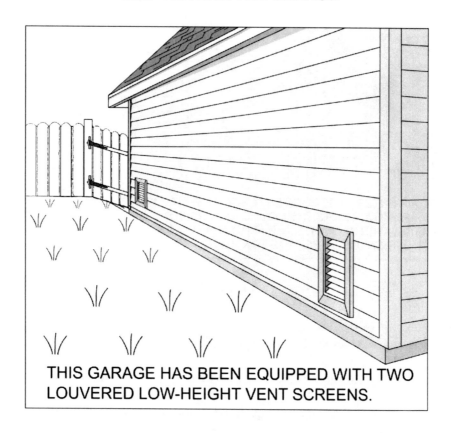

THIS GARAGE HAS BEEN EQUIPPED WITH TWO LOUVERED LOW-HEIGHT VENT SCREENS.

Fig. 26.3

Young lovers might 'pet' or 'make out' inside a car parked in a cold private garage with the garage door closed while the car engine runs. How foolish they are. Toxic fumes emanating from the car exhaust that have little chance to escape from the garage can kill! And that's the reason why low-height screened wall vent openings are needed for the garage.

26.4 ATTIC SPACES NEED VENTING

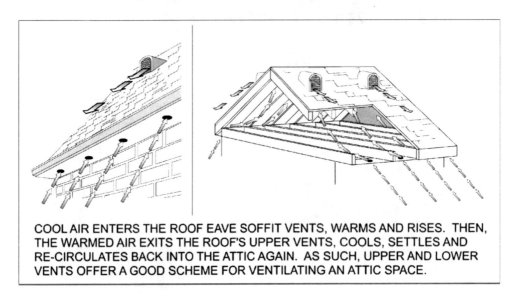

COOL AIR ENTERS THE ROOF EAVE SOFFIT VENTS, WARMS AND RISES. THEN, THE WARMED AIR EXITS THE ROOF'S UPPER VENTS, COOLS, SETTLES AND RE-CIRCULATES BACK INTO THE ATTIC AGAIN. AS SUCH, UPPER AND LOWER VENTS OFFER A GOOD SCHEME FOR VENTILATING AN ATTIC SPACE.

Fig. 26.4

Attics might be lacking adequate ventilation, or may be lacking ventilation altogether. Don't just assume that all attic spaces have been equipped with vents. Unfortunately, vents are frequently forgotten about. Because of this, there could be the occurrence of overheating during hot days and the formation of condensation on wood attic members during cool summer nights. Consequently, rot damage can eventually result. Adequate ventilation would need to be provided. And, in other attic spaces, perhaps there would be the need to simply increase attic ventilation.

26.5 EXHAUST VENTING IN ALL THE WRONG PLACES

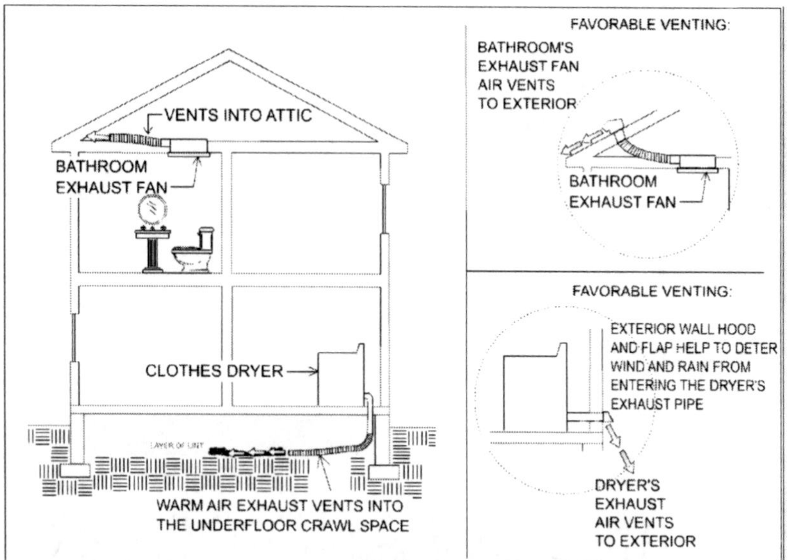

EXAMPLES OF INCORRECT VENTING OF A CLOTHES DRYER AND OF A BATHROOM EXHAUST FAN. NOTE THAT OFTENTIMES DRYERS ARE ALSO UNFAVORABLY EXHAUST-VENTED OUT TO THE ROOF. RUNS OF EXHAUST VENTING 20 FEET OR GREATER AND HAVING MORE THAN ONE BEND OF EXHAUST PIPE ALSO CONSTITUTE UNFAVORABLE VENTING.

Fig. 26.5

All exhaust venting should be examined not only for their flue condition, but also for where they go. Don't be surprised to learn that not all vent flues exhaust out to the exterior as they are supposed to do. Consider checking the exhausts for fuel-fired furnaces and hot water heaters, exhausts for the clothes dryer, the kitchen range hood fan and for some self-cleaning ovens which all require outdoor venting. You don't want carbon monoxide and carbon dioxide circulating in the house from fuel-fired heating plants because it's harmful to your health; nor do you want warm, moist air vented into crawl and attic spaces which can virtually weaken and destroy supportive wood members there.

Chapter 27

WINDOW AND DOOR

PROBLEMS

This part of the home inspection involves doing...opening, closing, locking, shaking windows and doors and more. Just to be thorough though, step back from each aperture to get an overview observation. Remember, these tests can be time-consuming, but the greater number of windows and doors which you demonstrate, the greater the number of problems will you likely encounter.   And, these kinds of problems do tally up.

27.1 COMMONLY FOUND WINDOW PROBLEMS

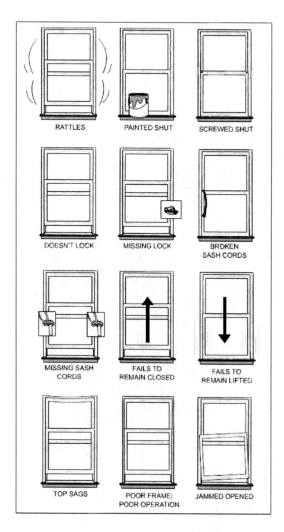

Fig. 27.1

A carpenter or window contractor should be engaged to make the remedial repairs.

27.2 COMMONLY FOUND DOOR PROBLEMS

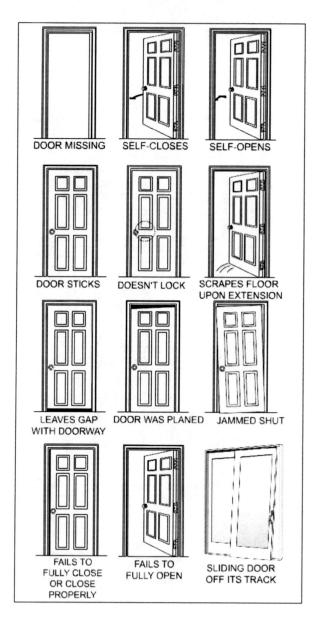

Fig. 27.2

Some of the example problems could be due to structural problems.

SUMMARIZING YOUR THOUGHTS ABOUT PURCHASING AN OLDER HOME AND MAKING A DECISION

A huge factor in what really matters in helping you make an intelligent decision about purchasing a home you have selected is its purchase price and what amount of money it would take for its repairs. With money, you can fix up a home, better its condition, and make it beautiful.

But, now, here's where its helpful to realize that the retrofitting cost estimates derived from your inspection findings can be broken down into 4 separate categories:

During the course of your home inspection, you will find items which need immediate repair: for example, the need to fix plumbing leaks, replace broken glazing, or rebuild a weak deck. You will also find items that will likely cause the homebuyer to face up to expenses within a few year period due to the aging process of the home (such as replacing an older asphalt shingle roof). Additionally, there are items of an indeterminate nature that come up in an inspection (as shown by evidences which one cannot readily conclude upon as to whether they are actually ongoing problems or summarizing them as definitely once existing problems). An example of this may be the observation of efflorescence along foundation wall lengths which typically indicates chronic water seepage problems - although no water has been observed to enter the underfloor location during the inspection. And finally, there are desirable or optional concerns discovered in an inspection which are especially important to you and which should not be overlooked but, instead, be estimated for. Sample cases of the latter-mentioned optional items relate to costs like decorating, adding a humidifier to a forced air heating system, modernizing an old-fashioned kitchen, or merely replacing old appliances. Move-in house cleaning service and re-landscaping are considered to be a part of that category, too.

Call in contractors to obtain cost estimates from them. Once the expenses are closely computed, you can best rate your feeling of the overall condition of the property. That's because you would be more comfortable in knowing what **immediate** estimated costs need to be spent, what estimated cost will be needed for **deferred maintenance**, what **"maybe"** costs are anticipated, and finally, what is the total estimated **optional** cost. Then, for example, you can say inside and out, the house is "reasonably well maintained" or is in a

405   Summary About an Older Home and Decision Making

"worn, run-down state" or perhaps is in "good -to- excellent condition." Of

course, in that rating, geological, legal- title and environmental concerns must be

taken into consideration. If there are many problems to be taken care of, weigh

these problems to your liking of the house, to your budget, and to your tolerance

level. Remember, the actions of getting good contractors, reviewing contracts

with them and supervising or overseeing the work could overbear you and this

should also be taken into account. But once you have done this analysis, you will

be able to make your home-buying decision wholeheartedly and, most

importantly, with confidence!

SUMMARIZING YOUR THOUGHTS ABOUT BUYING A NEW HOME AND MAKING A DECISION

Numerous defects and deficiencies can be found in a new house. Yet, the house can be considered to be in normal condition. As long as the builder attends to resolve the defects, deficiencies and other such conditions discovered, a new house can conclusively turn out very well. This assumes that the grounds are deemed to be geologically sound and that there are no hazardous wastes to be found. The idea is to avoid problem new houses that are really not fit for occupancy which have serious structural defects or which might involve items of legality or non-conformance. Indeed, avoid new homes constructed of poor workmanship and materials altogether.

EPILOGUE

By now, you have probably gotten a good feel of what you and the inspector should look for while examining a house for purchase. And with all this knowledge, you should be capable of performing a rather thorough examination of the premise. Keep in mind again that the more time that's being spent during the examination, the more items will be found. So, if you're really interested in a home, be sure not to just walk in and walk out with merely a cursory tour of the property.

I firmly believe that the intense and serious exercise in thoroughly examining a property for purchase engages you with necessary findings. And it is these findings which will ultimately assist you to make the determining decision as to whether there will be 'marriage' to (or the purchase of) the house or not.

If you do decide to spend the time required to accurately assess the house in question, then there's just a few more things to remember about your pre-purchase home inspection. First, findings can come in mighty handy. Besides the fact that they can help the homebuyer make the correct objective decision about the purchase as just mentioned, the findings can also serve as tools with which to negotiate a favorable contract price with the seller. Don't overuse the tools, however. They are to be used with discretion. For example, one lawyer client of mine who was armed with lots of information about his prospective home negotiated so much so that the seller refused to sell him the house altogether. His contentious approach essentially killed the deal.

Second, don't expect perfection. There is no house that's perfect, although many homes can be found to be in "excellent" condition. I noticed that a doctor client of mine who accompanied me while I was conducting an inspection for her became quite upset as the inspection time went by.

When I first sensed her discomfort and asked her what was troubling her, she stated that she thought she had selected a house that was in very good condition, but didn't expect the problems that were encountered during the inspection. It became upsetting to her that she would need to face the issues with the house and attempt to remedy them if she decided to go through with the purchase at hand. What she wanted was a near perfect house... and she was willing to pay for it since she didn't have the time to attend to all the repairs that needed to be instituted. In this case, she decided to buy the house regardless of the challenges posed. Her decision was carefully thought out, however, to prevent buyer's remorse. Another client of mine cancelled the sale of a top-shape condominium she was interested in buying simply because her long car failed to fit entirely into the parking space which was associated with the property. Regretfully for her, inspections which I since performed for her revealed that her subsequent choices of condominiums were not in as good condition as the first. Perhaps she should have purchased a new car instead.

And, finally, at the end of the inspection with a couple for whom I inspected a home, I was asked a question that I hear quite often. Upon being undecided about completing their purchase because of what the inspection had revealed, the couple asked me whether they should proceed with the purchase. I answered that question by telling them that the decision was strictly up to them. Specifically, their decision was dependent upon what their tolerance dictated. Sure, the house had problems, but they chose a house that was in overall good condition. And I additionally did indicate that if they really liked the house, they should consider buying it. The truth of the matter is that anything in less than stellar condition can generally get fixed. Most often, all it takes is the love of the home and such resources as time, money, ambition and patience. Indeed, the purchase of a home is not a one- size- fits- all endeavor. But once you find your "soul mate"- house, you can make the house a dream home and hopefully live in it happily ever after.

CPSIA information can be obtained at www.ICGtesting.com
Printed in the USA
BVOW06s2201190614

356903BV00002B/4/P